Less Web Development Cookbook

Over 110 practical recipes to help you write leaner, more efficient CSS code

Bass Jobsen

Amin Meyghani

[PACKT] open source*
PUBLISHING   community experience distilled

BIRMINGHAM - MUMBAI

Less Web Development Cookbook

First published: January 2015

Production reference: 1250115

Published by Packt Publishing Ltd.
Livery Place
35 Livery Street
Birmingham B3 2PB, UK.

ISBN 978-1-78398-148-9

www.packtpub.com

Credits

Authors
Bass Jobsen
Amin Meyghani

Reviewers
Fahad Ibnay Heylaal
Dave Poon
Steve Workman

Commissioning Editor
Ashwin Nair

Acquisition Editors
Richard Brookes-Bland
Richard Harvey

Content Development Editor
Akashdeep Kundu

Technical Editors
Shashank Desai
Novina Kewalramani
Mrunmayee Patil
Rikita Poojari

Copy Editors
Gladson Monteiro
Sarang Chari

Project Coordinator
Milton Dsouza

Proofreaders
Lauren E. Harkins
Paul Hindle
Amy Johnson

Indexer
Monica Ajmera Mehta

Production Coordinator
Conidon Miranda

Cover Work
Conidon Miranda

Foreword

I became interested in Less after starting work on a project to expand a complex web application that had just two large CSS files (one went over IE's limit for a number of selectors in a file), and it used a regex replacement for theme variables—it was a nightmare. There was no link between colors that were clearly visually linked and numbers that were clearly related, and the connection was not obvious and copy/pasted blocks of CSS, scattered throughout the file. At first, it looked manageable, but then as we made changes and fixed bugs, we found that changing something at one place meant having to find several other places where change was required. What was worse, perhaps, was that developers were just adding yet another more complex selector to override another specific place—ad infinitum—until there were older, simpler selectors that weren't even used anywhere. I thought there must be a better way and found Less, which is a superset of CSS, focused on fixing these kind of maintainability problems by making CSS more declarative. I started off with my involvement by porting Less.js to dotless and then became an integral part of the team, taking over from Alexis in maintaining and expanding Less.js to keep up with the demands of the ever-evolving WWW, third-party library usage, and new ideas for CSS management.

I still consider that the primary job of Less is to allow the web developer to have maintainable CSS in their project. For this, abstraction of variables, splitting them up into separate files, and abstraction of common selectors and properties is the most important task (though a long way from what Less can do). We do not implement every feature request but instead try and choose those that have the biggest impact. We are generally against a feature that just provides a different way of doing something. Sometimes this means the solution to problems is not the most obvious one. I hope this will encourage developers to create code with consistent patterns, and I would urge them to try and keep their Less code simple and consistent and ensure it follows the same kind of generally accepted maintainability approaches that are applied to more traditional programming languages. Where common problems would be better served with new Less features, I hope we identify them and always welcome input, discussions, and help to our Github repository. However, it was a recent aim of the project to enable plugins for Less so that projects that need it can implement their own extensions without burdening the core project with support, for instance, functions for 10 different color models.

One plugin I would really like to push people to use is Less-plugin-autoprefixer. In the future, older browsers will not be in use and old polyfills (such as SVG Gradient backgrounds) and prefixed properties will be, if not a thing of the past, a less common occurrence. By using this plugin, you can write your CSS in a forward-thinking way and do not have to bloat it with mixins for polyfills that will be repeated across every project you will work on.

The features most asked for, which I've implemented over the last couple of years, have tended to focus on using libraries. I think this reflects the rise of people using CSS frameworks such as Bootstrap to get a head start at the beginning of a project in order to avoid reimplementing the bare bones. This I think is very positive as it promotes reuse and reduces the number of ways in which fundamentals are done. The biggest problem that remains with libraries is around picking out the bits you want to keep and customizing the library into a project's particular need. Hopefully, Less' import reference feature, not Sass-like extension will help us with this.

As with any language, problems always present themselves out of nowhere, and it always helps to get a head start on good solutions. So keep your solutions maintainable and elegant and enjoy reading this book.

Luke Page

Technical Lead Developer, Scott Logic Ltd. (`http://uk.linkedin.com/pub/luke-page/35/81b/3b6`)

About the Author

Bass Jobsen has been programming for the Web since 1995, covering everything from C to PHP, and is always on the hunt to find the most accessible interfaces. Based in Orthen, the Netherlands, he has also written *Less Web Development Essentials*, *Packt Publishing*, which is a fast-paced tutorial that covers the fundamentals of Less (Leaner CSS) when used in web development.

Bass uses Less in his daily job for web design tasks, WordPress theme development, and other Twitter Bootstrap apps.

He is always happy to help those with questions (http://stackoverflow.com/users/1596547/bass-jobsen), and he writes a blog you can find at http://bassjobsen.weblogs.fm/.

Also, check out his Bootstrap WordPress starters theme (JBST) and other projects at GitHub (https://github.com/bassjobsen).

This book is for Colinda, Kiki, Dries, Wolf, and Leny.

Writing this book wasn't possible without the support of my family, Caroliene, and the people of Vivent. Richard Harvey is a patient and excellent motivator and critical reader. Akashdeep Kundu helped me to dot the i's and cross the t's. I'd also like to thank the reviewers of this book, Dave Poon, Steve Workman, and Fahad Heylaal, for their critical and valuable suggestions that made this book even better.

Last but not least, I should not forget to thank the Less core Team: Alexis Sellier (@cloudhead), Jon Schlinkert (@jonschlinkert), Luke Page (@lukeapage), Marcus Bointon (@Synchro), Mária Jurčovičová (@sommeri), Matthew Dean (@matthew-dean), Max Mikhailov (@seven-phases-max), and all the other contributors who have made coding Less possible in the first place.

Amin Meyghani is a designer and developer currently working at HD MADE (`http://hdmade.com/`), making automation tools, websites, and apps. He is also a lead developer at Flitti (`http://flitti.com/`), leading the team to make next-generation gamification apps. In addition to arts and technology, Amin has always been passionate about teaching. He takes advantage of every opportunity to share his knowledge with the world through books, blogs, or videos. You can find his works and blogs at `http://meyghani.com/`. When Amin is not coding, he is either enjoying Persian food or mastering his Persian calligraphy techniques.

I would like to thank my family for always supporting me and filling my life with love and hope. I owe them this book, as they have always been there for me even in the most difficult times.

About the Reviewers

Fahad Ibnay Heylaal is a developer who hails from Bangladesh and is currently living and working in Amsterdam. Mostly known for being the creator of Croogo (a CMS based on the CakePHP framework), he has progressed to become more of a frontend developer over the last couple of years. If he isn't coding, chances are high that he will be seen cycling around the beautiful canals of Amsterdam.

Dave Poon is a UX/UI designer, web developer, and entrepreneur based in Sydney. He graduated from Central Queensland University with a degree in multimedia studies and a master's degree in IT. He began his career as a freelance graphics and web designer in 1998 and currently works with web development agencies and medium-sized enterprises. He began his love affair with Drupal afterward and worked for a variety of companies using Drupal. Now, he is evangelizing good user experience and interaction design practices to start-ups and enterprises.

Currently, he is a design lead at Suncorp, one of the biggest financial institutions in Australia. He is the cofounder of Erlango (`http://erlango.com`), a digital product development and design startup located in Sydney and Hong Kong that creates user-centered digital products for clients and users. He is also the cofounder of SpikeNode (`http://spikenode.com`) which is, a platform for DevOps automation.

He is the author of *Drupal 7 Fields/CCK Beginner's Guide, Packt Publishing*.

Also, he is the technical reviewer of the books *Drupal Intranets with Open Atrium*, *Advanced Express Web Application Development*, and *Mastering Web Application Development with Express,* all by Packt Publishing.

I would like to thank my wife, Rita, for her endless patience and support. Without her, whatever I do would be meaningless.

I would also like to thank my father for his continued encouragement.

Steve Workman is a frontend web engineer and an organizer of the London Web Standards group. He is a champion at creating high-performance sites with the latest web technologies and making developers' lives easier with tools and new languages.

I'd like to thank the whole Less community for creating this great language and my wife, Emily, for always being there.

www.PacktPub.com

Support files, eBooks, discount offers, and more

For support files and downloads related to your book, please visit www.PacktPub.com.

Did you know that Packt offers eBook versions of every book published, with PDF and ePub files available? You can upgrade to the eBook version at www.PacktPub.com, and as a print book customer, you are entitled to a discount on the eBook copy. Get in touch with us at service@packtpub.com for more details.

At www.PacktPub.com, you can also read a collection of free technical articles, sign up for a range of free newsletters, and receive exclusive discounts and offers on Packt books and eBooks.

https://www2.packtpub.com/books/subscription/packtlib

Do you need instant solutions to your IT questions? PacktLib is Packt's online digital book library. Here, you can search, access, and read Packt's entire library of books.

Why subscribe?

- ▸ Fully searchable across every book published by Packt
- ▸ Copy and paste, print, and bookmark content
- ▸ On demand and accessible via a web browser

Free access for Packt account holders

If you have an account with Packt at www.PacktPub.com, you can use this to access PacktLib today and view 9 entirely free books. Simply use your login credentials for immediate access.

Table of Contents

Preface

CSS has dramatically changed since its very first emergence, and it is continuing to evolve. In particular, the emergence of CSS3 has added many new features to CSS, including gradients and animations. Along with this are many new opportunities to build websites using only CSS and HTML. Developers are no longer dependent on techniques such as Flash and other tricks to build interactive and fancy websites.

CSS3 has played an integral role in building responsive websites, where CSS media queries have made it possible to apply some styles dependent on the width of the browser's viewport only.

Despite this improvement, CSS is inherently, at its core, a simple style sheet language that lacks some fundamental programming features such as variables, functions, and operators. The need for more maintainable CSS, especially with the explosion of complex web apps, has made CSS preprocessors such as Less a necessity in enabling us to write more readable and manageable versions without breaking cross-browser compatibilities.

Although Less cannot magically change CSS, it certainly provides us with the tools to help structure, modularize, debug, and maintain small or large CSS projects more easily. By extending CSS with variables, functions, and mixins; nesting CSS selectors; and allowing you to follow the don't repeat yourself (DRY) principle of software programming, Less behaves more like a programming language in a way that CSS never was. Despite some of the programming characteristics of Less, you should not be put off by this; by being built as a superset of CSS, its features are implemented in the CSS way and it follows W3C standards where possible. Designers and developers who are familiar with CSS will find coding in Less very natural. Because Less fixes these shortcomings of CSS, the best time to start using Less is now!

In this book, you are going to explore the Less preprocessor, most of its core, and some of its less frequently used features. Through these very easy-to-follow and practical recipes, you will learn how to write more maintainable and scalable CSS. You will explore making components and structures through reusable mixins and extends. We will also learn about frameworks that are based on Less, exploring their features and how they can be seamlessly integrated into your own projects. In addition, you will learn how to use prebuilt mixin libraries for your current or upcoming projects. Finally, you will look at debugging techniques that have been available for other preprocessors and are now available to Less through source maps. By the end of this book, you will have an extended knowledge and a good understanding of the power of Less, its libraries, and the important features it has to offer to make writing your CSS more natural, productive, and intuitive.

What this book covers

Chapter 1, Getting to Grips with the Basics of Less, shows you how to install the Less compiler for client- and server-side usage. After the installation, you will be shown how to make use of the basic features of Less: using variables, mixins, operations, built-in functions, and namespaces; how to nest your rules will also be on the menu here!

Chapter 2, Debugging and Documenting Your Less Code, shows you how to debug your Less code using your CSS source maps and browser developer tools. You will also be introduced to style guides and learn how to properly comment your code.

Chapter 3, Using Variables and Mixins, covers the advanced usage of variables and mixins in Less. After reading this chapter, you will know how to use variables to create reusable Less code and use mixins to make your CSS properties interactive.

Chapter 4, Leveraging the Less Built-in Functions, explains the different types of built-in functions of Less. You will find examples of each type of function, including functions for color manipulation and mathematical operations.

Chapter 5, Extending and Referencing, shows you how to extend and reference selectors and properties to help you write better CSS and reduce the size of the compiled CSS code. You will learn to change the order of selectors and merge them.

Chapter 6, Advanced Less Coding, walks you through the process of parameterized mixins and shows you how to use guards. A guard can be used with as if-else statements and make it possible to construct interactive loops in Less.

Chapter 7, Leveraging Libraries with Prebuilt Mixins, explains how to install and use the libraries of prebuilt mixins. You will explore different libraries such as Less Elements, Less hats, and Preboot to build background gradients, grids, and animations in Less, among others.

Chapter 8, Building a Layout with Less, takes you through the process of creating a complete website layout with Less. The layout will be built with a responsive and semantic grid and will include a vertical menu. Finally, you will also learn how to use iconic fonts with Less.

Chapter 9, Using Bootstrap with Less, shows you how to customize Bootstrap and its components using Bootstrap's Less source files. You will also learn how to use Bootstrap's mixins to make semantic and reusable layouts and components.

Chapter 10, Less and WordPress, shows you how to use Less when theming your WordPress site. This includes examples of the Roots.io, SemanticUI, and JBST WordPress themes. You will be shown how to customize the WooCommerce plugins with Less along with integrating Less into your other WordPress themes and plugins.

Chapter 11, Compiling Less Real Time for Development Using Grunt, shows you how to set up a Less compiler using Grunt for real-time compilation. It will also show you how to use several Node modules for your Less development. By the end of this chapter, you will be very comfortable setting up a development environment with Grunt and its plugins.

What you need for this book

The latest version of Less.js can be downloaded for free from `http://www.lesscss.org/`. You will definitely need a text editor to write your code; however, it does not matter which text editor or operating system you use. You will also need a modern web browser, namely the latest versions of Mozilla Firefox, Google Chrome, or Microsoft Internet Explorer. Please note that some recipes, especially in the final chapter, require some basic familiarity with the command line. All the tools used in the last chapter are cross-platform and are available for free, so you should be fine using your favorite operating system. Grunt plugins can be found by visiting `http://gruntjs.com/plugins`.

Who this book is for

This book is mainly intended for web developers and designers who are comfortable with CSS and HTML. If you are someone with some experience with CSS, you will find the learning curve of understanding the Less syntax to be less steep. Although this book is beneficial to those who have had some experience with using Less, web developers and designers who would like to use this book as a gateway to learning the program can still benefit and harness its true power.

Sections

In this book, you will find several headings that appear frequently (Getting ready, How to do it, How it works, There's more, and See also).

To give clear instructions on how to complete a recipe, we use these sections as follows:

Getting ready

This section tells you what to expect in the recipe, and describes how to set up any software or any preliminary settings required for the recipe.

How to do it...

This section contains the steps required to follow the recipe.

How it works...

This section usually consists of a detailed explanation of what happened in the previous section.

There's more...

This section consists of additional information about the recipe in order to make the reader more knowledgeable about the recipe.

See also

This section provides helpful links to other useful information for the recipe.

Conventions

In this book, you will find a number of text styles that distinguish between different kinds of information. Here are some examples of these styles and an explanation of their meaning.

Code words in text, database table names, folder names, filenames, file extensions, pathnames, dummy URLs, user input, and Twitter handles are shown as follows: "To start the process, you will have to edit your `index.html` file."

A block of code is set as follows:

```
header {
  color: blue;
}
section {
  color: green;
}
footer {
  color: purple;
}
```

When we wish to draw your attention to a particular part of a code block, the relevant lines or items are set in bold:

```
<link rel="stylesheet/less" type="text/css"
  href="less/styles.less" />
<script type="text/javascript">less = { env: 'development'
  };</script>
<script src="less.js" type="text/javascript"></script>
```

Any command-line input or output is written as follows:

```
java -jar js.jar -f less-rhino-1.7.0.js lessc-rhino-1.7.0.js example.less
example.css
```

New terms and **important words** are shown in bold. Words that you see on the screen, for example, in menus or dialog boxes, appear in the text like this: "In the **Styles** tab of the **Developers Tools** page, you will find the rules that are applied while selecting a selector."

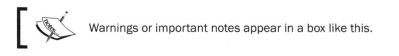

Warnings or important notes appear in a box like this.

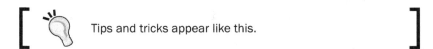

Tips and tricks appear like this.

Reader feedback

Feedback from our readers is always welcome. Let us know what you think about this book— what you liked or disliked. Reader feedback is important for us as it helps us develop titles that you will really get the most out of.

To send us general feedback, simply e-mail `feedback@packtpub.com`, and mention the book's title in the subject of your message.

If there is a topic that you have expertise in and you are interested in either writing or contributing to a book, see our author guide at `www.packtpub.com/authors`.

Customer support

Now that you are the proud owner of a Packt book, we have a number of things to help you to get the most from your purchase.

Downloading the example code

You can download the example code files from your account at `http://www.packtpub.com` for all the Packt Publishing books you have purchased. If you purchased this book elsewhere, you can visit `http://www.packtpub.com/support` and register to have the files e-mailed directly to you.

Downloading the color images of this book

We also provide you with a PDF file that has color images of the screenshots/diagrams used in this book. The color images will help you better understand the changes in the output. You can download this file from: `https://www.packtpub.com/sites/default/files/downloads/B01849_Coloredimages.pdf`.

Errata

Although we have taken every care to ensure the accuracy of our content, mistakes do happen. If you find a mistake in one of our books—maybe a mistake in the text or the code—we would be grateful if you could report this to us. By doing so, you can save other readers from frustration and help us improve subsequent versions of this book. If you find any errata, please report them by visiting `http://www.packtpub.com/submit-errata`, selecting your book, clicking on the **Errata Submission Form** link, and entering the details of your errata. Once your errata are verified, your submission will be accepted and the errata will be uploaded to our website or added to any list of existing errata under the Errata section of that title.

To view the previously submitted errata, go to `https://www.packtpub.com/books/content/support` and enter the name of the book in the search field. The required information will appear under the **Errata** section.

Piracy

Piracy of copyrighted material on the Internet is an ongoing problem across all media. At Packt, we take the protection of our copyright and licenses very seriously. If you come across any illegal copies of our works in any form on the Internet, please provide us with the location address or website name immediately so that we can pursue a remedy.

Please contact us at `copyright@packtpub.com` with a link to the suspected pirated material.

We appreciate your help in protecting our authors and our ability to bring you valuable content.

Questions

If you have a problem with any aspect of this book, you can contact us at `questions@packtpub.com`, and we will do our best to address the problem.

1
Getting to Grips with the Basics of Less

In this chapter, we will cover the following topics:

- ▶ Downloading, installing, and integrating `less.js`
- ▶ Installing the `lessc` compiler with `npm`
- ▶ Using `less.js` with Rhino
- ▶ Declaring variables with Less for commonly used values
- ▶ Setting the properties of CSS styles with mixins
- ▶ Writing more intuitive code and making inheritance clear with nested rules
- ▶ Creating complex relationships between properties
- ▶ Using the built-in functions of Less
- ▶ Using namespaces to make your code reusable and portable

Introduction

Leaner CSS (**Less**) is a preprocessor for CSS code. This chapter will guide you through the installation of Less. It can be used on the command line via `npm` (or Rhino) or downloaded as a script file for a web browser. Other third-party compilers are available too.

Although client-side compiling is not suitable for production, it is very useful to develop and test your code. A client-side compiler will run in any modern browser and show you the effect of your coding in real time. On the other hand, the server-side-compiled CSS code can be minified and used for production. Note that client-side compiling doesn't save the output and compiles your code again after each browser reload, while the output of the server-side compiler will be saved in a static CSS file.

You will also see that Less, in contrast to CSS, is a programming language for writing CSS more efficiently. It adds built-in functions, variables, and mixins with a lot more to offer to CSS, which helps you to meet the **Don't repeat yourself** (**DRY**) principle of software programming and reuse your code. Variables enable you to define the commonly used values only once, and mixins create the reusable blocks of code. You will work more effectively and find that you will spend less time on debugging and maintaining your projects.

Less extends the CSS language, which also means that valid CSS code is valid Less code. Whoever is familiar with CSS will find that the process of learning Less has a flat learning curve and is very intuitive.

After installing Less, the other recipes in this chapter will show you its basic features and how to use them to write a better, reusable, and more maintainable CSS code.

Downloading, installing, and integrating less.js

The client-side compiler `less.js` can be downloaded from `http://lesscss.org/`. You can use `less.js` in the browser, which is a great tool to get you started with Less, although it should only be used for development. For production usage, you should use precompiling. Precompiling with the `Node.js` compiler will be discussed in the *Installing the lessc compiler with npm* recipe.

Getting ready

You can download the latest version of `less.js` from `http://lesscss.org/` and copy this file into your working directory. You will also have to create the `index.html` and `project.less` files in the working directory. You can edit these files with any text editor of your choice.

You will have the following folder and file structure:

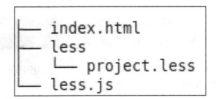

```
├── index.html
├── less
│   └── project.less
└── less.js
```

You will also need a modern web browser to inspect the results of your work.

It is not necessary to have a web server running. Navigating to the `index.html` file on your hard drive with your browser will be enough. However, this won't work for all browsers, so use Mozilla Firefox to be sure when you do not have a web server running. The examples in this book use `http://localhost/map/` and can be replaced with the path similar to `file:///map/` or `c:\map\`, depending on your situation.

How to do it...

1. To start the process, you will have to edit your `index.html` file. The `index.html` file should contain a valid HTML5 code and have references to the `project.less` and `less.js` files. After you edit it, the HTML file will look as follows:

```
<!DOCTYPE html>
<html>
  <head>
    <meta charset="utf-8">

    <link rel="stylesheet/less" type="text/css"
      href="project.less">
    <script src="less.js" type="text/javascript"></script>
  </head>
  <body>
  <header>the header</header>
    <section>this is a paragraph</section>
  <footer>the footer</footer>
  </body>
</html>
```

2. The HTML5 code from the preceding step contains a header, section, and footer. Now you can use Less to style these elements. Enter the following code into the `project.less` file to give each element a different font color:

```
header {
  color: blue;
}
section {
  color: green;
}
footer {
  color: purple;
}
```

3. Finally, you can inspect the result of your actions by opening the `index.html` file in your web browser.

The `less.js` compiler compiles the Less code in the `project.less` file linked with the following HTML code:

```
<link rel="stylesheet/less" type="text/css" href="project.less" />
```

Note that without setting the `rel="stylesheet/less"` attribute, the compiler does not recognize your code.

The reference to the `less.js` compiler should be included after the reference to the `project.less` file in the preceding code as follows:

```
<script src="less.js" type="text/javascript"></script>
```

Other Less files can be imported into `project.less` with the `@import` directive. All imports are compiled into CSS code. Also note that when using the server-side compiler, all of the compiled CSS code will be saved to the same file. The preceding code differs from the situation of linking more than one `.less` style sheet. When linking multiple `.less` style sheets, each file will be compiled independently and will not use variables and mixins defined in the other files.

The compiled CSS code will be injected into the HTML document and style your HTML elements according to normal CSS rules. When using Firefox's or Google Chrome's developer tools to inspect your source, you will find the compiled code as follows:

```
    Edit    style#le...-project < head < html

<!DOCTYPE html>
<html>
  <head>
    <meta charset="utf-8">
    <meta content="IE=edge,chrome=1" http-equiv="X-UA-Compatible">
    <title>Less example</title>
    <meta content="width=device-width, maximum-scale=1.0" name="viewport">
    <link href="firstproject.less" type="text/css" rel="stylesheet/less">
    <style id="less:book2-chapter1-project" type="text/css">
      1  header {
      2    color: blue;
      3  }
      4  section {
      5    color: green;
      6  }
      7  footer {
      8    color: purple;
      9  }
    </style>
    <script type="text/javascript" src="less-1.7.0.min.js">
  </head>
  <body>
```

The `less.js` file also has a watch function that checks your files for changes and reloads your browser views automatically when changes are found. It is pretty simple to use—add `#!watch` after the URL you want to open, which in this case means appending `#!watch` after `index.html`, and then reload the browser window.

There's more...

You can configure the `less.js` compiler by adding a `less = {}`; JavaScript object to your code using the following code:

```
<link rel="stylesheet/less" type="text/css"
  href="less/styles.less" />
<script type="text/javascript">less = { env: 'development'
  };</script>
<script src="less.js" type="text/javascript"></script>
```

In the preceding code, `less` is a global object used to parse the `env: 'development'` settings to `less.js`. Please refer to `http://lesscss.org/#client-side-usage-browser-options` to learn more about the settings that can be used with the `less.js` compiler.

Alternatively, these options can be set as data attributes on the `script` and `link` tags, as can be seen in the following example code from the Less website:

```
<script src="less.js" data-poll="1000"
  data-relative-urls="false"></script>
    <link data-dump-line-numbers="all" data-global-vars='{ myvar:
      "#ddffee", mystr: "\"quoted\"" }' rel="stylesheet/less"
        type="text/css" href="less/styles.less">
```

In this recipe, a local copy of the `less.js` compiler was used. Alternatively, you can also load the `less.js` compiler from **content delivery network** (**CDN**) or build it with **Bower**. To load `less.js` from CDN, you will have to add the following code to your `index.html` file:

```
<script src="//cdnjs.cloudflare.com/ajax/libs/less.js/2.x.x/
  less.min.js"></script>
```

If you aren't aware, Bower is a package manager for the Web. You can install Bower by running the following command in your console:

`npm install bower`

You can then run the following command to build `less.js` with Bower:

`bower install less`

See also

- ▸ More information about Bower can be found at `http://bower.io/`

Installing the lessc compiler with npm

For server-side compilation, Less comes with a command-line compiler for Node.js. The **node package manager** (**npm**) can be used to install the Less command-line compiler.

 Node is a platform built on Chrome's JavaScript runtime called V8, allowing you to easily create fast and scalable network applications.

Getting ready

If you have not installed Node.js and npm on your system yet, you will have to do this first. You can do this by following these steps:

1. Download the Node.js source code or a prebuilt installer for your platform from http://nodejs.org/download/.

2. Install Node.js, which includes npm, on your system.

In the *Installing Node and Grunt* recipe in *Chapter 11, Compiling Less Real Time for Development Using Grunt*, you can read about installing Node.js and npm on your system in more detail. After installing npm, you can simply run the following command:

```
npm install --global less
```

How to do it...

1. For this recipe, you will first need to create a simple Less file and save this file, which for instance might be example.less. You can try the following code in your example file:

```
@color: red;
.paint() {
  color: @color;
}
p {
  .paint();
}
```

2. After creating the Less file in the preceding format, you will need to save your file (which may be example.less or whatever filename you have chosen). If you have chosen example.less, you can run the following command in your command prompt:

```
lessc example.less
```

3. After running the `lessc` command, you will see it output the following CSS code in the console:

```
p {
  color: #ff0000;
}
```

How it works...

If you are new to Less, the example Less code used inside `example.less` may contain some syntax that is completely alien to you. The code defines a `@color` variable and a `paint()` mixin. The *Declaring variables with Less for commonly used values* recipe explains the basics of variables in Less, while the *Setting the properties of CSS styles with mixins* recipe does the same for mixins.

By default, the `lessc` compiler outputs to `stdout`. You can redirect the output to a CSS file with the following command:

```
lessc example.less > example.css
```

Running the `lessc` compiler without any parameters will give you a list of options for the compiler.

You can use the `-x` option to compress your output as follows:

```
lessc -x example.less > example.css
```

In a similar manner, you can use either the `--clean-css` option for a more involved minification, or the `--source-map` option to create a v3 CSS source map. In the *Using CSS source maps to debug your code* recipe in *Chapter 2, Debugging and Documenting your Less Code*, you can read more about CSS source maps and Less. Note that in version 2 of Less, the `--clean-css` option has been moved into a plugin. The usage is similar: just install the plugin (`npm install -g less-plugin-clean-css`), then make use of the `--clean-css` argument.

There's more...

There are many other third-party compilers for Less with a compressive list available at `http://lesscss.org/usage`.

With `grunt-contrib-less`, you can compile your code with Grunt. For Gulp, you can use `gulp-less`. The *Compiling style guides with Grunt* recipe in *Chapter 11, Compiling Less Real Time for Development Using Grunt*, shows you how to build a development workflow with the Grunt task runner.

In this recipe, you read about Grunt and Gulp, which are JavaScript task runners or build systems. Comparing with Grunt's build system, Gulp's build system is relatively new. Gulp uses streams and code over configuration, which makes it more simple and intuitive.

See also

▸ In *Chapter 11, Compiling Less Real Time for Development Using Grunt,* you can read all you want to know about Grunt

▸ To read more about Gulp, you can visit `http://gulpjs.com/`

▸ The Gulp Less plugin can be found at `https://github.com/plus3network/gulp-less`

Using less.js with Rhino

Less also runs inside Rhino, which is an open source implementation of JavaScript written entirely in Java. It is typically embedded into Java applications to provide scripting to end users. Rhino enables you to use the original `less.js` distribution in a pure JVM environment.

Getting ready

To use `less.js` inside Rhino, you will have to download and install Rhino from the following links:

▸ Download and install the latest version of Rhino from `https://developer.mozilla.org/en-US/docs/Mozilla/Projects/Rhino/Download_Rhino`

▸ Download the Rhino version of `less-rhino-x.x.x.js` and `lessc-rhino-x.x.x.js` from `https://github.com/less/less.js/tree/master/dist`

How to do it...

1. Open your text editor and create a file named `example.less`. The `example.less` file can contain, for instance, the following code:

```
@base-color: red;
h1 {
color: @base-color;
}
```

2. Now you can run the following command in your command prompt:

```
java -jar js.jar -f less-rhino-1.7.0.js lessc-rhino-1.7.0.js
example.less
```

3. The preceding command should output the following lines of CSS code:

```
h1 {
  color: #ff0000;
}
```

How it works...

Rhino enables Java to run the JavaScript code, while `js.jar` runs the Less compiler and generates the CSS output.

To write the output of a file, you will have to append the filename of the CSS files to the list of commands, as follows:

```
java -jar js.jar -f less-rhino-1.7.0.js lessc-rhino-1.7.0.js example.less example.css
```

You can also add options for the compiler. You can add the `-x` option to compress the output as follows:

```
java -jar js.jar -f less-rhino-1.7.0.js lessc-rhino-1.7.0.js -x example.less
```

The preceding command will then output the following line of CSS code:

```
h1{color:#f00}
```

There's more...

A Less compiler for Java has been built with Rhino. You can find out more information about this Less compiler for Java along with how to download it at `https://github.com/marceloverdijk/lesscss-java`.

Declaring variables with Less for commonly used values

Less allows you to use variables. You can assign a variable a value, which will be called a declaration. After a variable is declared, you can use the variable anywhere in your code to reference its value. Variables allow you to specify widely used values in a single place and then reuse them throughout your code. Defining once also means you have to edit it once when you want to change its value.

Getting ready

Open your text editor and create a file named `example.less`. Variables will start with `@` and will have a name with examples, including `@color`, `@size`, and `@tree`. To write the name, you are allowed to use any alphanumeric characters, underscores, and dashes. Using this as an elaborate example, `@this-is-variable-name-with-35-chars` is a valid variable name.

How to do it...

1. Start with creating a simple HTML5 file named `index.html`, as follows:

```html
<!DOCTYPE html>
<html>
  <head>
    <meta charset="utf-8">

    <title>Use variables in Less</title>

    <link rel="stylesheet/less" type="text/css"
      href="example.less">
    <script src="less.js" type="text/javascript"></script>
  </head>
  <body>
    <h1>Color your page with variables</h1>
    <p>Hello Less</p>
    <button>Click here</button>
  </body>
</html>
```

2. You then need to create the `example.less` file, which should contain the following code:

```less
@base-color: red;
h1 {
  color: @base-color;
}
p{
  color: @base-color;
}
button {
  color: @base-color;
}
```

3. After the first two steps, you will end up with the following folder and file structure:

```
├── index.html
├── less
│   └── example.less
└── less.js
```

4. After creating the files as described in the preceding steps, you can open `index.html` in your browser.

5. Now, change the first line of code `@base-color: red;` to `@base-color: green;` and reload your browser.

How it works...

As you can now see, changing the font color of the `h1`, `p`, and `button` text is easy as you change `@base-color` only once. The only thing you need to do is change the single line of the code: `@base-color: red;`. In the *Downloading, installing, and integrating less.js* recipe, you can read how to use the `watch` function of `less.js` to reload your browser automatically after changing and saving the `example.less` file.

Variables in Less are defined as the equivalent to statics in other programming languages. You assign a value to a variable once and use it everywhere in your code. To think of it in another way, this is like defining the value of the gravitational constant (for the force of gravity) or pi in your code. Both these values become constants once they are declared and so do not change at runtime. In fact, you can still change or redeclare them in Less, as explained in the *There's more...* section of this recipe.

You can assign any valid Less (or CSS) property value to a variable. Valid property values include the numbers, strings, lists, CSV lists, and escaped values. Strings and numbers can be used together to define values with units. For instance, the following code will show you a declaration for a length in pixels:

```
@length: 100px;
```

Other examples of valid variable declarations can be found in the following code:

```
@color: red;
@list: a b c d;
@csv-list: a, b, c, d;
@escaped-value: ~""dark@{color}";
```

There's more...

Less uses the **last declaration wins** and **lazy loading** rules, which play an important role and make redeclaration of a variable suitable for customization.

See also

▶ You can read more about the usages of redeclaration variables for customization in the *Redeclaring variables based on lazy loading* recipe in *Chapter 3, Using Variables and Mixins*

Setting the properties of CSS styles with mixins

In Less, mixins hold a set of properties that can be reused for different rulesets. The properties of a mixin are included in the ruleset. The mixin itself does not generate output to the final CSS. They look like normal classes (or an ID ruleset, starting with #). Although they are optional, most mixin declarations end with parentheses, which prevent the mixins from compiling into the source. A mixin with parentheses is called a **parametric mixin**. You can read more about parametric mixins in the *Using parametric mixins* recipe in *Chapter 3, Using Variables and Mixins*.

Getting ready

Open your text editor and create a file named `mixins.less`. In this file, define a mixin for rounded corners, as follows:

```
.rounded-corners() {
  border-radius: 5px;
}
```

You will also need an `index.html` file containing some HTML elements to which you can give rounded corners.

How to do it...

1. You first need to create a valid HTML5 document named `index.html` with the following elements:

```
<header>the header</header>
<p>this is a paragraph</p>
<footer>the footer</footer>
```

Make sure the `head` section of your `index.html` file also contains the following code:

```
<link rel="stylesheet/less" type="text/css"
  href="project.less">
<script src="less.js" type="text/javascript"></script>
```

Note that the preceding code references a Less file called `project.less` instead of `mixins.less`

2. After creating the `index.html` file, you can start writing your Less code, which will give the HTML elements rounded corners. Since mixins can be reused, it will be a good practice to write them in a separated file, enabling you to import the mixins in your other projects too.

3. Now, create your `project.less` file. This file imports the mixin(s) from the `mixins.less` file using the following code:

```
@import "mixins.less";
```

4. After creating the files, visit the `mixins.less` file. Here, write the following code:

```
.rounded-corners() {
  border-radius: 5px;
}
```

5. Following this edit, you can give an HTML element rounded corners by adding the `rounded-corners()` mixin call to its property list. Finally, your `project.less` file will look as shown in the following code:

```
@import "mixins.less";

@header-background-color: red;
@paragraph-background-color: orange;
@footer-background-color: green;

header {
  .rounded-corners();
  background-color: @header-background-color;
  color: contrast(@header-background-color);
}
p {
  .rounded-corners();
```

```
      background-color: @paragraph-background-color;
      color: contrast(@paragraph-background-color);
   }
   footer {
     .rounded-corners();
     background-color: @footer-background-color;
     color: contrast(@footer-background-color);
   }
```

How it works...

Every element has a background-color and color property set to make the rounded corners visible and the fonts readable. The color property is set with the built-in contrast function. You can read more about the built-in functions in the *Using the built-in functions of Less* recipe. When you open the index.html file, it looks like the following screenshot:

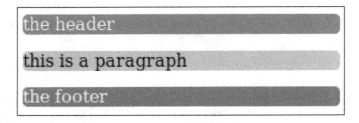

Less allows you to copy the properties of a class to another by simply adding the class to the property list. Consider the following example Less code:

```
.class1
{
  property1: value1;
}
.class 2
{
  .class1
  property2: value2;
}
```

The preceding Less code will compile into the following CSS code:

```
.class1 {
  property1: value1;
}
.class2 {
  property1: value1;
  property2: value2;
}
```

As you can see, the `property1` property is added to the `.class2` class, but `.class1` has also been compiled into the source. With parentheses, the `.class1` mixin is not compiled into the CSS source, so the following code will not be visible in the source:

```
.class1() {
  property1: value1;
}
```

There's more...

In the example code of this recipe, you set a `background-color` and `color` property for each element again. While using parametric mixins, as described in the *Using parametric mixins* recipe in *Chapter 3, Using Variables and Mixins*, you can write a second mixin to set these properties. The `roundedcorners()` mixin can be called from this particular mixin. The second mixin will then look like the following Less code:

```
.colored-and-rounded(@background-color: red) {
  .rounded-corners();
  background-color: @background-color;
  color: contrast(@background-color);
}
```

The `colored-and-rounded()` mixin can be added to the `mixins.less` file. Your `project.less` file will then look as follows:

```
@import "mixins.less";

@header-background-color: red;
@paragraph-background-color: orange;
@footer-background-color: green;

header {
  .colored-and-rounded();
}
p {
  .colored-and-rounded();
}
footer {
  .colored-and-rounded();
}
```

Writing more intuitive code and making inheritance clear with nested rules

HTML elements in the hierarchy of the **Document Object Model** (**DOM**) of HTML5 documents are nested while CSS, on the other hand, does not reflect this nested structure. Less makes nesting of CSS selectors possible. With the nested selectors being used, your code reflects the nested structure of HTML5.

Getting ready

To get started, you will need to create a valid HTML5 file, including some nested elements. Your HTML, for instance, may look like the following code:

```
<section role="main">
<h1>heading</h1>
<p>some content</p>
</section>
```

You will also have to create an empty Less file named `project.less`. Make sure the `head` section of your HTML5 document also contains the following code:

```
<link rel="stylesheet/less" type="text/css" href="project.less">
<script src="less.js" type="text/javascript"></script>
```

How to do it...

In CSS, the section with the nested `h1` and `p` elements can, for instance, be styled with the following CSS code:

```
section h1 {}
section p {}
```

However, with Less, you can style the same elements using the following Less code:

```
section {
  h1 {}
  p{}
}
```

How it works...

In the preceding example, nesting the selector mimics the nested structure of your HTML code. Nesting makes the code intuitive and so much easier to read and maintain. Less's code will also be more concise than its corresponding CSS code. You should use nesting with care; nesting too much will break your CSS code after small changes in your HTML. You should not try to nest your complete HTML structure, but nesting will be very useful to assign pseudo classes, such as `hover`, to your elements.

Note that the nested selectors in Less still compile to un-nested selectors in CSS.

To see how this works, use the following Less code:

```
section {
  h1 {font-size: 20em;}
  p{ padding: 0 10px;}
}
```

The preceding code will compile into the following CSS code:

```
section h1 {
  font-size: 20em;
}
section p {
  padding: 0 10px;
}
```

There's more...

Although nesting your selector can make your code more intuitive, it can equally break other things. For instance, considering **object-oriented CSS** (**OOCSS**) principles; these do not allow nesting of headings (`h1` to `h6`). Headings are considered to be built-in objects in OOCSS and so their appearance should be consistent across an entire site.

See also

- ▶ You can read more about OOCSS at `http://appendto.com/2014/04/oocss/`
- ▶ Read the presentation by *Nicole Sullivan* used to introduce OOCSS at `http://www.slideshare.net/stubbornella/object-oriented-css`

Creating complex relationships between properties

Less supports basic arithmetic operations. These operations, such as division (/), can be applied to any number, variable, or even color. They can be used to create complex relationships between properties.

Getting ready

You will first need to create a Less file named `project.less` and a valid HTML5 document named `index.html`. You should make sure the `head` section of the `index.html` file contains the following lines of code:

```
<link rel="stylesheet/less" type="text/css" href="project.less">
<script src="less.js" type="text/javascript"></script>
```

How to do it...

1. First create an HTML structure in the `index.html` file as follows:

```
<div class="container">
  <section role="main">Content</section>
  <aside role="complementary">Side bar</aside>
</div>
```

2. To set the width of the content and sidebar dependent on the width of the container, you can use the following Less code:

```
@basic-width: 800px;

.container {
  width: @basic-width;

  section {
    width: @basic-width * 2/3;
    background-color:red;
    color:white;
    float:left;
  }
  aside {
    width: @basic-width * 1/3;
    background-color: black;
    color: white;
```

```
        float: right;
    }

}
```

3. Now you can open the `index.html` file in your browser, which will look like the following screenshot:

Content	Side bar

> Note that browsers can use different algorithms to round the pixel values when you assign them with decimal numbers. This phenomenon has also been described as Sub-Pixel problems in CSS. You can read more about these sub-pixel problems in CSS at `http://ejohn.org/blog/sub-pixel-problems-in-css/`.

How it works...

In Less, you can operate numbers, variables, and colors. The compiler understands colors and units. Take a look at the following Less code:

```
@width: 50px;
@color: yellow;
p {
  width: @width * 50;
  color: @color + #111;
}
```

This will actually compile into the following CSS code:

```
p {
  width: 2500px;
  color: #ffff11;
}
```

The Less compiler accepts different types of color definitions. In Less, you can use the hexadecimal notation for **red, green, and blue** (**RGB**) values, the RGB functional notation, or one of the 148 color names defined in CSS3. A complete overview of the color definition can be found at `http://www.w3.org/TR/css3-color/` and `http://lesscss.org/functions/#color-definition`. When applying a basic operation on two or more colors, the compiler gives the result as a color even when different types of color definitions are used. As you can see, `yellow + #111` compiles into `#ffff11`.

When multiplying `50px` fifty times, the compiler automatically adds the `px` unit after the calculated result.

There's more...

In this recipe, you learned about some basic operations on colors. Less also has many built-in functions to define and manipulate colors. You can read more about Less's built-in color functions in *Chapter 4, Leveraging the Less Built-in Functions*.

See also

▶ At `http://meyerweb.com/eric/css/colors/`, you can find an overview of the 147 (or 148) color keywords

▶ Refer to `http://meyerweb.com/eric/thoughts/2014/06/19/rebeccapurple/` for color names, which are defined in the CSS3 module along with their corresponding numeric equivalents

Using the built-in functions of Less

Less has many built-in functions that can be leveraged for others, transforming colors, manipulating strings, or even performing mathematical operations.

Getting ready

Create a valid HTML document named `index.html` and an empty `project.less` file. Make sure your `index.html` HTML5 document has the following lines of code in its `head` section:

```
<link rel="stylesheet/less" type="text/css" href="project.less">
<script src="less.js" type="text/javascript"></script>
```

How to do it...

This recipe will show you how to use the `darken()` and `contrast()` built-in functions. Perform the following steps:

1. Start this recipe by creating a simple HTML structure in the `index.html` file, shown as follows:

    ```
    <div class="item color1">Text</div>
    <div class="item color2">Text</div>
    <div class="item color3">Text</div>
    <div class="item color4">Text</div>
    <div class="item color5">Text</div>
    ```

2. After creating the HTML page, add the following Less code to the `project.less` file:

```less
@start-color: white;
.color1 {
  background-color: @start-color;
  color: contrast(@start-color);
}
.color2 {
  @color: darken(@start-color, 25%);
  background-color: @color;
  color: contrast(@color);
}
.color3 {
  @color: darken(@start-color, 50%);
  background-color: @color;
  color: contrast(@color);
}
.color4 {
  @color: darken(@start-color, 75%);
  background-color: @color;
  color: contrast(@color);
}
.color5 {
  @color: darken(@start-color, 100%);
  background-color: @color;
  color: contrast(@color);
}
```

3. Now, open the `index.html` file in the browser and you will see the following output:

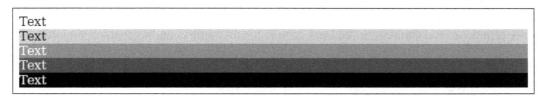

How it works...

Both the `darken()` and `contrast()` functions return a color. The `darken()` function returns a darker variant of the input color, and `contrast()` returns black or white, based on the highest contrast with the input color.

The `darken()` function ensures that a color is readable against a background, which will be useful to meet web accessibility requirements too. The `contrast()` function compares the **luma** value (also called luminosity that represents the brightness in an image) of a color and not the lightness.

There's more...

The built-in functions of Less can be grouped based on their input type. Refer to the following functions:

- The `string` functions can be used to manipulate strings. The `replace` function, which replaces the text in a string, is an example of a `string` function.

- The `type` functions, which include functions such as `isnumber()` and `iscolor()`, return a Boolean value. The `iscolor()` function returns `true` for values such as `#ff0` or `red` and `false` for all other kinds of input types.

- The `list` functions operate on values. Both comma and space-separated lists are supported. The only two functions in the group are `extract()` and `length()`. The group of mathematical functions contain functions for all kinds of mathematical operations, such as `sin()`, `round()`, and `pow()`.

- Finally, there are four groups of functions that can be used with colors:

  - Color definition functions
  - Color channel functions
  - Color operations functions
  - Color blending functions

You will also have to note that the example code in this recipe did not meet the DRY principle of software programming. When using guards, as described in the *Building loops leveraging mixins and guards* recipe in *Chapter 6, Advanced Less coding*, you can solve this issue of code repetition. You can rewrite the Less code to the following code, which uses a guard:

```
.shade(@color,@number) when (@number>0) {
.shade(@color,@number - 1);
@darkcolor: darken(@color,(25% * (@number - 1)));
.color@{number} {
  background-color: @darkcolor;
  color: contrast(@darkcolor);
  }
}
.shade(white,5);
```

A complete list of the built-in functions supported by Less can be found at `http://lesscss.org/functions/`.

Using namespaces to make your code reusable and portable

In programming languages, namespace is used to create a different scope for an object of a different origin. It prevents problems with such objects that have the same name. In Less, you can also create and use namespaces. They will help you to make your Less code more portable and reusable.

Getting ready

Open your text editor and create a file named `project.less`. If you don't use the command-line compiler, you will also have to create a valid HTML5 document, including the following lines of code in the `head` section:

```
<link rel="stylesheet/less" type="text/css" href="project.less">
<script src="less.js" type="text/javascript"></script>
```

How to do it...

1. Create two mixins with the same name in the `project.less` file. You can, for instance, use the following code to create two mixins called `mixin`:

```
.mixin(){
  color: red;
}
.mixin(){
  color: blue;
}
el {
  mixin
}
```

2. Now, compile the Less code you wrote in the `project.less` file and you will find that it will compile into the following code:

```
el {
color:red;
color:blue;
}
```

3. After compiling your code, you can use the following Less code to wrap the first mixin in a namespace called `#namespace`, as follows:

```
#namespace {
  .mixin(){
    color: red;
  }
}
.mixin(){
  color: blue;
}
```

4. Now the namespace `mixin`, can be utilized with the following Less code:

```
e1 {
  #namespace > mixin;
}
```

5. Finally, the Less code from the preceding step will compile into the following CSS code:

```
e1 {
  color: red;
}
```

How it works...

The Less compiler doesn't throw an error for mixins with the same (or conflicting) names. The compiler compiles every matching mixin into the CSS code. You can read more about matching mixins in the *Building loops leveraging mixins guards* recipe in *Chapter 6, Advanced Less coding*.

Namespaces prevent conflicting names. In Less, a namespace starts with # and the code for it should be wrapped between accolades. A typical namespace will look as follows:

```
#namespace {  .mixin(){}  }
```

Mixins inside a namespace can be called by adding the namespace before the mixin call, which you can see in the following code:

```
#namespace > mixin;
```

You can also use the following code; it will generate the same result as you have obtained in the preceding code:

```
#namespace mixin;
```

 Note that the > sign in the preceding code is optional. The > sign has the same meaning as in CSS. In CSS, the > sign means a child (must be an immediate child, not any descendant).

2
Debugging and Documenting Your Less Code

In this chapter, we will cover the following topics:

- ▶ Debugging your code with `less.js`
- ▶ Using CSS source maps to debug your code
- ▶ Using Chrome Developer Tools to debug your code
- ▶ Commenting your code in Less
- ▶ Building style guides with `tdcss.js`
- ▶ Building style guides with StyleDocco

Introduction

Less helps you to write better, reusable, and more readable CSS. While writing, you should check your syntax and solve the errors found while compiling your code. In the first recipe, you will learn how to do this. The final CSS code should be tested on different devices and browsers. Automated testing, as required for **test-driven development** (**TDD**), is not possible, but you can test your code in a browser. Although some tools that compare screen dumps have had the spot light recently, for more information, see `https://github.com/BBC-News/wraith` and `https://github.com/facebook/huxley`. In this chapter, you will learn how to find the Less code that generates the style rules for an HTML element in your page. A good code also contains constructive comments that make your code clearer for others. Adding comments to your code is covered in the *Commenting your code in Less* recipe. Finally, you will learn about two tools that can build style guides based on your code. Note that the style guide will show you the visual effect of your code.

Debugging your code with less.js

When compiling your Less code on the client side and running it in your browser, you won't see any syntax or compile errors in the default situation. The `less.js` file doesn't compile your code on errors. As a result, you will find your document with no styles. In this recipe, you will learn how to let `less.js` display errors and understand them.

Getting ready

For this recipe, you need a valid HTML document, a Less file, and the `less.js` compiler file ready.

How to do it...

1. Create the following folder and file structure:

```
├── index.html
├── js
│   └── less.js
└── less
    └── example.less
```

2. Edit the HTML5 file named `index.html` and make it look as follows:

```html
<!DOCTYPE html>
<html>
  <head>
    <meta charset="utf-8">
    <title>Use variables in Less</title>
    <link rel="stylesheet/less" type="text/css"
      href="less/example.less">
    <script type="text/javascript">var less = { env:
      'development' };</script>
    <script src="js/less.js"
      type="text/javascript"></script>
  </head>
  <body>
    <h1>How to display errors</h1>
  </body>
</html>
```

3. Edit your `example.less` file to style the `h1` element in the body, as follows:

```
h1 {
  color:red;
  font-size:3em;
}
```

4. Load the `index.html` file in your browser and find the `h1` colored red.

5. After creating the valid Less code in the `example.less` file, you can make it invalid by removing the last curly bracket. Now, when reloading the `index.html` file in your browser, you will see an error message, as shown in the following screenshot:

ParseError: missing closing `}`

in **example.less** on line 1, column 4:

```
1  h1 {
2  color:red;
```

How to display errors

How it works...

In your `index.html` file, a JavaScript `less` object has been created. This object allows you to set the options for the `less.js` compiler. The `env` option is set to `development` to allow the compiler to display the HTML error messages.

The Less compiler throws errors of different types, namely `ParseError`, `SyntaxError`, `NameError`, and `FileError`, described as follows:

> ▶ `FileError`: These errors are found while importing a file that does not exist. In Less, you can import other Less and CSS files with the `@import` directives.

> ▶ `SyntaxError`: This error occurs, for instance, if you declare a property that is not wrapped inside a selector block. Compiling the following code will throw a SyntaxError:

> ```
> The properties must be inside the selector blocks; they cannot
> be in the root error:
> color:red;
> p {
>    color: green;.
> }
> ```

> The preceding error is triggered by the `color:red;` declaration, which is not wrapped inside any selector block.

> ▶ `ParseError`: These errors can be triggered by the missing { and ; symbols, as seen in the *How to do it...* section of this recipe and other invalid code.

> ▶ `NameError`: These errors refer to the undefined mixins, classes, and variables. Using the following code, without declaring `@darkColor` elsewhere in your Less code, will break your code and the compiler throwing `NameError`. The `@darkColor` variable throws an undefined error:

> ```
> p {
>    color: @darkColor;
> }
> ```

There's more...

Not all possible errors will trigger an error. The compiler checks the syntax for parse errors but does not validate your code. The Less compiler does not check the property names to make sure they are the known CSS properties. Also, assigning the wrong type to a property does not throw any error. So, the following code will compile without throwing an error:

```
p {
  red: color;
  color: 10px;
  width:red;
}
```

Also note that declaring a mixin with the same name twice doesn't trigger an error. In fact, in Less, this is not an error at all. See the *Using namespaces to make your code reusable and portable* recipe in *Chapter 1, Getting to Grips with the Basics of Less*, for more information, as this recipe explains how namespaces can help you prevent the problems with regard to name conflicts of objects. If the compiler finds two or more matching mixins, all of them will be compiled.

Tools, such as CSSlint, described in the *Analyzing your code with CSS Lint* recipe in *Chapter 11, Compiling Less Real Time for Development Using Grunt*, can be used to validate your code for the property and property value typos and mismatches.

Finally, make sure you enable the syntax highlighting feature of the Less code in your editor when you are coding Less. Syntax highlighting with color-coded fonts makes this far more readable and will prevent typos and other syntax errors. If your favorite editor doesn't support Less, try to highlight your code as CSS.

See also

▶ To analyze your compiled CSS, you can also use the online version of CSSlint, which can be found at `http://csslint.net/`.

▶ Also, check the blog post about the syntax highlighting in Less at `http://www.hongkiat.com/blog/less-tips-tools/`. This blog post shows you how to install the Less syntax highlighting feature into Sublime Text 2 and Notepad++.

Using CSS source maps to debug your code

The Less compiler merges the different Less source files into a single CSS file. This file has been minified in most cases. When you are inspecting the source of the CSS files with the developer tools of your browser, you cannot relate the style effects to your original Less code. The CSS source maps solve this problem by mapping the combined/minified file back to its unbuilt state.

Getting ready

Currently, the `less.js` client-side compiler does not support the `SourceMap` option, so you will need the command-line compiler `lessc` to generate CSS source maps. The *Installing the lessc compiler with npm* recipe in *Chapter 1, Getting to Grips with the Basics of Less*, shows you how to use the command-line compiler. Note that this recipe also requires you to use the latest version of Google Chrome or the Mozilla Firefox web browser. The developer tools of both browsers support CSS source maps now.

How to do it...

1. Create the following folder and file structure:

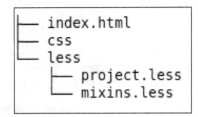

```
├── index.html
├── css
└── less
    ├── project.less
    └── mixins.less
```

2. Then, edit the HTML5 file named `index.html` and make it look as follows:

```html
<!DOCTYPE html>
<html>
  <head>
    <meta charset="utf-8">
    <title>Use CSS Source Maps in Less</title>
    <link rel="stylesheet" type="text/css"
      href="css/project.css">
  </head>
  <body>
    <h1>The style rules for this heading are defined in
      mixins.less</h1>
  </body>
</html>
```

3. Thirdly, edit your `project.less` file to style the `h1` element in the body, as follows:

```less
h1 {
  .heading(2em);
  .shadow();
}
```

4. Then, edit your `mixins.less` file to create the mixins used in the `project.less` file, as follows:

```less
.heading(@font-size:4em)
{
  color:navy;
  font-size: @font-size;
}
.shadow() {
  text-shadow: 2px 2px #ff0000;
}
```

5. Now, compile your CSS by running the following command in the command-line prompt:

```
lessc --source-map less/project.less --source-map-less-inline=true
css/project.css
```

6. Finally, load the `index.html` file in your browser and inspect your code with the browser's **Developer Tools** option (using Google Chrome).

7. After executing the preceding steps, you will find that your CSS style rules are now mapped to their origin source file, as can be seen in the following screenshot:

How it works...

Source maps were introduced to map the minified JavaScript to its source of origin since v3 of the CSS source map protocol also has support for CSS. The Less compiler generates the CSS source map and adds a reference to the CSS file, as follows:

```
/*# sourceMappingURL=project.css.map */
```

The `-source-map-less-inline` option, which is used when compiling the CSS code with the command-line compiler, adds a copy of the Less files to the `project.css.map` source map file.

CSS source maps were originally designed to work exclusively with minified code. You can test this by adding the `-x` option to the `compile` command. Currently, the `-clean-css` option or plugin does not work together with CSS source maps.

There's more...

In Google developer tools, you can click on Less file link in the **Sources** panel to open the source file, as shown in the following screenshot:

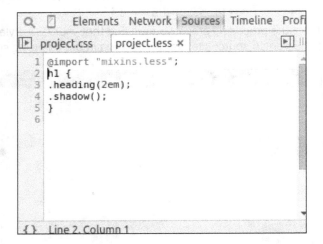

Support for CSS source maps makes Google Chrome also suitable for live editing and the saving of your Less files. In *Chapter 11, Compiling Less Real Time for Development Using Grunt*, you can read how to use Grunt in combination with Google Chrome for live editing your files.

See also

- ▶ Chrome's instruction about working with the CSS preprocessor can be found at `https://developer.chrome.com/devtools/docs/css-preprocessors`. These instructions also include live editing of your Less source files.

- ▶ Version 29 of Mozilla Firefox will add support for CSS source maps. More information on this topic can be found at `https://hacks.mozilla.org/2014/02/live-editing-sass-and-less-in-the-firefox-developer-tools/`.

- ▶ Also, Internet Explorer will follow and add CSS source map support in version 11.

Using Chrome Developer Tools to debug your code

Nowadays, all major browsers have built-in developer tools, which can help you debug and test your code. You can use this tool to see the effect of your style rules or find unused CSS code. Most developer tools also add the performance test tools. The CSS source panel will give you insight into how CSS's precedence rules influence your style rules.

Getting ready

In this recipe, all you need to use is the Google Chrome browser.

How to do it...

1. Create the following folder and file structure:

```
├── index.html
├── js
│   └── less.min.js
└── less
    └── project.less
```

2. Your `index.html` file can, for instance, look as follows:

```
<!DOCTYPE html>
<html>
  <head>
    <meta charset="utf-8">
    <title>Browser Developer Tools</title>
    <link rel="stylesheet/less" type="text/css"
      href="less/project.less">
    <script src="less/less.min.js"
      type="text/javascript"></script>
  </head>
  <body>
    <h1>Less Example</h1>
    <header><h1>an other heading</h1></header>
    <footer id="content-footer"><span>&copy; 2014 Packt
      Publishing</span></footer>
  </body>
</html>
```

3. In the `less/project.less` file, write the following Less code:

```
h1 {
    font-size: 2em;
    color: tomato;
}
header {
  h1 {
    font-size: 1em;
  }
}

#content-footer {
  span {
    font-family:"Times New Roman", Times, serif;
  }
}
```

4. Now, open the `index.html` file in your browser, right-click on the **an other heading** text with your mouse, and click on the **Inspect** element.

In the **Styles** tab of the **Developers Tools** page, you will now find the following:

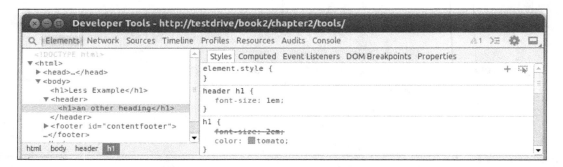

In the **Styles** tab, you can disable the `font-size` property of the `header h1{}` selector by unchecking it. You can also add a `color` property to the `header h1{}` selector and set this property's value to `green`.

As you can see in the preceding screenshot, the **Styles** rules are not linked to the Less file of origin. In the *Writing more intuitive code and making inheritance clear with nested rules* recipe in *Chapter 1, Getting to Grips with the Basics of Less*, you will find out how to map style rules to the source files of their origin.

How it works...

The styles that are applied to a selector are determined by the **cascading, inheritance**, and **precedence** rules, as described at `http://www.w3.org/TR/CSS2/cascade.html`.

In the **Styles** tab of the **Developers Tools** page, you will find the rules that are applied while selecting a selector. Style rules, which are overruled by others, are crossed out. For the `header h1{}` selector, you will find that its `color` property is set by the style rules for `h1` in the `project.less` file, while the `font-size` property is set by the rules for `header h1{}`.

You will also find that you cannot overwrite the `font` face of the `span` tag inside the `footer` tag with a `footer span{}` selector; this is due to the `#contentfooter span {}` selector having a higher precedence.

The browser tools can help make the applying of styles clearer. Nesting of selectors, as described in the *Writing more intuitive code and making inheritance clear with nested rules* recipe in *Chapter 1, Getting to Grips with the Basics of Less*, will also help you meet this rule more intuitively.

There's more...

In the recipe in *Chapter 11, Compiling Less Real Time for Development Using Grunt*, you will learn to remove the unused CSS code automatically. Chrome Developer Tools also have an audit function. In Chrome's **Developer Tools** page, visit the **Audits** tab and run the **Web Page Performance** option. Add, for instance, the following unused code to your `project.less` file:

```
#notinuse {
    color: green;
}
```

Upon adding the preceding code, you will find that 25 percent of your code is unused, as shown in the following screenshot:

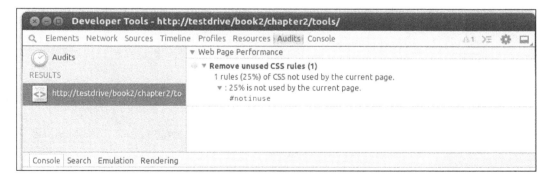

The developer tools of Mozilla Firefox also have an option to validate your CSS. You can validate both the code of the current URL and local CSS files. This option only opens the URL or file into the online CSS validator at `http://jigsaw.w3.org/css-validator/validator`. W3C CSS Validation Service itself is a useful tool to remember.

Google Chrome does not offer any CSS validation, but you can download a plugin from `https://chrome.google.com/webstore/detail/validate-page-css/hmjfaiddfmhjabcagledbpoppaapacnp?hl=en`, which can be used to validate your CSS code.

See also

 ▶ At `http://devtoolsecrets.com/`, you can find a great overview of tips and tricks for the developer tools of major browsers

Commenting your code in Less

Commenting your code will help you and others to better understand the code. If you or someone else have to change your code, maybe after a long period since the code was written, the comments should clarify what a block of code does and why it was added in the first place.

Getting ready

In this recipe, you will need a randomly chosen Less file without a comment. If you don't have such a file, you can create one yourself.

How to do it...

1. Open your Less file.
2. Then, start adding comments.

   Both Less and CSS allow you to use block-level comments that start with /* and end with */. The following code will show you an example of a block-level comment:

   ```
   /*
   * Example code for Less Cookbook
   * copyright 2014 by Bass Jobsen
   */
   ```

   In contrast to CSS, Less allows single-line comments. A single-line comment starts with //, as shown in the following example code:

   ```
   @menuColor: red; //sets the background color for the menu
   ```

Note that you cannot nest two or more block-level comments. Nesting a single-line comment inside a block-level comment is allowed in Less.

How it works...

Good comments are important to write high quality code. Less's code is reusable, but you can't reuse something if you don't know what it does. Try to keep your comments short, clear, and meaningful by using one-liners, if possible.

In most cases, comments should only describe the reason you added some code and not what the code does. Besides adding a comment to your code, it is important to use clear and meaningful names for classes, variables, and mixins. Refer to the following code:

```
//sets the background color of the menu
.mixin45(@a:@defaulta) {
  background-color: @a;
}
```

The preceding code should be replaced with this code:

```
//sets the background color of the menu to give more attention
.menu-backgroundcolor(@background-color:@menubackgroundcolor) {
  background-color: @background-color;
}
```

The Less compiler does not compile the single-line comment into the CSS code. Block-level and single-line comments wrapped inside a block-level comment are preserved and compiled into the final CSS code.

 Block-level comments written between /*! and */ (note the added ! mark) are not removed either by the -x compress or the clean-css option. You can use this type of comment, for instance, to add copyrights at the beginning of your code.

Browsers don't read comments, so the clean-css minifier used by Less removes all the comments from the CSS code. This means the compress option of the compiler removes all the comments, too.

In version 2 of Less, the clean-css option has been moved into a plugin.

There's more...

Although browsers don't read your Less or CSS comments, other tools can read and use them. **StyleDocco** uses the specially formatted comments in your Less code to generate documentation and style guide documents from your Less files automatically. You can read more about StyleDocco in the *Building style guides with StyleDocco* in this chapter and *Compiling style guides with Grunt* recipes in *Chapter 11, Compiling Less Real Time for Development Using Grunt*.

See also

In 2013, Lukas Eder (`https://twitter.com/lukaseder`) wrote a blog entitled *The Golden Rules of Code Documentation*. You can apply most of these rules to your Less code, too. This blog can be found at `http://architects.dzone.com/articles/golden-rules-code`.

Building style guides with tdcss.js

Jakob Løkke Madsen (`https://twitter.com/jakobloekke`) promotes test-driven CSS. Madsen wrote the `tdcss.js` framework, which is a simple style guide tool. The `tdcss.js` framework depends only on jQuery and is especially well-suited to adopt a test-driven approach to CSS styling. You can also use the `tdcss.js` framework to build a regular online style guide. In TDD, tests are written to test the functional blocks of code and match the specification. After this, you can write the code that should meet the test. In test-driven CSS, the style guide is your test. After making changes in your Less code, all the user interface elements in your style guide will look as required.

Getting ready

Download the `tdcss.js` files from `https://github.com/jakobloekke/tdcss.js/archive/master.zip`. Unzip this file in your working directory, which will create a folder named `tdcss.js-master`.

How to do it...

1. Create the following folder and file structure:

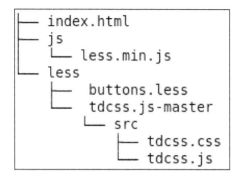

```
├── index.html
├── js
│   └── less.min.js
└── less
    ├── buttons.less
    └── tdcss.js-master
        └── src
            ├── tdcss.css
            └── tdcss.js
```

2. Edit your `less/buttons.less` file to style some buttons:

```less
@stop-color: red;
@wait-color: orange;
@go-color: green;

.btn {
  padding: 0 30px;
  font-size: 2em;

  &.stop {
    background-color: @stop-color;
    color: contrast(@stop-color);
  }

  &.wait {
    background-color: @wait-color;
    color: contrast(@wait-color);
  }

  &.go {
    background-color: @go-color;
    color: contrast(@go-color);
  }
}
```

3. Edit the HTML5 file named `styleguide.html`, and make it look as follows:

```html
<!DOCTYPE html>
<html>
  <head>
    <meta charset="utf-8">
    <title>Style guide</title>
    <link rel="stylesheet/less" type="text/css"
      href="less/buttons.less">
    <script src="js/less.min.js"
      type="text/javascript"></script>
    <!-- TDCSS -->
    <link rel="stylesheet" href="tdcss.js-master/src/tdcss.css"
      type="text/css" media="screen">
    <script type="text/javascript"
      src="https://code.jquery.com/jquery-2.1.1.min.js">
        </script>
    <script type="text/javascript" src="tdcss.js-
      master/src/tdcss.js"></script>
    <script type="text/javascript">
      $(function(){
        $("#tdcss").tdcss();
      })
    </script>
  </head>
  <body>
    <div id="tdcss">

      <!-- # Button styles -->
      <!-- & Collection of buttons. -->
      <!-- : Stop button -->
      <button class="btn stop">Stop</button>
      <!-- : Wait button -->
      <button class="btn wait">Wait</button>
      <!-- : Go button -->
      <button class="btn go">Go</button>

    </div>
  </body>
</html>
```

4. Now, you can load the `styleguide.html` file in your browser.

Finally, you will have a style guide as shown in the following screenshot:

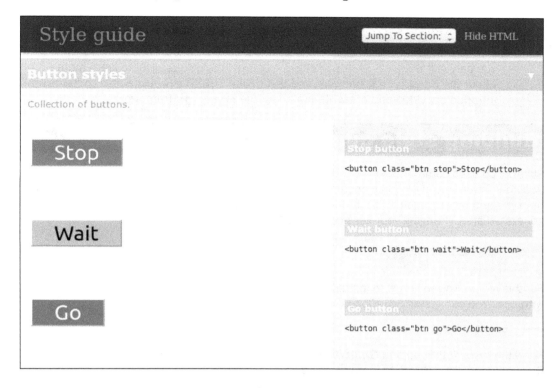

How it works...

Style guides built with the `tdcss.js` framework are not generated automatically.

The `styleguide.html` file contains styled user interface elements. You can group and describe these elements with HTML comments. All user interface elements should be wrapped inside `<div id="tdcss"></div>` tags.

The following HTML comments can then be used to build your style guide:

- To create a section, use the `<!-- # Section name -->` comment style
- Descriptive text can be added everywhere in your document with `<!-- & Descriptive text -->`
- Finally, the HTML code of your elements should be preceded with `<!-- : Element title -->`

The `tdcss.js` framework built the style guide on the basis of the preceding HTML comments.

See also

▶ Read the *Building style guides with StyleDocco* recipe to learn how to generate style guides automatically based on the comments in your Less code.

▶ You can visit `http://jakobloekke.github.io/tdcss.js/` to learn more about the `tdcss.js` framework and test-driven CSS. This website also contains an introductory video and presentation about the `tdcss.js` framework.

Building style guides with StyleDocco

StyleDocco uses comments formatted in **Markdown** in your Less code to generate documentation and style guide documents from your Less files automatically. Style guides can help you and others, such as content developers, to make sure correct styles are used and generated after changing your Less code base.

Getting ready

For this recipe, you will have to install StyleDocco. This requires `Node.js` and can be installed with `npm`. You can install StyleDocco with the following command:

```
npm install styledocco
```

Read the *Installing Node and Grunt* recipe in *Chapter 11, Compiling Less Real Time for Development Using Grunt*, to learn more about `Node.js` and `npm`.

Markdown is a plain text formatting syntax that can be easily converted into HTML. **Stackoverflow** (`http://stackoverflow.com/`), a popular developer forum, uses Markdown for comments and asking questions. Markdown is readable, easy-to-learn, and does not require any special software. If you are not familiar with Markdown, you can learn it in about 10 minutes at `http://markdowntutorial.com/`.

How to do it...

1. Create a single Less file named `less/button.less` and write the following code in it:

```
@stop-color: red;
@wait-color: orange;
@go-color: green;

.btn
{
```

```less
    padding: 0 30px;
    font-size: 2em;

    /* Stop button

      <button class="btn stop">Stop</button>

    */
    &.stop {
      background-color: @stop-color;
      color: contrast(@stop-color);
    }
    /* Wait button

      <button class="btn wait">Wait</button>

    */
    &.wait {
      background-color: @wait-color;
      color: contrast(@wait-color);
    }
    /* Go button

      <button class="btn go">Go</button>

    */
    &.go {
      background-color: @go-color;
      color: contrast(@go-color);
    }
  }
```

2. Now, run the following command in your command-line prompt:

```
styledocco -n "My buttons" -s less/*.less
```

3. Open `docs/index.html` in your web browser and click on the **buttons** tab in the topmost navigation bar.

Finally, you will have a style guide as shown in the following screenshot:

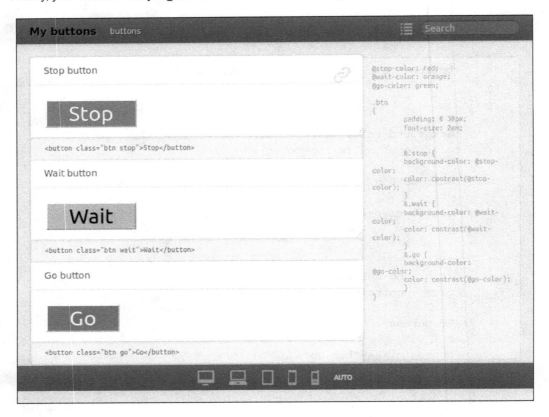

How it works...

StyleDocco reads the filenames of Less files and Markdown comments to generate your style guide automatically in the `docs/` folder. You can use the `-n` option to give your style guide a different name.

Try to avoid indents in your Markdown comments because StyleDocco can interpret them wrong. In Markdown, code is written with indentation or in ``` ``` ``` code ``` ``` ``` blocks.

There's more...

After adding the formatted comments to your Less files, StyleDocco can run automatically, and you can generate a new style guide every time your code is changed. The *Compiling style guides with Grunt* recipe in *Chapter 11, Compiling Less Real Time for Development Using Grunt*, describes how you can integrate StyleDocco in a Grunt development workflow.

See also

- ▸ You can find the complete documentation of StyleDocco at `http://jacobrask.github.io/styledocco/`.

3
Using Variables and Mixins

In this chapter, you will learn about the following:

- ▶ Deriving a set of variables from a single base variable
- ▶ Value escaping with the ~"value" syntax
- ▶ Using variable interpolation
- ▶ Redeclaring variables based on lazy loading
- ▶ Using mixins to set properties
- ▶ Declaring a class and mixin at once
- ▶ Using selectors inside mixins
- ▶ Using parametric mixins

Introduction

Less extends CSS with variables and mixins, which helps you to write reusable code. The recipes in this chapter show you how to use variables and mixins. You will see and learn that meeting the DRY principle of software programming can be accomplished with Less. Variables allow you to set and edit the commonly used values only once, and mixins can be reused to set the properties of more than one CSS style.

In this chapter, you will learn how to use and declare variables in Less. Less uses **lazy loading** for variables, which means they do not have to be declared before being used. Less also uses the **last declaration wins** rule when declaring the same variable more than once in your code. The last declaration wins rule means that the last assigned value will be used at the point of initialization. Both features make it easy to override a variable at the end of your code. In this way, the customization of your code becomes easy. You will also learn how to escape values when assigning variables and how to apply variable interpolation in your Less code.

In addition, you'll be introduced to mixins, which enable you to reuse the mixin properties from the existing styles. These mixins will become more flexible and reusable when parameterized. Parametric mixins accept arguments that can be used to set the properties dynamically based on these arguments.

Deriving a set of variables from a single base variable

In Less, variables can be used to set other variables. This allows you to create sets of variables derived from a single variable. For instance, a variable set can define a color palette or a set of related dimensions. Mathematical operations, as described in the *Creating complex relationships between properties* recipe in *Chapter 1, Getting to Grips with the Basics of Less*, and the Less built-in functions, as described in *Chapter 4, Leveraging the Less Built-in Functions*, can be used to assign the derived variables.

Getting ready

In this recipe, you will change the look of a simple layout by changing one single variable value. You will need a valid HTML5 document that should include the less.js compiler and a Less file called project.less.

How to do it...

1. You will first need to create a simple HTML5 file named index.html, as follows:

```
<!DOCTYPE html>
<html>
  <head>
    <meta charset="utf-8">

    <title>Use variables in Less</title>
```

```
    <link rel="stylesheet/less" type="text/css"
      href="less/project.less">
    <script src="js/less.js"
      type="text/javascript"></script>
  </head>
  <body>
    <header>
      <h1>Page Title</h1>
    </header>
    <nav>
      <ul>
        <li>Menu item 1</li>
        <li>Menu item 2</li>
        <li>Menu item 3</li>
      </ul>
    </nav>
    <article>
      <h1>Article title</h1>
      <p>Article content</p>

    </article>
    <aside>Additional Information</aside>
    <footer>Copyright &copy; 2014 Packt Publishing</footer>
  </body>
</html>
```

2. After creating and editing your layout in the `index.html` file, you can create the Less code to style your layout in the `less/project.less` file, as follows:

```
@base-width:800px;
@base-color: Tomato;
@dark-color: darken(@base-color, 20%);
@light-color: lighten(@base-color, 20%);
@inverse-color: spin(@base-color, 180);

* {
  -webkit-box-sizing: border-box;
  -moz-box-sizing: border-box;
  box-sizing: border-box;
}
*:before,
*:after {
```

```
      -webkit-box-sizing: border-box;
      -moz-box-sizing: border-box;
      box-sizing: border-box;
   }

   header {
      width: @base-width;
      background-color: @base-color;
      h1 {
         color: contrast(@base-color);
      }
   }
```

3. Now, you can load the index.html file in your browser.

4. Change the @base-color to purple, green, or blue. Reload your browser to see the effect of changing the @base-color variable.

The layout from the preceding steps will look as shown in the following screenshot:

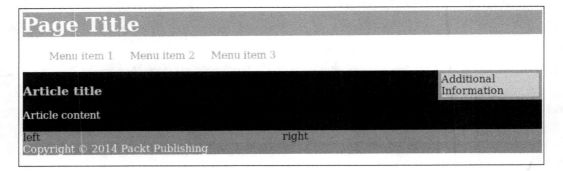

How it works...

The Less code in the project.less file declares two base variables, @base-width and @base-color, respectively. The @base-width variable is used to set the width of the article and the side element with mathematical operations but is not used to derive a new variable.

Note that the Less code starts with resetting the box-sizing model using the Less code that is shown as follows:

```
* {
   -webkit-box-sizing: border-box;
   -moz-box-sizing: border-box;
   box-sizing: border-box;
}
```

```
*:before,
*:after {
  -webkit-box-sizing: border-box;
  -moz-box-sizing: border-box;
  box-sizing: border-box;
}
```

By default, browsers use the content-box box-sizing model. In the content-box model, the widths of the HTML elements do not include the width of borders and padding. The preceding code calculates the percentage-based width complex. For instance, two HTML elements of a 50 percent width with a border of 1 pixel width will get a total width of 2 * 50% + 4 px, which is greater than 100 percent.

The border-box box-sizing model includes borders and padding when calculating the width of an HTML element. This model allows you to add borders and padding without breaking your layout and use percentage-based widths easily.

Most libraries and the CSS frameworks use a mixin to set the `box-sizing` model. The vendor prefix for the `box-sizing` model can also be automated using an `autoprefix` postprocessor.

The second base variable, called `@base-color`, is used to derivate a set of variables, which define the other colors used in this layout.

At the beginning of the Less code, the following color variables are derived from the `@base-color` variable:

```
@dark-color: darken(@base-color, 20%);
@light-color: lighten(@base-color, 20%);
@inverse-color: spin(@base-color, 180);
```

The `darken()`, `lighten()`, and `spin()` functions are built-in functions of Less, which are discussed in more detail in *Chapter 4, Leveraging the Less Built-in Functions*.

Further, in the Less code, you see the `@border-color` variable derived from the `@inverse-color` variable. Since the `@inverse-color` variable was derived from the `@base-color` variable already, changing the `@base-color` variable will also change the `@border-color` variable. Also note that the `border` property finally has been set with the following code:

```
border: ~"5px solid @{border-color}";
```

The preceding line of the Less code uses the string interpolation to replace the value assigned to the `@border-color` variable with the `@{border-color}` placeholder in the string. The `~"value"` syntax reads the values between the quotes as parameters and returns the string without the surrounding quotes, as discussed in the *Value escaping with the ~"value" syntax* recipe, and the `~"value"` syntax.

See also

▶ In this chapter, you will read about variables and mixins. Basically, mixins are used to set property values and are not used to set variables. However, in some situations, you can use a mixin to set a variable because the variables set inside a mixin are only available in the scope of the caller. You can read more about assigning variables with mixins in the *Using mixins as functions* recipe in *Chapter 6, Advanced Less Coding*.

▶ The Bootstrap 1pxdeep theme is an excellent example of defining derivate variables. This theme defines color palettes for Bootstrap 3 based on a single @seed-color variable. You can find a demonstration of this theme at http://rriepe.github. io/1pxdeep/. A WordPress theme based on 1pxdeep can be found at http://wordpress.org/themes/jbst-1pxdeep.

Value escaping with the ~"value" syntax

The ~"value" syntax for value escaping can be used to assign a value to a property that is not recognized by Less. Less only accepts a valid CSS syntax for property values.

Getting ready

For this recipe, you will have to create a gradient.less file and an index.html file, which load the Less file and less.js compiler with the following code in the head section:

```
<link rel="stylesheet/less" type="text/css" href="gradient.less">
<script src="less.js" type="text/javascript"></script>
```

How to do it...

1. Write the following Less code into your gradient.less file:

```
.gradient {
  background-image:linear-gradient(to bottom, red, yellow);
  background-repeat: repeat-x;
  filter: ~"-progid:DXImageTransform.Microsoft.gradient
    (startColorStr='#ffff0000', EndColorStr='#ffffff00')";
}
```

2. Add some header elements to your index.html file, as follows:

```
<header><h1>Page header</h1></header>
<section><header><h2>Article header</h2></header></section>
```

3. Now, apply the gradient to the `header` element written in the preceding step by appending the following Less code to the `gradient.less` file:

```
header {
  color: white;
  .gradient;
}
```

4. Finally, open your `index.html` file in your browser. The final result should look like the following screenshot:

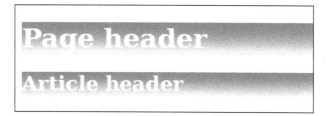

How it works...

Since version 10, MS Internet Explorer only supports standard gradient backgrounds. Earlier versions of IE support the `filter` or `ms-filter` property with a function as the value. A function such as `-progid:DXImageTransform.Microsoft.gradient()`, used as a property value, can't be compiled by Less since the syntax is not valid CSS. The `~"value"` syntax allows you to set your property to any string value without compiler errors. The `~"value"` syntax returns everything between the quotes except for the surrounding quotes themselves. The only exception is variables, which are set to their assigned values first. The latest will be called variable interpolation; you can read more about this in the *Using variable interpolation* recipe. To illustrate the preceding description, consider the following Less code:

```
selector
{
  @variable: "value";
  property1: "value";
  property2: ~"value";
  property3: ~"@{variable}";
}
```

The preceding Less code will compile into the following CSS code:

```
selector {
  property1: "value";
  property2: value;
  property3: value;
}
```

There's more...

The `~"value"` syntax is similar to the `e()` built-in function, except that the `e()` built-in function can also accept another built-in function as an argument. The `e()` function allows you, for instance, to use the following Less code:

```
e(%("ms:somefunction(%$)",lighten(red,10%)));
```

The preceding code will compile into the following CSS code:

```
ms:somefunction(#ff3333);
```

 You can read more about Less's built-in function in *Chapter 4, Leveraging the Less Built-in Functions*.

Also note that this recipe adds the `filter` property to support older versions of IE. To support gradient backgrounds for older versions of other browsers, you will have to add more vendor prefixes to your code. You can create a mixin for this purpose, which, for instance, will look like the following code:

```
.vertical-gradient(@startcolor: red; @endcolor: yellow) {
  background-color: @startcolor; /* fallback color if gradients
    are not supported */
  background-image: -webkit-linear-gradient(top, @startcolor,
    @endcolor); /* For Chrome and Safari */
  background-image: -moz-linear-gradient(top, @startcolor,
    @endcolor); /* For Firefox (3.6 to 15) */
  background-image: -o-linear-gradient(top, @startcolor,
    @endcolor); /* For Opera (11.1 to 12.0) */
  background-image: linear-gradient(to bottom, @startcolor,
    @endcolor; /* Standard syntax */
  filter: e(%("progid:DXImageTransform.Microsoft.gradient
    (startColorstr='%d', endColorstr='%d', GradientType=0)",
      argb(@startcolor),argb(@endcolor))); /* IE9 and down */
}
```

You should note that the preceding `.vertical-gradient()` mixin still does not cover all possible browsers. You should add vendor prefixes to your mixins for the browsers that you will have to support in accordance with your requirements. For gradients, the `-ms-` and older `webkit` prefixes are also available. Since version 2 of Less, you can use the `autoprefix` plugin to add the vendor prefixes automatically. Also, in *Chapter 11, Compiling Less Real time for Development Using Grunt*, you can read how to add vendor prefixes with Grunt. Both postprocessors are based on PostCSS's `autoprefix` plugin. The PostCSS `autoprefix` plugin only adds the prefixes and not the polyfills. When using these autoprefix plugins with the preceding gradient code, the `filter` property that supports the older version of the Internet Explorer browser is not added to your final CSS code. Instead of trying to find the right prefixes for the most antique browsers, you could also consider to use graceful degradation.

Finally, the ~"value" syntax can also be used to set the variable values and selector names. Variable assignment can look similar to @variable: ~"value";. Although it will be possible to use the ~"value" syntax to dynamically construct your selectors, doing this will be depreciated. Alternatively, you can use the selector interpolation to build your selectors dynamically, as discussed in the *There's more...* section of the *Using variable interpolation* recipe.

You cannot use the ~"value" syntax to write properties and values. The ~"color: red"; code will additionally throw an error. Also, it is not possible to use the ~"value" syntax with operations. So, for instance, ~"2" + 2; will throw an error, too, since the syntax returns a string.

See also

> ▶ Even when using Less, the support gradients for the older browser will soon become complex. An online tool found at http://www.colorzilla.com/gradient-editor/ can help you find and understand the right vendor prefixes. You can build your mixins using the code examples from the online gradient editor.

> ▶ Many mixin libraries that are discussed in *Chapter 5, Extending and Referencing,* also provide you with the mixins to declare background gradients.

> ▶ Finally, the Less code of Bootstrap, as discussed in *Chapter 9, Using Twitter Bootstrap with Less,* contains a set of namespaced gradient mixins, too.

Using variable interpolation

People who program in PHP, Perl, or Ruby will already be familiar with variable interpolation. Variable interpolation is the use of variables in strings where the compiler replaces the variable with the value that has been assigned to it.

Getting ready

For this recipe, you will have to create an example.less file. To see what happens, you can compile this file on the client side or server side. For server-side compiling, you should have the lessc compiler installed, as described in the *Installing the lessc compiler with npm* recipe in *Chapter 1, Getting to Grips with the Basics of Less.* For client-side compiling, you will have to create an index.html file, which loads the Less file and the less.js compiler with the following code in the head section:

```
<link rel="stylesheet/less" type="text/css"
  href="less/example.less">
<script src="less.js" type="text/javascript"></script>
```

When you inspect the results in your browser, you will also need an example.png background image.

How to do it...

1. Write the following Less code into the `example.less` file:

    ```less
    @thickness: "thick";
    @position: top;
    @path: "../images";

    .selector {
      border-@{position}: ~"@{thickness} double red";
      background: url("@{path}/example.png");
    }
    ```

2. Compile the `example.less` file into the CSS code using the following command:

    ```
    lessc example.less
    ```

    Alternatively, load the `index.html` file in your browser for client-site compiling.

    In both cases, you will find that the Less code will be compiled into the following CSS code:

    ```css
    .selector {
      border-top: thick double red;
      background: url("../images/example.png");
    }
    ```

How it works...

With variable interpolation, variables inside the string, which are the subject of interpolation, are written with accolades around their name. So, for instance, the variable will be written as `@{variable}`. The string itself is written between double or single quotes. Less compiles the string in Less into the string in CSS, which also means that the resulting CSS code is outputted with surrounding quotes, too. The `~"value"` syntax, as described in the *Value escaping with the ~"value" syntax* recipe, can be used to remove these surrounding quotes.

Variable interpolation can not only be applied on variable values, but also on selector names, property names, URLs, and `@import` statements. Variable interpolation to dynamically create selector names, also called selector interpolation, will be discussed in the *There's more...* section.

Note that the interpolation automatically removes the surrounding quotes of the interpolated variable itself. This means that `url("@{path}/example.png");` does not compile into `url(""../images""/example.png");`.

There's more...

Currently, Less only allows you to use variable interpolation in the import directives when the variable has been defined in the root or current scope. For this reason, the following code will work well:

```
@path: "../../less/";"
@import "@{path}code.less";
```

With the `@path: "../../less/";` Less code declared in the `variables.less` file, the following code won't compile and will result in a `NameError` variable. The `@{path}` error is an undefined error. This can be seen when compiling the Less code, as follows:

```
@import "variables.less";
@import "@{path}code.less";
```

As mentioned in the *How it works...* section, selectors can be built with interpolation. Consider the following Less code, for instance:

```
@class: ~".myclass";
@{class} {
  @color: white;
}
```

The preceding code will be compile into the following CSS code, as follows:

```
.myclass {
  color: white;
}
```

Alternatively, the preceding code can be written with the `~"value"` syntax, as follows:

```
@class: ".myclass";
~"@class" { }
```

The last way of the selector interpolation has been depreciated.

See also

▶ In the *Building loops, leveraging mixin guards* recipe in *Chapter 6, Advanced Less Coding*, you will find an example of dynamically generating style rules based on string interpolation and guards

Redeclaring variables based on lazy loading

When working with variables in Less, you have to realize that the last declaration wins and that Less uses lazy loading. The theoretical aspect of lazy loading is that the variables are initialized at the point at which they are used. Coding Less means you can use variables before you declare them. You can declare these variables later. When you declare a variable with the same name twice, the last declared value will be used everywhere in your code.

Getting ready

For this recipe, you will have to create an `example.less` and `index.html` file, which load the Less file and `less.js` compiler with the following code in the `head` section:

```
<link rel="stylesheet/less" type="text/css" href="example.less">
<script src="less.js" type="text/javascript"></script>
```

How to do it...

The easiest way to understand both the last declaration wins rule and lazy loading is to perform the following steps:

1. Write the following code into the `example.less` file:

```
@color: red;
p {
  color: @color;
}
@color: green;
@color: blue;
```

2. After creating your Less file, add a `p` HTML element containing some text to the `index.html` file, as follows:

```
<p>Colored text</p>
```

3. After creating both the files in the preceding steps, load `index.html` in your browser. Now, you will find your text is colored blue. In your browser, it will look like what is shown in the following screenshot:

Colored text

4. Remove the `@color: blue;` line in the `example.less` file and you will find your text is green after you reload your browser.

5. Finally, remove the `@color: red;` line in the `example.less` file and you will also find the text is colored green after reloading.

How it works...

If you declare a variable more than once in the same scope, all the variables will use the last set of values due to the last declaration wins rule. Consider the following example code:

```
@color: red;
p {
  color: @color;
}
@color: blue;
```

The preceding Less code will be compiled into the following CSS code:

```
p {
  color: blue;
}
```

Lazy loading means that in the Less code, you can use a variable before it has been declared. The following code will give you an example of lazy loading:

```
p {
  color: @color;
}
@color: blue;
```

The preceding Less code will be compiled into the following CSS code:

```
p {
  color: blue;
}
```

There's more...

In the preceding *How it works...* section, you read that the last declaration wins rule will be applied only for variables in the same scope. This means that the variable declaration in Less is not global. Mixins and classes in Less have their own scope. Please try the operation we are performing with the following code:

```
:
.mixin-with-its-own-scope() {
  color: @color;
  @color: red;
}
p {
  .mixin-with-its-own-scope;
}
@color: yellow;
```

You will find that the preceding Less code will compile into the following CSS code:

```
p {
  color: #ff0000;
}
```

Note that the `#ff0000;` value equals the hexadecimal representation of the red color. Since version 2 of Less, colors are no longer compiled into their hexadecimal representation. In the preceding code, `@color: red;` is declared inside the scope of the `.mixin-with-its-own-scope()` mixin. Within the scope of mixins, the last declaration wins and lazy loading rules are applied.

As you have seen, you can easily override a variable in Less by putting the definition after it. For this reason, you don't have to define the default variables in Less. The default variables assign a value for the variables that are not already set. Also note that using a variable which has not been set will result in a `NameError` error.

Both last declaration wins and lazy loading play an important role in Less. Every variable can be declared again at the end of the code and can affect the preceding code. Redeclaration of variables makes customization of frameworks, such as Bootstrap 3, possible in the first place and easy in the second place.

See also

> ► In *Chapter 9, Using Twitter Bootstrap with Less*, you can read more about the customization of Bootstrap 3 with Less

Using mixins to set properties

In Less, mixins can be used to set the properties of a CSS style. The same mixin can be used to set more than one CSS style. On the official Less site, they call this **mix-in properties from existing styles**. Looking at mixins this way will make mixins nothing else than just a common style. In contrast to normal styles, mixins are not compiled in the final CSS.

Getting ready

1. For this recipe, you will have to create a `project.less` file and an `index.html` file, which load the Less file and `less.js` compiler with the following code in the `head` section:

```
<link rel="stylesheet/less" type="text/css"
  href="less/project.less">
<script src="less.js" type="text/javascript"></script>
```

2. Although not required, it is a good practice to define your mixins in a separate file. For this reason, create a file named `mixins.less`. This file should be imported in your `project.less` file with the following code:

    ```
    @import "less/mixins.less";
    ```

3. Finally, you should end up with the following folder and file structure:

    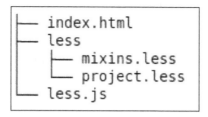

    ```
    ├── index.html
    ├── less
    │   ├── mixins.less
    │   └── project.less
    └── less.js
    ```

How to do it...

In this recipe, you will rotate an HTML element by performing the following steps:

1. First, create a mixin to rotate the HTML elements with the following code in the `mixins.less` file:

    ```
    .rotate(@degrees: 180deg) {
      -webkit-transform: rotate(@degrees);
      -moz-transform: rotate(@degrees);
      -ms-transform: rotate(@degrees);
      -o-transform: rotate(@degrees);
      transform: rotate(@degrees);
    }
    ```

2. Now, add some HTML code to your `index.html` file and include the following HTML code:

    ```
    <div class="upsidedown">Text upsidedow</div>
    ```

3. Finally, your `project.less` file should look as follows:

    ```
    @import "less/mixins.less";
    .upsidedown {
      .rotate;
    }
    ```

4. After creating the files from the preceding step, you can load the `index.html` file in your browser.

How it works...

In the preceding Less code, the call to the `.rotate` mixin inside the `.upsidedown` class copied or "mixined" the properties from the `.rotate` mixin into the `.upsidedown` class. You can see this in the following Less code:

```
.upsidedown {
  .rotate;
}
```

The preceding code will be compiled into the following CSS code:

```
.upsidedown {
  -webkit-transform: rotate(180deg);
  -ms-transform: rotate(180deg);
  transform: rotate(180deg);
}
```

The `.rotate` mixin itself is not compiled into the CSS code. Notice that the parentheses after the mixin's name in the `mixins.less` file are not required in this situation. However, when you leave out the parentheses, the mixins will be compiled into the CSS as any normal class would.

After creating a mixin, you can reuse and apply it on any CSS selector in your Less code. You can apply the `.rotate` mixin instance on the `body` element or on every `div` element, as in the following Less code:

```
body {
  background-color: red;
  .rotate;
}
div {
  .rotate;
}
```

There's more...

In this recipe, the `.rotate` mixin has been used to set the so-called vendor prefixes. An example of such a vendor prefix is the `-webkit-transform` property. Vendor-specific rules or prefixes were introduced in CSS3. These rules allow browsers to implement the proprietary CSS properties that would otherwise have no working standard (and may never actually become the standard). The vendor prefixes are for any CSS rule that has not yet been standardized as a part of the web standard process. The use of vendor prefixes will make your CSS code more complex. As you have seen, setting the vendor prefixes with the mixins enable you to define these rules only once. Changing and maintaining your code will be a lot easier now.

Some libraries with prebuilt mixins, as discussed in *Chapter 4, Leveraging the Less Built-in Functions*, offer you single-line declarations for the properties that require vendor prefixes. In the *Automatically prefix your code with Grunt* recipe in *Chapter 11, Compiling Less Real Time for Development Using Grunt*, you can read how to append the vendor prefixes automatically to your code. Since version 2 of Less, you can also use the Less autoprefix plugin.

You can consult the `Can I use` database to find out which vendor prefixes you should use for a CSS3 property. This database provides the compatibility tables for the support of HTML5, CSS3, and SVG.

See also

▶ The `Can I use` database can be found at `http://caniuse.com/`
▶ The Less autoprefix plugin can be found at `https://github.com/less/less-plugin-autoprefix`

Declaring a class and mixin at once

Mixins are not compiled into the final CSS code. In some situations, it will be useful to define a class with the same name and properties as the mixin. In this recipe, a `clearfix` mixin is used as an example.

Getting ready

For this recipe, you will have to create the `clearfix.less` and `index.html` files, which load the Less file and `less.js` compiler with the following code in the `head` section:

```
<link rel="stylesheet/less" type="text/css" href="clearfix.less">
<script src="less.js" type="text/javascript"></script>
```

How to do it...

1. Open the `index.html` file with your favorite text editor and write the following HTML structure into it:

```
<div class="row">
  <div class="column">C1</div>
  <div class="column">C2</div>
</div>
<div>positioned under the row</div>
<br>
<div class="clearfix">
  <div class="column">C1</div>
  <div class="column">C2</div>
```

```
</div>
<div>positioned under the row</div>
```

2. Now, open the `clearfix.less` file and add the following code to make what you are doing visible:

```
div {
  border: 1px dashed red;
  padding:10px;
}
```

3. Let your `div.column` elements float with the following Less code in the `clearfix.less` file:

```
.column {
  width:200px;
  float:left;
}
```

4. Open the `index.html` file in your browser. See that in the default situation, the float is not cleared and the **positioned under the row** text is not underneath the columns, but on the right-hand side of the columns. In your browser, it will look like what is shown in the following screenshot:

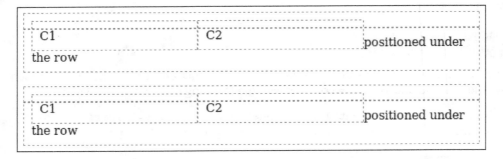

5. Add the `.clearfix` mixin to the `clearfix.less` file using the following code:

```
.clearfix() {
  &:before,
  &:after {
    content: " ";
    display: table;
  }
  &:after {
    clear: both;
  }
}
```

6. Finally, mix the `clearfix` properties into the `row` class with the following Less code in the `clearfix.less` file:

```
.row {
  .clearfix;
}
```

Then, create a `.clearfix` class in your CSS code, leveraging the Less code as follows:

```
.clearfix {
  .clearfix();
}
```

7. Inspect the result of your coding by opening the `index.html` file in your browser. You will find your page looking like what is shown in the following screenshot:

C1	C2

positioned under the row

C1	C2

positioned under the row

How it works...

A `clearfix` method is a way for HTML elements to automatically clear themselves without additional markup. The `clearfix` properties are frequently used in layouts with floated elements. In this recipe, **micro clearfix hack** by Nicolas Gallagher is used; more information can be found at `http://nicolasgallagher.com/micro-clearfix-hack/`. The same `clearfix` method is used by Bootstrap.

As you can see, the preceding code enables you to use the `clearfix` code in two different ways. Firstly, the `.clearfix` code is used as a mixin in Less to clearfix every element with the `.row` class. Secondly, a `.clearfix` class is compiled into the CSS code, which enables you to add a `class="clearfix"` attribute to your HTML elements.

There's more...

The method described in this recipe is mostly used to keep the organization of a Less code base's file structure clear and clean. Mixins can be grouped in a file or namespace; such a group should only contain mixins that are not compiled into the CSS. Grouped mixins are portable and can be easily reused for different projects. For the project itself, it will be useful to have the ability to use the class in your HTML code and compiled in your CSS code. The compiled Less code of this recipe allows you to use, for instance, the following HTML code:

```
<div class="clearfix"></div>
```

Other than keeping your files well-organized, there is a reason why you need to declare the .clearfix class without parentheses, which can be mixed in and will provide an output, too.

Bootstrap 3 uses the same strategy (and the clearfix mixin) as used in this recipe. Bootstrap developers can use the .clearfix class in their Bootstrap templates. On the other hand, when using Bootstrap as a mixin library, the .clearfix() mixin will be available. You can read more about Bootstrap and Less in *Chapter 9, Using Twitter Bootstrap with Less*.

See also

- ▶ At http://css-tricks.com/snippets/css/clear-fix/, you can read how the way to implement the clearfix hack has evolved over time

Using selectors inside mixins

Mixins in Less can not only contain properties, but also selectors. This recipe will show you how to leverage selectors inside mixins.

Getting ready

For this recipe, you will have to create a coloredlinks.less file and an index.html file, which load the Less file and less.js compiler with the following code in the head section:

```
<link rel="stylesheet/less" type="text/css"
  href="coloredlinks.less">
<script src="less.js" type="text/javascript"></script>
```

How to do it...

In this recipe, you will create a mixin that gives a color and appends an icon or symbol to your hyperlinks by performing the following steps:

1. Start this recipe by adding the `.colored-links` mixin to the `coloredlinks.less` file, as follows:

```
.colored-links() {
  a {
    color:green;
    &::after {
      content: "\2764";
    }
  }
}
```

2. Now, add the following HTML code to the `index.html` file:

```
<header>the header</header>
<section>
<p>this is a paragraph<br><a href="">Link 1</a> <a
  href="">Link 1</a></p></section>
<footer>
  <a href="">Link 1</a> <a href="">Link 1</a>
</footer>
```

3. After editing the `coloredlinks.less` and `index.html` files, you can add the CSS selector, which styles the hyperlinks in the `footer` element, to the Less code in the `coloredlinks.less` files, as follows:

```
footer {
.colored-links;
}
```

4. Finally, open the `index.html` file in your browser and you will find that the hyperlinks in the `footer` element have a green color and the ♥ symbol appended. The following screenshot shows how the page should look:

the header

this is a paragraph
Link 1 Link 1

♥Link 1♥ Link 1♥

How it works...

The following Less code creates the CSS code that appends some content after a hyperlink automatically:

```
footer {
  .colored-links;
}
```

The preceding Less code will compile into CSS, as follows:

```
footer a {
  color: green;
}
footer a::after {
  content: "\2764";
}
```

As you can see, the `.colored-links` mixin mixes all its content, including selectors, into the `footer` selector.

The `&` sign before the `::after` pseudo class is a reference to the parent selector (in this case, the `a` selector). You can read more about referencing the parent selector in the *Referencing parent selectors with the & operator* recipe in *Chapter 5, Extending and Referencing*.

There's more...

While working on this recipe, you have likely realized that the possibilities of mixins are nearly endless. Code can be reused in different projects and to copy a mixin to another project. Also, styling your links the same way will be easy now. Namespaced mixins, as discussed in the *Using namespaces to make your code reusable and portable* recipe in *Chapter 1, Getting to Grips with the Basics of Less*, will make your code more portable.

Also note that you can't always overwrite the other styles defined in your project. The Less code compiles into normal CSS code. Your CSS code will follow all specificity, inheritance, and cascade rules. The `.coloredlinks` mixin won't work if other rules with a higher specificity are applied on the `footer` element, too. A `body footer a {}` selector defined elsewhere in your project will overrule the styles set by the `footer` selector in this recipe. Also, in case your footer has, for instance, an `id` attribute such as `id="site-footer"`, all style rules for the `#site-footer a` selector will have a higher precedence. Less does not influence the CSS rules for specificity, inheritance, and cascades.

The *Building style guides with tdcss.js* and *Building style guides with StyleDocco* recipes in *Chapter 2, Debugging and Documenting Your Less Code*, will give you another use case of using selectors inside mixins. In this recipe, mixins are used containing the `&.selector` selectors inside them. The `&.selector` selectors select the parent selector with the `.selector` class.

See also

> ► You can read more about referencing the parent selector in the *Referencing parent selectors with the & operator* recipe in *Chapter 5, Extending and Referencing*

Using parametric mixins

Mixins can be used with parameters, which make them more flexible and reusable.

Getting ready

For this recipe, you will have to create the following file and folder structure:

```
├── index.html
├── less
│   └── project.less
└── less.js
```

You can edit these files with your favorite text editor and inspect the results with your web browser.

How to do it...

In this recipe, you will leverage a simple mixin to set the border radius of the HTML elements by performing the following steps:

1. You first need to create a valid HTML5 document named `index.html` with the following elements:

```
<header>the header</header>
<p>this is a paragraph</p>
<footer>the footer</footer>
```

Make sure the `head` section of your `index.html` file also contains the following code:

```
<link rel="stylesheet/less" type="text/css"
  href="project.less">
<script src="less.js" type="text/javascript"></script>
```

2. Open the `project.less` file with your text editor and write the following mixins into it:

```
.rounded-corners(@radius) {
  border-radius: @radius;
  border: 3px solid red;
  background-color: navy;
   padding:10px;
  color: white;
}
```

3. Finally, add the following Less code into the `project.less` file to give your HTML elements rounded corners with different radii:

```
header {
  .rounded-corners(10px);
}
p {
  .rounded-corners(20px);
}
footer {
  .rounded-corners(30px);
}
```

4. Open the `index.html` file in your browser and you will see the result shown in the following screenshot:

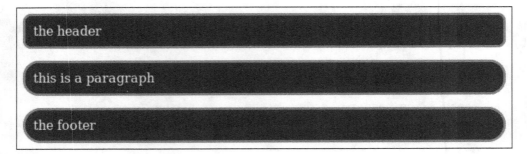

How it works...

The `@radius` parameter accepts the value and makes it available for the local scope of the `.rounded-corners` mixin. The preceding steps enable you to use the `@radius` variable, which contains the values assigned by the caller, inside the mixins. A user who is familiar with the programming functions will find that mixins act in a way similar to the functions in programming languages.

Your code can call the same mixins more than once, and parameters make them flexible. Depending on the input parameter, the output will differ, and finally, set different values for your properties.

There's more...

The mixin in this recipe accepts only one parameter, but mixins in Less can accept more than one, or better theoretically, an endless number of parameters. You can read more about this in the *Using mixins with multiple and named variables* recipe in *Chapter 6, Advanced Less Coding*.

Nearly all the major browsers support the `border-radius` property, which is part of the CSS3 specification. MS Internet Explorer Version 8 and below does not support this `border-radius` property. The **progressive internet explorer** (**PIE**) project makes IE 6-8 capable of rendering several of the most useful CSS3 decoration features, including the `border-radius` feature. More information about the PIE project can be found at `http://css3pie.com/`. Alternatively, popular projects such as Twitter's Bootstrap simply don't support the `border-radius` property for the older versions of IE. The strategy to skip some advanced functionalities for the older browser is called graceful degradation. Graceful degradation may not break the basic functionalities of your website or application. To find out which browsers support a CSS property, you can seek the counsel of the `Can I use` database.

See also

▶ The `Can I use` database can be found at `http://caniuse.com/`

▶ More information about Bootstrap's support for older browsers can be found at `http://getbootstrap.com/getting-started/#support`

▶ More information about graceful degradation versus progressive enhancement can be found at `http://www.w3.org/wiki/Graceful_degredation_versus_progressive_enhancement`

4

Leveraging the Less Built-in Functions

In this chapter, you will learn the following topics:

- ► Converting units with the `convert()` function
- ► Using the `default()` function
- ► Embedding images with data URIs
- ► Formatting strings
- ► Replacing a text within a string
- ► Working with lists
- ► Using mathematical functions
- ► Using the `color()` function
- ► Evaluating the type of a value
- ► Creating color objects with RGB values
- ► Getting information about a color
- ► Creating a color variant with the `darken()` and `lighten()` functions
- ► Creating overlays of two colors with Less

Introduction

In this chapter, you will learn how to use the Less built-in functions. Less provides you many built-in functions, which enable you to perform instant mathematical and color operations to set your CSS property's values. From the *Using the built-in functions of Less* recipe in *Chapter 1, Getting to Grips with the Basics of Less*, you can learn that the built-in functions are grouped based on their return (and input) type. The Less built-in functions work just like the functions in function programming. The built-in functions return a computed value to its caller based on the function arguments set by the caller.

Converting units with the convert() function

This recipe will show you how to work with units in Less. Less allows you to work with values and units as defined in CSS3.

Getting ready

For this recipe, you will need a text editor and a Less compiler. In *Chapter 1, Getting to Grips with the Basics of Less*, we learned how to use and install the `less.js` client-side or command-line `lessc` compiler. We will need those skills for this recipe.

How to do it...

1. Use a Less compiler to compile the following Less code into the CSS code:

```
.distance {
  centimeters: convert(10mm,cm);
  inches: convert(10mm,in);
  pixels: convert(10mm,px);
  points: convert(10mm,pt);
  picas: convert(10mm,pc);
}
```

2. You will find that the Less code compiles into the CSS code, as follows:

```
.distance{
  centimeters: 1cm;
  inches: 0.39370079in;
  pixels: 37.79527559px;
  points: 28.34645669pt;
  picas: 2.36220472pc;
}
```

How it works...

As can be seen in the *Creating complex relationships between properties* recipe in *Chapter 1, Getting to Grips with the Basics of Less*, the Less compiler understands colors and units. The built-in `convert()` function makes it possible to covert units of the same type. You can't only convert different units for distance; CSS also defines units for time, frequency, angles, and resolution.

For instance, angle can be defined in the `deg`, `grad`, `rad`, and `turn` units, which can be seen while compiling the following Less code:

```
.angles {
  gradians: convert(180deg, grad);
  radians: convert(180deg, rad);
  turns: convert(180deg, turn);
}
```

The preceding Less code will compile into the following CSS code:

```
.angles {
  gradians: 200grad;
  radians: 3.14159265rad;
  turns: 0.5turn;
}
```

Note that a full circle contains 360 degrees, 200 gradians, 1 turn, and 2 pi radians.

There's more...

The built-in `convert()` function does not work with font-relative lengths (the `em`, `ex`, `ch`, and `rem` units). Also, converting units of different types is not possible. For this reason, the `convert(10mm,grad);` Less code will compile into the `10mm` CSS code.

Less only accepts units defined in CSS3. The `convert(3600s,h)` code won't compile into `1h` but remains `3600s`. This is because CSS3 only defines milliseconds (`ms`) and seconds (`s`), and time, minutes, and hours are not defined.

See also

▶ A complete overview of units of distances, degrees, and time can be found at http://www.w3.org/TR/css3-values/

Using the default() function

The built-in `default()` function plays a special role when leveraging mixins, especially mixin guards.

Getting ready

For this recipe, you will have to know something about parameterized mixins. You also need to be aware of what guards are and how to use them. You can find both in the *Using mixin guards* recipe in *Chapter 6, Advanced Less Coding*. You will also need a Less compiler, as discussed in *Chapter 1, Getting to Grips with the Basics of Less*.

How to do it...

1. Use the command-line `lessc` compiler to compile the following Less code:

```less
.mixin(1) {
  property: 1 * 2;
}
.mixin(2) {
  property: 2 * 3;
}
.mixin(@a) when (default()) {
  property: @a;
}
one {
  .mixin(1);
}
five {
  .mixin(5);
}
```

2. The preceding Less code compiles into CSS, which looks like the following code:

```css
one {
  property: 2;
}
five {
  property: 5;
}
```

How it works...

The `default()` function returns `true` for the situation if no other mixin matches. Note that the `default()` function can only be used in the parametric mixin guards. Also, as mentioned in the *Using namespaces to make your code reusable and portable* recipe in *Chapter 1, Getting to Grips with the Basics of Less*, the Less compiler compiles all the matching mixins and does not throw an error when no matching mixins are found.

There's more...

The `default()` function can also be used with logical guard operations. The following Less code will show you how to use the `default()` function together with the `not` keyword:

```
.mixin(@value) when not(default())
```

The `.mixin()` mixin in the preceding code will only be compiled into the CSS code when at least one other `.mixin()` mixin matches. A use case of using the `default()` function with the `not` keyword can be found when evaluating the following Less code:

```
.mixin(@value) when (iscolor(@value)){
  background-color: @value;
}
.mixin(@value) when not(default()) {
  color: contrast(@value);
}
```

With the preceding mixins, the `test {mixin(black);}` code will compile into the following CSS code:

```
test {
  background-color: #000000;
  color: #ffffff;
}
```

For instance, the `test {.mixin(5);}` code does not compile anything into the CSS code.

Multiple usages of the `default()` function for the same mixins are allowed. However, when these calls conflict with each other, an `Ambiguous use of `default()` found` error will be thrown by the compiler.

The following code will show you a valid usage of the multiple `default()` function:

```
.mixin(red){color:darkred;}
.mixin(@a) when (iscolor(@a)) and (default()) {color: @a}
.mixin(@a) when not (iscolor(@a)) and (default()) { display: none;
  }
```

See also

The deployment of the code in this recipe also leverages other built-in functions. More information about the `contrast()` function can be found in the *Creating a color variant with the darken() and lighten() functions* recipe. The `iscolor()` function is a built-in function grouped in the `type` functions. The `type` functions return `true` when their input value meets the `type` function. This is explained in more detail in the *Evaluating the type of a value* recipe.

Embedding images with data URIs

In this recipe, you will set the background images for HTML elements with data URIs. Data URIs don't link to images, creating extra HTTP requests, but write down their content into the CSS file.

Getting ready

For this recipe, you can use the command-line `lessc` or the client-side `less.js` compiler, as described in *Chapter 1, Getting to Grips with the Basics of Less*. You will also need a Less file, which can be edited with your favorite text editor. Finally, you will need an example image, for instance, a PNG file named `image.png`.

How to do it

1. Create a `project.less` file in the same directory as your `image.png` file and write the following Less code into it:

   ```
   div {
   background-image: data-uri('image.png');
   }
   ```

2. Now compile the Less code into CSS code using the following command:

   ```
   lessc project.less
   ```

3. Finally, you will find the compiled CSS will look like the following code:

   ```
   div {
     background-image:
       url("data:image/png;base64,iVBORw0KGgoAAAANSUh=");
   }
   ```

How it works...

The background-image CSS property should be set to a URI. The function notation for an URI is `url()`. Note that the URI not only contains URL, but also data URIs. The data URI is inline the content of the file into the CSS code. The `data-uri()` function can be called with an optional MIME-type string, such as `image/png;base64`, followed by the URL of the file to inline. Note that the `base64` part of this string sets the encoding type of the inlined content of the files. Setting the encoding type is not required. The inline code that is not encoded by `base64` should be the URL encode. In Less, you can use the `escape()` function for URL encoding.

Sder browsers don't support data URIs. Internet Explorer supports data URIs since Version 8. In this version of Internet Explorer, the data URI may not contain more than 32,768 bytes. The `IEcompat` option in Less enables you to use the `data-uri()` function for IE8 too. When the data exceeds the limit, 32,768 bytes, the compiler falls back to the `url()` syntax to link the image.

The Less compiler neither validates the MIME type string, nor checks whether the URL content matches the set MIME type. However, if the URL does not exist, it throws a `RuntimeError: error evaluating function `data-uri`: ENOENT, no such file or directory` error. If no MIME type string has been set, the file extension of the URL will be used to determine the MIME type.

There's more...

For small images, using data URIs seems a good or better alternative for image sprites, as described in the *Leveraging sprite images with Pre* recipe in *Chapter 7, Leveraging Libraries with Prebuilt Mixins*. The preceding recipe should be read with care because of the investigation reported that on some mobile views, a data URI is on average six times slower than using a binary source. Other situations can be solved using an icon font, such as **Font Awesome**. Font Awesome can be found at `http://fortawesome.github.io/Font-Awesome/`.

Background images with the data URI should only be used for images, which are a part of the outcome. Technically, there is no reason not to define all the images of your website as an inline image with a data URI. However, for accessibility proposals, functional and semantically important images should always be provided with the `img` tags in the document markup because screen readers will ignore the background images. Also, some devices running in a high contrast mode and many printers will disable the background images. For this reason, you should also set an alternative background color for situations when the image is unavailable.

You might have noticed that the number of bytes of the base 64-encoded URI is mostly larger than the number of bytes of the original image. Base 64-encoded data can be compressed very well. So, when using the HTTP compression for your website, the side effect of the larger number of bytes can be eliminated.

See also

▶ More information on the usage of URIs in CSS can be found at
`http://www.w3.org/TR/CSS21/syndata.html#value-def-uri`.

▶ Some background information about the usage of the HTTP compression with
`gzip` or `deflate` for your website can be found at `http://css-tricks.com/`
`snippets/htaccess/active-gzip-compression/`. For Apache, you can enable
the compression via `.htaccess`. The IIS users should use the `web.config` file.

▶ More information about the load time of data URIs by Peter McLachlan can be found
at `http://www.mobify.com/blog/data-uris-are-slow-on-mobile/`.

Formatting strings

With the `%()` function, you can format strings in Less. This function is very similar to the
`printf` function found in other programming languages.

Getting ready

For this recipe, you will only need a Less compiler. You can use the command line `lessc` or
the client-side `less.js` compiler and inspect the results in your browser. We have covered
the installation part of these compilers in *Chapter 1, Getting to Grips with the Basics of Less*.

How to do it...

1. To find out how to use the `%()` function, you can compile the following Less code
   and inspect the compiled CSS code:

```
formattedstrings {
    quotesincluded: %("Open the %a file","../less.txt");
    quotesincludedescaped: %("Open the %A file","../less.txt");
    quotesremoved: %("Open the %s file","../less.txt");
    quotesremovedescaped: %("Open the %S file","../less.txt");
}
```

2. After compiling the preceding Less code, your compiled CSS code will look like
   the following:

```
formattedstrings {
    quotesincluded: "Open the "../less.txt" file";
    quotesincludedescaped: "Open the %22..%2Fless.txt%22 file";
    quotesremoved: "Open the ../less.txt file";
    quotesremovedescaped: "Open the ..%2Fless.txt file";
}
```

How it works...

The `%()` function should be called with a string containing one or more placeholders followed by the remaining arguments, containing expressions to replace the placeholders. Placeholders start with a `%` sign and should have one of the following syntaxes: `%a`, `%A`, `%d`, `%D`, `%s`, or `%S`. A placeholder can contain any kind of argument, such as string, numbers, colors, and the escaped values. Currently, there is no difference between the interpretation or usage of `%a` and `%d` or between their capitalized versions. Both the `%a` and `%d` placeholders are replaced with the content, including the surrounding quotes. The `%s` placeholders are replaced without quotes; note that this placeholder cannot contain colors. The uppercase placeholders, `%A`, `%D`, and `%S`, work in the same way as their lowercase versions. However, special characters are replaced with their utf-8 escape code.

There's more...

Some sources mention that the `%d` and `%D` placeholders should be used for numbers. These sources expect that maybe newer versions of Less will have a different format for numbers. A preferred way of using `%d` and `%D` for number placeholders is not confirmed by the Less core team.

Replacing a text within a string

The built-in `replace()` function enables you to replace a text within a string. In this recipe, you will use this function to create a mixin that sets your retina image's background URLs automatically based on the filename (URL) of your original image. High-density devices have more than one screen pixel per CSS pixel. For this reason, you should use images with a higher number of pixels on such devices to get a sharp image projection.

Getting ready

For this recipe, you will use the client-side `less.js` compiler, as described in *Chapter 1, Getting to Grips with the Basics of Less*. You will also need a text editor to create and edit your HTML and Less files, an image editor to edit an image file, and a square example image, which is wider than 100 px.

How to do it...

1. Open your square example image with an image editor and resize the file to 200 px x 200 px and save the resized file to `example@2x.png`. Then resize the image to 100 px x 100 px and save this file as `example.png`.

2. Create a `project.less` file and write the following Less code into it:

```
.img-retina(@file; @width: auto; @height: auto;) {
  background-image: url("@{file}");
  @media
  only screen and (-webkit-min-device-pixel-ratio: 2),
  only screen and (   min--moz-device-pixel-ratio: 2),
  only screen and (     -o-min-device-pixel-ratio: 2/1),
  only screen and (        min-device-pixel-ratio: 2),
  only screen and (                min-resolution: 192dpi),
  only screen and (                min-resolution: 2dppx) {
    background-image: e(%('url("%s")',replace(@file,
      "\.([a-zA-Z]{3,4})$","@2x.$1")));
    @size: ~"@{width} @{height}";
    -webkit-background-size: @size;
    background-size: @size;
  }
}

body {
  .img-retina('example.png', 100px, 100px);
}
```

3. Create `project.html`, which links the `less.js` compiler and the `project.less` file from step 2 with the following HTML code:

```
<link rel="stylesheet/less" type="text/css"
  href="less/project.less">
<script src="js/less.js" type="text/javascript"></script>
```

4. Inspect the results in your browser and whether they are available on a high resolution device.

How it works...

As already said, the built-in `replace()` function enables you to replace a text within a string. The `replace()` function accepts the following four parameters:

- ▶ The first parameter contains a string to search and replace in
- ▶ The second parameter sets a regular expression (or string) to search for
- ▶ The third parameter contains a string that replaces the matched pattern
- ▶ The last optional parameter can be used to set regular expression flags

In this recipe, the `replace(@file, "\.([a-zA-Z]{3,4})$", "@2x.$1")` code is used to replace the `.png` text in the filename with the `@2x.png` text. The preceding code will result in a new filename: `example@2x.png`. The replaced filename is used to set the background image with the `url()` syntax. Alternatively, the `data-uri()` function, as explained in the *Embedding images with data URIs* recipe, can be used to inline this image.

The basic concept of a retina image is that you're taking an image with double the amount of pixels of your original image and displaying this image with the CSS pixel width of the original image. High-density devices have more than one screen pixel per CSS pixel. An iPhone or iPad has four screen pixels per CSS pixel and therefore has a device-pixel-ratio of 2.

There's more...

As you know, Less is written in JavaScript. Those who are familiar with JavaScript may wonder, "Can I also use native JavaScript functions?" Especially in this recipe, you will find the Less `replace()` function very similar to the JavaScript `String.replace()` function. The answer to the first question is yes; currently, Less compilers allow you to use native JavaScript calls. JavaScript calls should be placed between batesticks. Consider the following Less code:

```
@image: "../image.png";
.class {
  @image_2x: `@{image}.replace("image","image@2x")`;
  background-image: url("@{image_2x}");
}
```

The preceding Less code will compile into the following Less code:

```
.class {
  background-image: url("../image@2x.png");
}
```

Although the preceding usage of JavaScript will give you the desired result, using JavaScript in your Less code has been depreciated. Future versions of Less may not support the usage of the native JavaScript. Also, compilers written in other languages cannot compile the JavaScript code. Avoiding the native JavaScript will keep your code clean and portable.

While Apple devices have a device-pixel-ratio of 2, there are many other high-density devices with a different device-pixel-ratio. The media queries used in this recipe are based on an article at `http://css-tricks.com/` by Chris Coyier. Other strategies, which take different device-pixel-ration into account too, should be used now. Also, in future, prebuilt mixin libraries, as described in *Chapter 7, Leveraging Libraries with Prebuilt Mixins*, will provide you with mixins for retina images.

See also

- The *A pixel is not a pixel is not a pixel* blog post by Peter-Paul Koch in 2010 explains the difference between the device and CSS pixels very well. This blog post can be found at `http://www.quirksmode.org/blog/archives/2010/04/a_pixel_is_not.html`.

- Brett Jankord wrote about *Cross Browser Retina/High Resolution Media Queries* in 2012, which can be found at `http://brettjankord.com/2012/11/28/cross-browser-retinahigh-resolution-media-queries/`.

- Some basic information about regular expressions and the available flags can be found at `https://developer.mozilla.org/en-US/docs/Web/JavaScript/Guide/Regular_Expressions`.

- Read how to test retina display on the Chrome browser at `http://www.gee.web.id/2014/09/how-test-retina-display-on-chrome.html`.

Working with lists

In Less and CSS, list is a comma or space-separated collection of values. The `length()` function returns the number of elements in the list, while the `extract ()` function will give you the value of a given position in the list.

Getting ready

In this recipe, you will learn how to use the `extract()` and `length()` functions with CSS lists. To demonstrate these functions, a mixin guard will be used to create a loop with recursion. You can read more about loops with recursion in the *Using mixin guards* recipe in *Chapter 6, Advanced Less Coding*. You can use the client-side `less.js` compiler or the command-line `lessc` compiler, as explained in *Chapter 1, Getting to Grips with the Basics of Less*, to compile the Less code.

How to do it...

1. Write and compile the following Less code:

```
@sizes: "small","medium","large";
.build(@number) when (@number > 0) {
  .build(@number - 1);
  @class: e(%(".%s",extract(@sizes, @number)));
  @{class} {
    width: 100px * @number;
  }
}
.build(length(@sizes));
```

2. After compiling the preceding Less code, you will end up with the following CSS code:

```css
.small {
  width: 100px;
}
.medium {
  width: 200px;
}
.large {
  width: 300px;
}
```

How it works...

You have used lists in CSS before, maybe without even realizing it. Lists are, for instance, property values for margins and padding, as shown in the following code:

```
margin: 0 10px 20px 0;
```

Many shorthand property values are lists. Also, the recent additions to CSS3 add some new properties with the list values. So, for the background image property, you can assign more than one image by separating the URLs with a comma.

The `extract()` and `length()` functions get the values and the length of a CSV list. Together, these functions can be used to iterate over the CSV list as arrays. When using the `extract()` function, you should note that the first position has the index 1 and not 0.

Less enables you to assign any list of values; you can, for instance, use the following code to create a list of written numbers:

```
@numbers: "one", "two", "three";
```

Note that in the preceding code, the quotes around the values are optional.

There's more...

The return value of the `extract()` function acts as an assigned value. So, for instance, it can be used with operations and other built-in functions, as in the following Less code:

```less
@border: 1px solid red;
div.bordered {
  border: @border;
  background-color: lighten(extract(@border,3),20%);
  padding: extract(@border,1) * 10;
}
```

The preceding code will compile into the following CSS code:

```css
div.bordered {
  border: 1px solid #ff0000;
  background-color: #ff6666;
  padding: 10px;
}
```

Using mathematical functions

Frequently used mathematical functions are also available in Less. These functions include, among others, functions for rounding and trigonometry. In this recipe, you will create a list of colors, which covers the visible spectrum, using the `sin()` and `floor()` functions.

Getting ready

In this recipe, you will compile the Less code using the client-side `less.js` compiler, as described in the *Downloading, installing, and integrating less.js* recipe in *Chapter 1, Getting to Grips with the Basics of Less*. Finally, you will inspect the result in your browser. You will also need a text editor to edit your Less and HTML files.

How to do it...

1. Create a Less file named `rainbow.less` and write the following Less code into it:

```less
.rainbow(@number,@frequency:0) when (@number > 0)
{
  .setfrequency() when (@frequency = 0) {
    @frequency: 5 / @number;
  }
  .setfrequency;

  .rainbow(@number - 1, @frequency);

  @red: floor(sin(@frequency * (@number - 1) + 0) * 127 +
    128);
  @green: floor(sin(@frequency * (@number - 1) + 2) * 127 +
    128);
  @blue: floor(sin(@frequency * (@number - 1) + 4) * 127 +
    128);

  @classname: e(%(".color-%a",@number));
  @{classname} {
```

```
      background-color: rgb(@red,@green,@blue);
      height:30px;
   }
}
.rainbow(12);
```

2. Create an `index.html` file, which will link the `less.js` compiler and the `rainbow.less` file from step 2 with the following HTML code:

```
<link rel="stylesheet/less" type="text/css"
  href="rainbow.less">
<script src="less.js" type="text/javascript"></script>
```

This `index.html` will have the following HTML code in its `body` part:

```
<div class="color-1"></div>
<div class="color-2"></div>
<div class="color-3"></div>
<div class="color-4"></div>
<div class="color-5"></div>
<div class="color-6"></div>
<div class="color-7"></div>
<div class="color-8"></div>
<div class="color-9"></div>
<div class="color-10"></div>
<div class="color-11"></div>
<div class="color-12"></div>
```

3. Inspect the results in your browser. In your browser, you will find twelve colored `div` elements, which look like the following screenshot:

How it works...

Less has a built-in function for commonly used mathematical calculations. In this recipe, `sin()` and `floor()` functions are used. The `sin()` function of course calculates a sine function and the `floor()` function returns the next lowest integer. The code in this recipe uses three sine waves with a different phase to calculate the RGB values of the colors. The channel values in the `rgb()` function are set by an integer, so the results are rounded first with the `floor()` function.

There's more...

As made clear in the *Replacing a text within a string* recipe, native JavaScript math functions, such as the `Math.floor()` function, can also be used when put between quotes; however, to keep your code clean and portable, you should only use the built-in Less math functions.

See also

▶   The code used in this recipe is inspired by a blog post written by Markandey Singh. You can find his original post and the JavaScript code at `http://www.markandey. com/2012/04/how-to-generate-rainbow-colors.html`.

▶   A complete list of the built-in mathematical functions can be found at `http://lesscss.org/functions/#math-functions`.

Using the color() function

The Less colors are defined in the same way as in CSS; `color` is a color keyword, an RGB hex value, or the equivalent triplet of the numerical RGB values.

Getting ready

For this recipe, you can use your favorite text editor and the command-line `lessc` compiler, as described in the *Installing the lessc compiler with npm* recipe in *Chapter 1, Getting to Grips with the Basics of Less*.

How to do it...

1. Write the following code into a Less file and compile this file with the command-line `lessc` compiler:

```
colors {
  color1: color("red");
  color2: color("#ff0000");
  color3: color("#f00");
}
```

2. The preceding Less code will compile into the following CSS code:

```
colors {
  color1: #ff0000;
  color2: #ff0000;
  color3: #ff0000;
}
```

How it works...

The `color()` function converts a string into a color, as defined by CSS. Colors are compiled into six-digit hex values. These values start with a # symbol followed by a triplet of hexadecimal numbers between 0 and 255.

The `color()` function can also have another built-in function as an argument when this function provides a valid color value. So, for instance, `color(%("#"%s,"f00"));` will compile into `#ff0000;`.

There's more...

Although the `color()` function removes quotes in most cases, the `color()` function is not just a wrapper of the ~"value" syntax or the `e()` function. Note that the ~"blue" syntax will be compiled into the unquoted blue string, while the `color("blue");` call will compile into the #0000ff color value. Also, the `iscolor()` function evaluates `false` for ~"blue", as can be seen in the compiled CSS code in the *Evaluating the type of a value* recipe. Last but not least, the `color()` function is more strict and throws an argument that is a color keyword or 3/6 digit hex (for example, the #FFF error for invalid color values).

The color definition functions and other color functions, as described in the *Creating color objects with RGB values* recipe, already return a color type and should not be wrapped in the `color()` function. On the other hand, when you have colors or color names defined as `string`, which you want to use as the function argument for built-in color functions, you should covert them to colors first, leveraging the `color()` function. The latest can be seen in the following example code:

```
@colors: "red", "blue", "yellow";

.lighten(@i: 1) when (@i <= length(@colors)) {

  .lighten(@i + 1);

  @color: e(extract(@colors, @i));

  .light@{color} {

    color: lighten(color(@color), 10%);

  }

}

.lighten();
```

The `lighten()` function in the preceding code requires a color, as an argument throws an error for other argument types. You should note that in the preceding example, the quotes around the values of `@colors` are not required. When you drop these quotes, you do not need both the `e()` and `color()` functions too.

See also

▶ A complete overview of CSS Color Module Level 3 can be found at `http://www.w3.org/TR/2011/REC-css3-color-20110607/`.

▶ The CSS3 modules extend 16 basic color keywords in CSS with a lot of color keywords. A complete list of the color keywords contain 147 color names now and is the same as the SVG 1.0 color keyword names, which can be found at `http://www.w3.org/TR/SVG/types.html#ColorKeywords`.

▶ You can also look up these color keywords in the color equivalents table at `http://meyerweb.com/eric/css/colors/`. This table also includes the HSL definitions of these colors.

Evaluating the type of a value

The built-in functions are grouped as the type functions that can be used to evaluate the type of a value. The result can be used to match mixins based on the value type.

Getting ready

For this recipe, you will need a text editor and the command-line `lessc` compiler ready, as described in the *Installing the lessc compiler with npm* recipe in *Chapter 1, Getting to Grips with the Basics of Less*.

How to do it...

1. Write the following code into a Less file and compile this file with the command-line `lessc` compiler:

```
color-tstt(@color,@test-number) when (iscolor(@color))
{
  result-@{test-number}: %("%a is a color",@color);
}
.color-test(@color,@test-number) when (default())
{
  result-@{test-number}: %("%a is Not a color",@color);
}
test {
  .color-test(blue,1);
  .color-test("blue",2);
  .color-test(color("blue"),3);
  .color-test(~"blue",4);
}
```

2. The preceding Less code will compile into the following CSS code:

```
test {
  result-1: "#0000ff is a color";
  result-2: ""blue" is Not a color";
  result-3: "#0000ff is a color";
  result-4: "blue is Not a color";
}
```

How it works...

The Less code of this recipe contains two mixins with the same name. The first mixin is only compiled when the `iscolor()` condition matches, or in other words, evaluates `true` for the input parameter. These conditional mixins are also called mixin guards and are explained in more detail in the *Using mixin guards* recipe in *Chapter 6, Advanced Less Coding* recipe.

Colors in Less are not strings, but a special color type defined as a color keyword, an RGB hex value, or the equivalent triplet of the numerical RGB values. The `iscolor()` function returns `false` for strings or other invalid color values. The *Using the color() function* recipe describes how to convert a string to a color with the built-in `color()` function. Also, other built-in color definitions and color functions will evaluate as `true`. For instance, the `iscolor(rgb(255,0,56))`; call will return `true`. Note that `transparent` is a valid color keyword. User agents should compute this keyword as `rgba(0,0,0,0)`. See the *There's more...* section of the *Creating color objects with RGB values* recipe for more information about the `rgba()` color definition function.

There's more...

Besides the `iscolor()` function, Less has other eight built-in functions, so-called `is` or type-checking functions, namely the `isnumber()`, `isstring()`, `iskeyword()`, `isurl()`, `ispixel()`, `isem()`, `ispercentage()`, and `isunit()` functions. All these functions, except the `isunit()` function, accept a single argument. The arguments for the `isunit()` function are a value and a unit type, and this function evaluates to `true` when the value is a number in the specified units. The following code will show you some examples of the usage of the `is` functions:

```
iskeyword(keyword); //true
isunit(1px,em); //false
```

Creating color objects with RGB values

In this recipe, you will create some color objects with the `rgb()` color definition function.

Getting ready

For this recipe, you can use your favorite text editor and the command-line `lessc` compiler, as described in the *Installing the lessc compiler with npm* recipe in *Chapter 1, Getting to Grips with the Basics of Less*. Also, looking at the color equivalents table at `http://meyerweb.com/eric/css/colors/` will be useful. This table will give you an insight into the relation between the different color definitions available in CSS3.

How to do it...

1. Create a `colors.less` file and write down the following Less code into it:

```
colors {
    color1: rgb(255,0,0); //red
    color2: rgb(100%,0,0); //red
    color3: rgb(255,255,0); //yellow
    color4: rgb(100%,100%,0); //yellow
    color5: rgb(255,99,71); //tomato
    color6: rgb(100%,38.8%,27.8%); //tomato
}
```

2. After the compilation of the preceding Less code, your final CSS code will look like the following code:

```
colors {
    color1: #ff0000;
    color2: #ff0000;
    color3: #ffff00;
    color4: #ffff00;
    color5: #ff6347;
    color6: #ff6347;
}
```

How it works...

The `rgb()` color definition has been defined in CSS and Less. The `rgb()` color definition function in Less accepts a triplet of numbers or percentages as arguments. The three numbers of the triplet are called channels mostly. The numbers in the triplet define the red, green, and blue color components. Each of the channels can vary between 0 and 255 (or 0 and 100 percent). The RGB notation allows you to define $2\text{^}24 = 16777216$ different colors. You can easily convert the notation from hexadecimal to RGB by calculating the decimal equivalent of the hexadecimal number or vice versa. The hexadecimal value for the `tomato` color is `#ff6347`; the first number of the triplet `ff` defines red, and the `ff` hexadecimal value is equal to 255 decimal. The next number of the triplet (green) `63` hexadecimal equals 99 ($16*6 + 3$) decimal. Finally, the green component of the triplet has `47` hexadecimal, which is equal to 71 in the decimal notation. Putting the preceding data together makes it clear that `#ff6347` is equal to `rgb(255,99,71);`. The percentage numbers can be found as the decimal value divided by 255 times 100 percent, or of course, for hexadecimal numbers, the hexadecimal number divided by `ff` times 100 percent. So again, for the `tomato` color, you will find the `rgb(100%,38.8%,27.8%);` notation.

CSS3 extends the `rgb` notation with the `rgba` notation. The `rgba` notation works the same way as `rgb`; besides, there is an additional alpha (`a`) channel. The alpha value in this notation will be a fraction between 0 and 1 and can be used to set the opacity of a color. An alpha of 1 correspondence with an opaque color and an alpha of 0 will be invisible. In Less, `rgba` colors are assigned with the `rgba()` function. The `rgba()` function in Less also accepts a percentage for the alpha channel argument. The effect of the opacity can be made visible with the following HTML loaded in your browser:

```
<div style="background-color:white;">
  <div style="padding:10px;
    background-color:rgba(255,0,0,0.5);color:white;">text</div>
</div>
```

As you can see, `red` with an opacity of 50 percent on the `white` background will look similar to pink. Of course, you can rewrite the inline styles in the preceding HTML example into the Less code. In Less, your code will look like the following code:

```
div {
  background-color: white;
  div {
    padding: 10px;
    background-color: rgba(255,0,0,50%); // red
    color: white;
  }
}
```

There's more...

In case you want to create a transparent color, you can use the built-in `red()`, `green()`, and `blue()` functions to get the input values for the `rgba()` function. The following example code shows how to use these functions to create a transparent color:

```
.rgba-background(@color; @alpha: 50%){

  background-color: rgba(red(@color), green(@color), blue(@color),
    @alpha);

}

div.red {

  .rgba-background(red);

}
```

The preceding Less code will compile into the CSS code as follows:

```
div.red {

  background-color: rgba(255, 0, 0, 0.5);

}
```

Less provides more functions to define colors. The `hsl()` color function defines numerical **hue, saturation, lightness** (**HSL**) colors as a complement to the numerical RGB colors. The HSL color definition also exists in CSS3. People have claimed that the HSL colors are more intuitive than the RGB colors (refer to *Yay for HSLa* by Chris Coyier at `http://css-tricks.com/yay-for-hsla/`). The HSL definition also works as a triplet (hue, saturation, and lightness). The first value of this triplet is the hue. The hue has been defined as an angle of the color circle with 0 degree (and 360 degrees) being red, 120 degrees representing green, and blue found at 240 degrees. The second value describes the saturation as a percentage, where `100%` is full saturation and `0%` is a shade of gray. The third and last value is also a percentage and represents the lightness. A lightness percentage of `50%` can be seen as *normal* lightness, `0%` lightness is black, and then of course, `100%` lightness should be white.

To get more of a grip on the HSL color, you can load and inspect the following HTML code into your browser:

```
<div style="background-color:hsl(240,100%,25%);">dark blue</div>
<div style="background-color:hsl(240,100%,50%);">blue</div>
<div style="background-color:hsl(240,100%,75%);">light blue</div>
<br>
<div style="background-color:hsl(240,25%,50%);">dark blue</div>
<div style="background-color:hsl(240,50%,50%);">blue</div>
<div style="background-color:hsl(240,100%,50%);">light blue</div>
```

In your browser, the preceding code output will look like what is shown in the following screenshot:

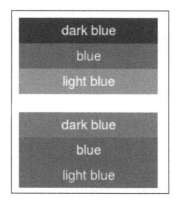

The preceding HTML example will show you that creating different shades of blue can be accomplished by varying the saturation or lightness of the channel values.

Note that the shades of the same color in the SVG 1.0 color keyword names are not related to HSL and are defined with different hue values, as can be seen in the blue range as follows:

- **light blue**: `hsl(195,53.3%,79%)`
- **blue**: `hsl(240,100%,50%)`
- **dark blue**: `hsl(240,100%,27.3%)`

The `hsla()` function adds an alpha channel to the HSL definition to define transparency. The alpha range is from 0 to 100 percent, and it can also be set with a fraction between 0 and 1.

In Less, you can also use some other color definition functions, which are not defined in CSS3. The HSV, also called HSB, color space is just like HSL. It's a cylindrical coordinate representation of points in an RGB color model. HSV is used by Adobe Photoshop and the popular open source alternative GIMP for color pickers and other built-in color algorithms. In Less, HSV colors can be defined with the `hsv()` function. Using the same color definition for your designs, your Less code will make it easier to match them. The `hsv()` function also has a variant that enables you to set the transparency with an alpha channel value, the `hsva()` function, with alpha as a percentage between 0-100 or number 0-1.

Finally, there is the `argb()` function in Less. The `argb()` function defines a color in the `#aarrggbb` hexadecimal format. This `#aarrggbb` hexadecimal format, with alpha for transparency between `00` (0) and `ff` (255), is used in Internet Explorer, .NET, and Android development.

In Less, you can convert RGB into ARGB with the following code:

```
argb(rgba(0, 0, 255, 0.5)); //blue, with 50% transparency
```

This conversion will compile into the CSS code, as follows:

```
#800000ff;
```

Note that ARGB is not defined in CSS3, so you can't use the `argb()` function to assign a CSS property. A use case for the `argb()` function can be found in Bootstrap's gradient mixins, which assigns a background gradient for Internet Explorer 8 and earlier versions with the following code:

```
filter: e(%("progid:DXImageTransform.Microsoft.gradient
  (startColorstr='%d', endColorstr='%d', GradientType=1)",
    argb(@start-color),argb(@end-color))); // IE9 and down
```

Finally, you will have to pay some attention to the compiled output of the color definitions. If possible, colors are compiled in your CSS code with the RGB hexadecimal format (#rrggbb), the color names; three-digit hexadecimal representation; and `rgb()`, `hsl()`, and `hsv()` functions compile into the #rrggbb representation. Colors with an alpha channel cannot be written in a hexadecimal triplet and will compile into the `rgba(r,g,b,a);` representation, unless `alpha = 1`. If `alpha = 1`, your color will compile in the #rrggbb format too. The only exception of the preceding code is the `argb()` color definition, which will always compile into the #aarrggbb hexadecimal representation.

See also

▸ The formulas to convert HSL color to RGB colors and vice versa can be found at
   `http://www.w3.org/TR/2011/REC-css3-color-20110607/#hsl-color`

Getting information about a color

As you can read in the recipe, colors are defined with different channels. Less provides you with some functions to get information about a channel that belongs to a certain color definition.

Getting ready

This recipe will only give you a small piece of example Less code. You can compile this example Less code with the client-side or server-side compiler, as described in *Chapter 1, Getting to Grips with the Basics of Less*, and inspect the compiled CSS code.

How to do it...

1. Compile the following Less code into CSS using a Less compiler:

```
hsv {
  hsvvalue: hsvvalue(hsv(90, 100%, 50%));
  color: hsv(90, 100%, 50%);
}
rgb {
  hsvvalue: hsvvalue(#408000);
}
```

2. You will find that the preceding Less code will compile into the following CSS code:

```
hsv {
  hsvvalue: 50%;
  color: #408000;
}
rgb {
  hsvvalue: 50%;
}
```

How it works...

Colors are defined with channels; the value set by the channel depends on the color definition. RGB colors have a red, green, and blue channel, and HSL colors have a hue, saturation, and lightness channel. Less provides you with some built-in color function, which will give you information (or the value set) about a channel.

For RGB colors, the functions are `red()`, `green()`, and `blue()`, and for HSL colors, `hue()`, `saturation()`, and `lightness()`. As you can guess now, for HSV colors, the `hsvhue()`, `hsvsaturation()`, and `hsvvalue()` functions are available.

The example code in this recipe shows you that the input parameter of these functions should be a valid color, but this color can be defined with any definition.

Both the `hsvvalue(hsv(90, 100%, 50.2%));` and `hsvvalue(#408000)` functions return 50%. Also, the `red(hsv(90, 100%, 50.2%));` and `red(#408000);` functions will return 64 (note that the result is 64.005 for the HSV color definition). Of course, these results do not differ due to `hsv(90, 100%, 50.2%)` and `#408000`. There are different ways to define the same color.

The channel functions convert a color into the corresponding color space before they find the channel value that should be returned.

The color channel functions, as described, can also be used for mixin guards, as explained in detail in the *Using mixin guards* recipe in *Chapter 6, Advanced Less Coding* recipe.

Creating a lighter variant of a color will be easy in the HSL color space. You will only have to increase the lightness of a color. If you only have the hexadecimal representation or even only the color name for your input color, you can compile the following code to find your lighter color variant:

```
@inputcolor: darkgreen;

p {

  color: hsl(hue(@inputcolor),saturation(@inputcolor),
    lightness(@inputcolor) + 20% ); // lighter green

}
```

You will find that the preceding code will compile into `#00ca00`; indeed. In the *Creating color a variant with the darken() and lighten() functions* recipe, you will learn more about the color operation functions of Less. These color operations also include the `lighten()` function, which will make the preceding `lighten` operation a lot easier. The `lighten('darkgreen',20%);` code will compile into the `#00ca00` hexadecimal RGB code.

Other functions, which give some information about a color, are the `luma()` and `luminance()` functions. The `luma()` function returns the perceptual brightness of a color object. The perceptual brightness of a color plays an important role for contrast with other colors. High color contrasts will help visually disabled people. For this reason, the implementation of the `luma()` function follows the recommendations in **Web Content Accessibility Guidelines** (**WCAG**) 2.0 by W3C. The same calculation is used for the built-in `contrast()` function. Note that the `luma()` function has been changed since Less v1.7; it now uses gamma correction. The `luminance()` function calculates perceptual brightness without gamma correction in the same way as the `luma()` function did before Less 1.7 for backward-compatibility reasons.

See also

▶ The recommended calculation for the relative luminance by W3C can be found at `http://www.w3.org/TR/2008/REC-WCAG20-20081211/#relativeluminancedef`

▶ Some background information and links for further reading about the gamma correction of colors can be found at `http://www.colormatters.com/the-power-of-gamma`

Creating a color variant with the darken() and lighten() functions

In this recipe, you will compile some shades of green into CSS with the Less color operation functions.

Getting ready

You will need a valid HTML5 document, which includes the `less.js` compiler and a Less file called `project.less`. Note that the *Using the built-in functions of Less* recipe in *Chapter 1, Getting to Grips with the Basics of Less*, will show you an example of how to darken colors with the `darken()` built-in function.

How to do it...

1. Write the following HTML code into your HTML5 file:

```
<div>
   <div class="green">Shades of green</div>
</div>
```

2. Open the `project.less` file with your text editor and write the following Less code into it:

```
@start-color: green;
div.green {
   background-color: @start-color;
   color: contrast(@start-color);
   border: e(%("5px solid %a",darken(@start-color,10%)));
   &:hover {
      background-color: fadeout( @start-color ,50%);
   }
}
```

3. Don't forget to link the `project.less` file in the `head` section of your HTML5 document with the following line of code:

```
<link rel="stylesheet/less" type="text/css"
   href="less/project.less">
```

4. Open the HTML5 file in your browser and you will see something that looks like the following screenshot:

Shades of green

How it works...

Except for the `contrast()` function, the color operation function, such as the `darken()` and `fadeout()` functions, used in this recipe changes the saturation, lightness, or transparency of your colors in the HSL(A) color space. More information about the HSL color space definition can be found in the *Creating color objects with RGB values* recipe. The `darken()` function will decrease the lightness channel of the color in the HSL space, and so the `desaturation()` function will decrease the value of the saturation channel. The `fadeout()` and `fadein()` functions change the value of the alpha channel, which sets the transparency of your color.

Each color operation function should be called with two arguments: the first argument should be a valid color and the second argument a percentage used to increase or decrease the channel value. Note that the percentage of the second argument will be used to increase or decrease the channel value with the absolute value of this argument, which means that if you set the second argument to `10%`, the channel value will change to the current percentage plus or minus 10 percent and not to 10 percent of the current value.

The color you operate on doesn't have to be defined in the HSL color space already; each valid color is converted to the HSL space before it is operated on. The color operation functions return a color in the `#rrggbb` hexadecimal notation, unless there is an `alpha < 1` condition. Transparent colors, with `alpha < 1`, are returned in the `rgba()` color definition.

Note that if you convert the colors to the HSL color space yourself, it is easy to see what happens.

The named color `green` can be defined in the HSL color space with the `hsl(120,100%,25.1%);` notation. Darken this color by 10 percent by calling `darken(green,10%);`. This will decrease the lightness channel by 10 percent which results into the color `hsl(120,100%,15.1%);`. Now, you can compile the following Less code and find out that both `hsl(120,100%,15.1%);` and `darken(green,10%);` will compile into `#004d00`:

```
colors {
  color1: hsl(120,100%,35.1%);
  color2: darken(green,10%);
}
```

There's more...

The `contrast()` function is also grouped into the color operation functions. The `contrast()` function returns a light or a dark color (white and black by default), depending on the input color. Based on the `luma()` function, as described in the *Getting information about a color* recipe, the `contrast()` function calculates and returns the color that has the highest contrast with the input color. The `contrast()` function can, for instance, be used to set your font color in relation to the background color; if your background color changes, the font also automatically changes to the color with the highest contrast. Using the font colors with high contrasts keeps your website readable and meets the web accessibility guidelines.

Creating overlays of two colors with Less

In this recipe, you will create an overlay of two colors with the built-in `overlay()` color-blending function.

Getting ready

The best way to compile the Less code in this recipe is by using the client-side `less.js` compiler, as described in the *Downloading, installing, and integrating less.js* recipe in *Chapter 1, Getting to Grips with the Basics of Less*, and inspecting the result in your browser. You will also have to create an HTML5 document named `index.html` and a `less/blending.less` file.

How to do it...

1. Edit the HTML5 file called `index.html` and make it look as follows:

```
<!DOCTYPE html>
<html>
  <head>
    <meta charset="utf-8">
    <title>Use variables in Less</title>
    <link rel="stylesheet/less" type="text/css"
      href="less/blending.less">
    <script type="text/javascript">var less = { env:
      'development' };</script>
    <script src="js/less.js"
      type="text/javascript"></script>
  </head>
  <body>
    <h1>How to display errors</h1>
  </body>
</html>
```

2. Edit your `blending.less` file to style the `div` elements, as follows:

```
h1 {
  color:red;
  font-size:3em;
}
```

3. Load the `index.html` file in your browser and the result of the `overlay()` color-blending function.

4. Now, vary the input color and color operation function in the `blending.less` file and inspect the results in your browser. Other blending or color operations are the `multiply()`, `screen()`, `softlight()`, `hardlight()`, `difference()`, `exculsion()`, `average()`, and `negation()` functions.

How it works...

As already mentioned, the built-in color-blending functions are: `multiply()`, `screen()`, `overlay()`, `softlight()`, `hardlight()`, `difference()`, `exculsion()`, `average()`, and `negation()` functions. These functions operate on the RGB channels of the colors and don't influence the transparency.

Every color operation function accepts two valid colors as input; the color should be valid but can use any kind of color definition available in Less. Compile the following Less code:

```
overlay(yellow,hsl(240,100%,50%,50%));
overlay(yellow,hsl(240,100%,50%));
overlay(yellow,blue);
```

The output of the preceding code will be three times the same as `#ffff00;` (yellow). The `overlay` function has been illustrated in the following screenshot:

Note that blue and yellow do not compile into green, as you have learned in primary school. Define yellow with an `alpha < 1` operation on a blue background to get a visual green color. You will also have noticed that the result of this `overlay` function is equal to one of the input colors (yellow). The `overlay()` function performs a `multiply()` blending operation when the first color is a light color and a screen blending operation otherwise. Yellow is a light color, so multiply both the colors. In this case, `ffff00` times `0000ff` is `ffff00` again. The `multiply()` function returns darker colors. The counterpart of the `multiply()` function is the `screen()` function, which returns lighter functions. Other color-blending functions in Less are as follows:

- `softlight()`: This function is similar to the `overlay()` function, but it uses only a fraction of the color, which soft-highlights the other color

- `hardlight()`: This function preforms an `overlay()` function with the second argument to determine whether a multiply or screen operation should be done

- `difference()`: This function subtracts the second input color from the first input color (note that the negative values are inverted)

- ▸ `exculsion()`: The performance of this function is the same operation as the `difference()` function but with a lower contrast
- ▸ `average()`: This function indeed computes the average of each color channel by channel
- ▸ `negation()`: This function has the opposite effect to the `difference()` function, which means subtracting the first input color from the second input color (note that the negative values are inverted)

There's more...

The Less blending color functions are similar to the blending function found in image editors, such as Photoshop or the open source alternative GIMP. The similarity between these functions makes it easier to match the colors of your design in Less and so finally in your compiled CSS. Read this with care; because of this similarity, it does not always mean that the functions (and results) are identical.

See also

GIMP is **GNU Image Manipulation Program**. It is a freely distributed piece of software for tasks such as photo retouching, image composition, and image authoring. It works on many operating systems and in many languages. You can find more information and download GIMP for free from `http://www.gimp.org/`.

5

Extending and Referencing

In this chapter, we will cover the following topics:

- ▶ Referencing parent selectors with the `&` operator
- ▶ Referencing to the parent selector more than once
- ▶ Changing the selecting order with the `&` operator
- ▶ Using `extend` to merge selectors
- ▶ Using `extend` inside a ruleset
- ▶ Extending with the `all` keyword
- ▶ Extending with media queries
- ▶ Using `extend` to reduce the compiled CSS size
- ▶ Using `extend` as an alternative for a mixin

Introduction

In Less, you can use the `&` sign as a reference to the parent selector in the case of nested selectors. This reference can not only be used to create style rules for the CSS pseudo classes, but can also be used in combination with Less's `:extend()` pseudo class. This pseudo class merges the attached class with all the appearances of the classes to extend. In this chapter, you will find some use cases of the `&` sign referencing in Less, and you will learn how to use the `:extend()` pseudo class.

Note that this chapter only handles the referencing and merging of selectors. Less also enables you to merge property values. The merging of property values will be described in the *Aggregating values under a single property* recipe in *Chapter 6, Advanced Less Coding*.

Referencing parent selectors with the & operator

In the *Writing more intuitive code and make inheritance clear with nested rules* recipe in *Chapter 1, Getting to Grips with the Basics of Less*, you can read how to use nested style rules in Less. Inside nested rules, you can use the & sign to reference the current parent selector. In this recipe, you will learn how to use the & parent referencing sign. An important use case for the & parent referencing sign is the nested declaration of pseudo classes for a selector. Some well-known pseudo classes are `:hover`, `:focus`, and `:link`.

Getting ready

You can compile the Less code in this recipe with the command-line `lessc` compiler, as described in the *Installing the lessc compiler with npm* recipe in *Chapter 1, Getting to Grips with the Basics of Less*. Alternatively, you can include the file that has your Less code together with the `less.js` compiler into a `button.html` file and inspect the results in your browser. More information about how to use the `less.js` compiler for client-side compiling can be found in the *Downloading, installing, and integrating less.js* recipe in *Chapter 1, Getting to Grips with the Basics of Less*.

How to do it...

1. Create a `button.less` file that will contain the following Less code:

```
button {

    color: white;

    border: 2px solid white;

    background-color: blue;



    &:hover,

    &:focus,

    &:active {

        background-color:red;
```

```
    }


    &:visited {

      background-color:green;

    }

  }
```

2. The `button.html` file should include the `button.less` file from step 1 and the `less.js` compiler. The HTML code in this `button.html` file should look similar to what is shown in the following code:

```
<!DOCTYPE html>
<html>
  <head>
    <meta charset="utf-8">

    <title>Button example</title>

    <link rel="stylesheet/less" type="text/css"
      href="less/button.less">
      <script src="js/less.js"
        type="text/javascript"></script>
  </head>
    <button>Button</button>
  <body>
</html>
```

3. Finally, load the `button.html` file in your browser and hover and click on the blue button with your mouse.

How it works...

In this recipe, the `&` parent referencing sign was used to set a different background color for the hover and focus states of the `button` element.

When inspecting the compiled CSS code, you will find that it will look like the following code:

```
button {

  color: white;

  border: 2px solid white;

  background-color: blue;

}

button:hover,

button:focus,

button:active {

  background-color: red;

}

button:visited {

  background-color: green;

}
```

You can see that the & operator has been replaced with the parent selector to build new selectors, such as the `button:hover` selector, in the compiled CSS code.

There's more...

Although the & parent referencing is commonly used with pseudo classes and elements, it also has some other use cases.

In the *Building style guides with StyleDocco* recipe in *Chapter 2, Debugging and Documenting Your Less Code*, you can read how to append class names to a selector with the & parent referencing sign. The following Less code is an example of how to append class names:

```
div {
&.class1 {
  color: red;
}
```

```
&.class2 {
  color: yellow;
}
}
```

The preceding Less code will compile into CSS, as follows:

```
div.class1 {
  color: red;
}
div.class2 {
  color: yellow;
}
```

 Watch out to use spaces after the & sign because the & class will compile into selector.class (meaning the selectors that have the .class class), while & .class will compile into a selector's .class class (meaning elements that have the .class class inside the selector and don't require an & sign at all).

The & parent referencing sign can even be used to produce repetitive class names. Consider the following Less code that uses the **Block Element Modifier** (**BEM**) methodology:

```
.label {
  &--success {
    color:darkgreen;
  }
  &--error {
    color:darkred;
  }
}
```

The preceding Less code will compile into the following CSS code:

```
.label--success {

  color: darkgreen;

}

.label--error {

  color: darkred;

}
```

Finally, the & parent selector can also be used to create child and sibling selectors that refer to the same parent. You will see some examples of this in the *Referencing to the parent selector more than once* recipe.

See also

▶ Read more about pseudo class selectors at `http://css-tricks.com/pseudo-class-selectors/`

▶ Also, read Organizing CSS: **Object-Oriented CSS (OOCSS)**, **Scalable and Modular Architecture for CSS (SMACSS)**, and BEM by Matt Stauffer at `http://mattstauffer.co/blog/organizing-css-oocss-smacss-and-bem`

Referencing to the parent selector more than once

The & parent referencing sign can be used multiple times in the same selector to reference the same parent. For instance, multiple parent references can be used to construct child and sibling combinatory selectors.

Getting ready

You can compile the Less code in this recipe with the command-line `lessc` compiler, as described in the *Installing the lessc compiler with npm* recipe in *Chapter 1, Getting to Grips with the Basics of Less*.

How to do it...

1. Write the following Less code into a file and compile this file with the command-line `lessc` compiler:

```
p {
  color: green;
  & + & {
    color: red;
  }
}
```

2. You will find that the preceding Less code will be compiled into the CSS code, as shown in the following code:

```css
p {
  color: green;
}
p + p {
  color: red;
}
```

How it works...

The compiler replaces the `&` + `&` code with `p` + `p`. The + sign creates an adjacent sibling combinatory selector in CSS. The selector selects a `p` HTML element directly after another `p` HTML element. The style effect of the Less code in this recipe can be made visible with the following HTML code, which should display all appearances of the green text in green and red text in red when loaded in the browser:

```html
<div>
  <p>green</p>
  <p>red</p>
  <p>red</p>
</div>

<div>
  <p>green</p>
</div>
```

There's more...

Note that the `&` parent referencing sign references all the parents and not just its nearest ancestors. This way all the parents are referenced, which can be seen when compiling the following Less code:

```less
section {
  p {
    & + & {
      property: value;
    }
  }
}
```

The preceding Less code will compile into the following CSS code:

```
section p + section p {
  property: value;
}
```

To understand why all the parents are referenced in the example shown before, you will have to realize what nesting means. The basics of nesting are explained in the following example. In fact, there is no functional difference between the following two pieces of code:

```
//nested
selector1 {
  selector2 {
    property: value;
  }
}
//without nesting
selector1 selector2 {
  property: value;
}
```

Both versions of the preceding Less code will compile into the CSS code as follows:

```
selector1 selector2 {
  property: value;
}
```

When the & operator only references it's nearest parent, the following code will compile into something unwanted or at least unexpected:

```
//nested
footer {
  a {
    property: value;
    &:hover {color:red;}
  }
}
```

Not referencing the footer selector in the preceding code should compile into the a:hover selector, which will select all the a elements instead of only the a elements in the footer element. By referencing, all the parents in the Less code will compile into the footer a:hover selector as intended. Also, the :extend() pseudo class extends all the parents; see the *Using extend inside a ruleset* recipe of this chapter.

See also

▸ You can read more about child and sibling selectors in CSS at
http://css-tricks.com/child-and-sibling-selectors/

Changing the selecting order with the & operator

The CSS selectors are pattern-matching rules that determine which style rules apply to the elements in the document tree. As can be read in the *Referencing parent selectors with the & operator* recipe, the & operator can be used inside nested rules in Less. Placing the & parent reference at the end of a selector inside a nested rule gives you the opportunity to change the selecting order.

Getting ready

For client-side compiling, you will have to create an `index.html` file that will load the `example.less` file and the `less.js` compiler with the following code in the `head` section:

```
<link rel="stylesheet/less" type="text/css"
  href="less/example.less">
<script src="js/less.js" type="text/javascript"></script>
```

How to do it...

1. Create an `example.less` file and write the following Less code into it:

```
p{
  font-size: 2em;
  color: darkgreen;

  footer & {
    font-size: 1em;
    color: darkred;
  }
}
```

2. Create an `index.html` file. This should contain the following HTML code in the `body` section:

```
<article>
  <p>First paragraph</p>
  <p>Second paragraph</p>
</article>
<footer>
  <p>Footer paragraph</p>
</footer>
```

3. Finally, load the `index.html` file in your favorite web browser. In your browser, you will see what is shown in the following screenshot:

How it works...

In this recipe, you created the Less code that styles the `p` elements in your HTML document, all in the same way. The same styles are also applied to the `p` elements inside the footer element, except for a smaller font size.

After inspecting, you will find that the Less code in this recipe will compile into the CSS code, as shown in this code:

```css
p {
  font-size: 2em;
  color: darkgreen;
}
footer p {
  font-size: 1em;
  color: darkred;
}
```

As you can see, the `footer` selector and the Less code compiles into the footer p selector. Changing the selecting order this way enables you to apply the differences in styles only when the parent selector matches a certain condition. Code duplication for the referenced selectors is not needed, which makes your code easier to maintain.

There's more...

A while ago in 2008, Paul Irish introduced the conditional classes of `<html>` as an alternative for conditional style sheets. With these conditional classes, the HTML tag of your document will look like the following code:

```
<!--[if lt IE 7]>      <html class="ie6"> <![endif]-->
<!--[if IE 7]>         <html class="ie7"> <![endif]-->
<!--[if IE 8]>         <html class="ie8"> <![endif]-->
<!--[if gt IE 8]><!--> <html>             <!--<![endif]-->
```

When using these conditional classes of `<html>`, no additional HTTP requests to load a browser-specific style sheet are needed. All the CSS code can be added to a single file.

Now consider the following CSS code:

```
div.foo { color: inherit;}
.ie6 div.foo { color: #ff8000; }
```

The Less code to compile the preceding CSS code can be easily written now, leveraging the technique with the & operator to change the selecting order, as follows:

```
div.foo {
  color: inherit;}
  .ie6 & {
    color: #ff8000;
    }
}
```

The **Modernizr** tool is a JavaScript library that detects HTML5 and CSS3 features in the user's browser. After detecting the features, Modernizr also adds condition classes to the `body` tag in your HTML document. For this reason, the changing selecting order technique can also be used together with Modernizr.

See also

▸ Conditional Stylesheets vs CSS Hacks? Answer: Neither! by Paul Irish can be read at `http://www.paulirish.com/2008/conditional-stylesheets-vs-css-hacks-answer-neither/`

▸ The Modernizr JavaScript library can be found at `http://modernizr.com/`

Using extend to merge selectors

The `:extend()` pseudo class has been added to Less to merge selectors. In contrast to using a mixin to set the properties, the `:extend()` pseudo class can also be applied for composite selectors. Merging selectors with the `:extend()` pseudo class reduces the number of sectors that have the same properties in the compiled CSS code. Merged selectors reduce the size of your final CSS code.

Getting ready

In this recipe, you will compile two pieces of the Less code to see how the `:extend()` pseudo class works.

You can compile the Less code in this recipe with the command-line `lessc` compiler, as described in the *Installing the lessc compiler with npm* recipe in *Chapter 1, Getting to Grips with the Basics of Less*. You can edit the code in this recipe with your favorite text editor.

How to do it...

1. The `:extend()` pseudo class can be put directly on a selector, as shown in the following Less code:

```
.class1{
  property: value;
}
.class2:extend(.class1){};
```

2. Write the preceding Less code into a file and compile this file with the command-line `lessc` compiler. You will find that the Less code will compile into the following CSS code:

```
.class1,

.class2 {

  property: value;

}
```

How it works...

The `:extend()` syntax is attached to a selector and looks like a pseudo class in CSS with one or more selectors as parameters. In this recipe, the `:extend()` selector will apply the extending selector (`.class2`) on to the `.class1` class. The `.class2` class will be applied on appearances of the `.class1` class. By default, nested appearances and appearances inside media declarations of the `.class1` class are not taken into account. Read the *Using extend inside a ruleset* recipe to find out how to extend nested selectors, and read the *Extending with media queries* recipe to get a grip on extending inside media declarations.

There's more...

The `:extend()` pseudo class can be put on a selector together with other pseudo classes, but the `:extend()` pseudo class should always be added at the end of the selector. So, `.selector:hover:extend(){}` will be a valid Less code in contrast to the `.selector:extend():hover{}` code, which will be invalid.

Less allows you to put multiple `:extend()` pseudo classes on the same selector, as shown in the following Less code:

```
.selector:extend(.class1):extend(.class2) {}
```

Note that the preceding Less code can also be written as follows:

```
.selector:extend(.class1, .class2) {}
```

In case you apply the `:extend()` selector on the same ruleset more than once, Less doesn't remove duplicates, as shown in the following Less code:

```
.class1,
.class2 {
  color: black;
}
.class3:extend(.class1,.class2){};
```

The preceding Less code will compile into the following CSS code:

```
.class1,
.class2,
.class3,
.class3 {
  color: black;
}
```

The `.class3` class has been compiled twice in the CSS code.

Using extend inside a ruleset

In most use cases, the `:extend()` pseudo class will be put on the selector using the `&` parent referencing sign, as described in the *Referencing parent selectors with the & operator* recipe.

Getting ready

You can compile the Less code in this recipe with the command-line `lessc` compiler, as described in the *Installing the lessc compiler with npm* recipe in *Chapter 1, Getting to Grips with the Basics of Less*. You can edit the code in this recipe with your favorite text editor.

How to do it...

Write the following Less code into a file and compile this file with the command-line `lessc` compiler:

```less
.class1{
  property: value;
}
.class2 {
  &:extend(.class1);
}
```

You will find that the Less code will compile into the following CSS code:

```css
.class1, class2{
  property: value;
}
```

There's more...

A common use case to use the `:extend()` pseudo class was shown in this recipe. This is to avoid the base or double CSS classes in the HTML markup. Because of the classes being merged, you only have to reference the extended class, as discussed in the following example.

Assume you will need variations of buttons with different background colors. In that case, you can define the following code in Less:

```less
.button {
  border: 1px solid black;
}
.button-red {
  background-color: red;
}
```

The compiled CSS code of the preceding Less code can be used with the following HTML snippet:

```
<button class="button button-red">
```

The preceding HTML snippet can be reduced to the following HTML code, without the .button class, when the .button-red class extends the .button class in Less:

```
<button class="button-red">
```

The Less code for the reduced HTML code will look like the following code:

```
.button {
  border: 1px solid black;
}
.button-red {
  &:extend(.button);
  background-color: red;
}
```

Note that Less provides you with different solutions that can be compiled into different CSS code with the same style effects. In most cases, there is no best solution; the solution to choose depends on the requirements of your project or even personal preferences. Some methodologies for writing CSS are OOCSS, SMACSS, and BEM. These methodologies will help you to structure and write more maintainable CSS code.

The preceding question to create different colored buttons can also be solved with the & parent referencing sign, as described in the *Referencing parent selectors with the & operator* recipe. When using only the & operator, the classes can be merged with the following code:

```
.button {
  border: 1px solid black;
  &-red {
    background-color: red;
  }
}
```

The preceding Less code will compile into the CSS code with separated classes for each button variation, but the same border property will be repeated for each class. If the number of different button variations grows, the size of the compiled CSS code will also increase due to the repeating border property declaration.

Finally, you should know that in the case of nesting, extending can become complicated due to the :extend() pseudo class, which has been applied on all the parents. Also, read the *There's more...* section of the *Referencing to the parent selector more than once* recipe for an explanation of this behavior.

Consider the following Less code, which also makes use of the `all` keyword:

```
.class1 {
    .class2 {color:red}
}
div > div:extend(.class2 all){}
```

The preceding Less code will be compiled into the following CSS code:

```
.class1 .class2,
.class1 div > div {
  color: #ff0000;
}
```

The `.class1 div > div` selector is not what is expected in most cases. The desired `div > div` selector can be compiled with the `div > div:extend(.class 1 .class2 all){}` Less code.

See also

▸ In some cases, the `:extend()` pseudo class can be used to reduce the CSS size, but this is not always true

▸ The *An Introduction To Object Oriented CSS (OOCSS)* article can be found at `http://www.smashingmagazine.com/2011/12/12/an-introduction-to-object-oriented-css-oocss/`

▸ Learn more about SMACSS at `https://smacss.com/` and get introduced to the BEM methodology at `https://bem.info/`

▸ Also, read *Organizing CSS: OOCSS, SMACSS, and BEM* by Matt Stauffer at `http://mattstauffer.co/blog/organizing-css-oocss-smacss-and-bem`

Extending with the all keyword

The `all` keyword can be added at the end of the `extend` argument to match all the instances of the selector. In this recipe, you can find that all the instances of a selector include merged and nested selectors. The `all` keyword can also be used to extend pseudo classes that are nested with the `&:pseudoclass` syntax, as discussed in the *Referencing parent selectors with the & operator* recipe.

Getting ready

You can compile the Less code in this recipe with the command-line `lessc` compiler, as described in the *Installing the lessc compiler with npm* recipe in *Chapter 1, Getting to Grips with the Basics of Less*. Use your favorite text editor to create and edit an example Less file called `all.less`.

How to do it...

1. Write the following Less code into an `all.less` file:

```
a.red-link {
  color:red;
  &:hover {
    color: lighten(red,20%);
  }
}
a.another:extend(a.red-link){}
a.another-withhover:extend(a.red-link all){}
.link--error:extend(.red-link){}
.link-all--error:extend(.red-link all){}
```

2. Compile the preceding code with the following command:

```
lessc all.less
```

3. Finally, you will find that the preceding Less code compiles into the CSS code, as follows:

```
a.red-link,

a.another,

a.another-withhover,

a.link-all--error {

  color: red;

}

a.red-link:hover,

a.another-withhover:hover,
```

```
a.link-all--error:hover {

  color: #ff6666;

}
```

How it works...

Unless the `all` keyword is used, only selectors that have an exact match are extended. When extending without the `all` keyword, as in the `a.another:extend(a.red-link){}` code, only the exactly matched `a.red-link` selector will compile into the CSS code. With the `all` keyword, Less also matches selectors that match parts of other selectors. In this recipe, the extended `.red-link` selector in the `.greenlink:extend(.red-link){}` code did not match the `a.red-link` selector. When using the `all` keyword, the preceding selectors will match because the `.red-link` selector matches the `.red-link` part of the `a.red-link` selector.

You also saw that when using the `all` keyword, the `&:hover {}` code was compiled into the CSS code. To understand this, you will have to realize that the `&` operator only adds a reference to the parent. So consider the following Less code:

```
.class{
  &:hover{}
}
```

Note that the preceding code, except from the parent reference, does not differ from the following Less code:

```
.class:hover {}
```

When extending with the `all` keyword, the `.class` selector will match the `.class` part of the `.class:hover` selector.

There's more...

The `all` keyword can also be applied in situations where the selectors describe child and sibling relations. An example of such a situation can be seen when considering the following Less code:

```
header p.red {
  color: red;
}
.red-paragraph:extend(p.red all){};
```

The preceding Less code will be compiled into the following CSS code:

```
header p.red,
header .red-paragraph {
  color: red;
}
```

Also, in the preceding Less example, note that the `header p.red` selector does not differ from the Less code with the `p` and `.red` selectors nested, as in the following code:

```
header {
  p {
    &.red {
      color: red;
    }
  }
}
```

Now, it will also be easier to understand that the compiled CSS code of the `.class1:extend(.red all) {}` Less code will be different from the compiled `.class1:extend(header p.red all) {}` Less code. The latest situation when compiling the `.class1:extend(header p.red all) {}` code can be compared to the mixin of the `.red` class into `.class1`. The use of the `:extend()` pseudo class as an alternative to mixins will be described in more detail in the *Using extend as an alternative for a mixin* recipe.

Finally, note that when extending more than one selector, you will have to add the `all` keyword after each selector. This can be seen in the following example code:

```
selector:extend {.class1 all, .class2 all}{}
```

See also

- ▶ Nesting can make extending more complicated, as described in the *There's more...* section of the *Using extend inside a ruleset* recipe

Extending with media queries

The CSS media queries help you to display the same content in a different way, depending on device properties, such as screen width or pixel ratio. The CSS media queries play an important role in responsive web design. In Less, `@media` declarations for the media queries have their own scope. This secluded scope in Less also influences how the `:extend()` pseudo class works inside media queries. This recipe tells why and how the `:extend()` pseudo class works differently when used inside a `@media` declaration.

Getting ready

In this recipe, you will compile some example Less code. You can use the command-line `lessc` compiler, as described in the *Installing the lessc compiler with npm* in *Chapter 1, Getting to Grips with the Basics of Less*, to compile this Less code. Otherwise, you can also use the client-side `less.js` compiler, as described in the *Downloading, installing, and integrating less.js* recipe in *Chapter 1, Getting to Grips with the Basics of Less*, to see the effect of the media queries in your browsers. The media queries in this recipe set conditions for the screen width of the device. You can make the effect of these media queries visible by resizing the window (screen width) of your browser.

How to do it...

1. Write the following Less code into an `extend-media.less` file:

```less
.base-font {
  font-family: Arial;
}
@media all {    .base-color {
  color: green;
  }
  p.base-class {
    &:extend(.base-font, .base-color, .base-border);
    font-size: 2em;

    @media (min-width: 768px) {
      &.base-border {
        border: 1px solid black;
      }
    }
  }
}
```

2. Compile the preceding Less code from step 1 with the command-line compiler, or include the `extend-media.less` and `less.js` files into an `index.html` file and load this file in your browser. The `index.html` should contain the following lines of code in the `head` section:

```
<link rel="stylesheet/less" type="text/css"
  href="extendmedia.less">
<script src="less.js" type="text/javascript"></script>
```

3. Now inspect the result and find that the `p.base-class` selector does not extend the `.base-font` selector as well as the `.base-border` selector.

4. Finally, rewrite your Less code by removing the `&:extend(.basefont, .maincolor, .mainborder);` line of code and add a new selector to the main scope that extends the `p.base-class-extended` selector with the `.base-font`, `.base-color`, and `.base-border` selectors. Your Less code should look like the following code:

```less
.base-font {

  font-family: Arial;

}

@media all {

  .base-color {

    color: green;

  }

  .base-class {

    font-size: 2em;

    @media (min-width: 768px) {

      &.base-border {

        border: 1px solid black;

      }

    }
```

```
          }

      }

    .base-class-extended:extend(.base-font, .base-color,
      .base-class.base-border) {}
```

How it works...

As you can see in the first step of this recipe, the `:extend()` pseudo class is used inside a `media` declaration. You can only extend selectors inside the same media declaration; all selectors outside the scope of the media declaration are ignored. Nevertheless, selectors inside the `media` declarations can be extended from the main scope, as is shown in the last step.

There's more...

Note that in step 4, the `.base-class-extended` selector was extended with `.base-class.base-border`, which results in the following compiled CSS code:

```
@media all and (min-width: 768px) {

  .base-class.base-border,

  .base-class-extended {

    border: 1px solid black;

  }

}
```

From the preceding code, what follows is that the `.base-border` class is not required to style the border for elements within the `.base-class-extended` class.

See also

▶ The media queries are also used to build responsive grids, as described in the *Creating responsive grids* recipe in *Chapter 8, Building a Layout with Less*

Using extend to reduce the compiled CSS size

In this recipe, you will see how to use Less's :extend() pseudo class to reduce the size of the compiled CSS code.

Getting ready

You can compile the Less code in this recipe with the command-line lessc compiler, as described in the *Installing the lessc compiler with npm* recipe in *Chapter 1, Getting to Grips with the Basics of Less*. Use your favorite text editor to create and edit the Less files used in this recipe.

How to do it...

1. Write the following Less code into a Less file and compile this file with the command-line lessc compiler:

```less
.mixin() {
  property1: value;
  property2: value;
}
.class1 {
  .mixin;
}
.class2 {
  .mixin;
}
```

2. You will find that the preceding Less code will compile into the following CSS code:

```css
.class1 {
  property1: value;
  property2: value;
}
.class2 {
  property1: value;
  property2: value;
}
```

3. Now rewrite your Less code, leveraging Less's `:extend()` pseudo class. Your Less code will now look as follows:

```
.mixin {
  property1: value;
  property2: value;
}
.class1:extend(.mixin){}
.class2:extend(.mixin){}
```

4. Finally, compare the compiled CSS code shown in the following code with the compiled CSS code from the step 2 of this recipe:

```
.mixin,
.class1,
.class2 {
  property1: value;
  property2: value;
}
```

How it works...

To reduce the CSS size in this recipe, the mixin was changed into a class by removing the parenthesis from the code. You saw that the Less code rewritten with Less's `:extend()` pseudo class compiles into a list with three merged classes. All the classes in this list set the same properties and values. The Less's `:extend()` pseudo class helps not to repeat the same properties and values and only write them out in the CSS code once.

There's more...

Using the Less's `:extend()` pseudo class shown in this recipe does not reduce the size of the CSS code in all situations. Consider the situation in the *There's more...* section of the *Using extend inside a ruleset* recipe. The code in this section uses the Less's `:extend()` pseudo class to avoid the base classes. If the number of properties of your base class is small in relation to the number of classes and states that extend this base class, the total size of your CSS will increase when extending this base class. An example of this situation can be found in the Less code of Bootstrap. Bootstrap, which will be discussed in *Chapter 9, Using Bootstrap with Less,* uses a base class for the styling of buttons, panels, and labels, among others. Consider an example code to see what happens. Compile the following Less code:

```
.base-class {
  color: red;
```

```less
    &:hover,
    &:focus {
        background-color: lightgreen;
    }
}

.green {
  &:extend(.base-class all);
  background-color: green;
}
```

When evaluating the compiled CSS code, you will find relatively long lists of selectors, such as the ones shown in the following compiled CSS code:

```css
.base-class:hover,
.base-class:focus,
.green:hover,
.green:focus {
  background-color: lightgreen;
}
```

The total size of the CSS code increases due to the long list of selectors. Less will give you solutions to extend the CSS syntax, but you still have to choose how to deploy these solutions. Finding the best solution depends on your requirements.

Also note that your class names in Less are compiled completely into the CSS code, and long class names will increase the size of the CSS code. On the other hand, short, meaningless class names will make your Less code unreadable and difficult to maintain.

Before you take your code in production, you should always compress your compiled CSS code.

See also

▶ Besides the default option of compiler, you can also use the Clean CSS plugin for Less to compress the CSS output from Less. More information about how to install and use this plugin can be found at `https://github.com/less/less-plugin-clean-css`

Using extend as an alternative for a mixin

Currently, Less accepts only simple selectors as a mixin. In this recipe, you will see how the `:extend()` pseudo class can be used to mix the nested or child selectors. Using the `:extend()` pseudo class as a mixin will have the same style effect, but the compiled CSS code will be different. The `:extend()` pseudo class merges selectors, and mixins add copy or property to the selector.

Getting ready

In this recipe, you will only compile a small piece of Less code. You can use the command-line `lessc` compiler, as described in the *Installing the lessc compiler with npm* in *Chapter 1, Getting to Grips with the Basics of Less.*

How to do it...

1. Write some Less code that styles a `button` element inside a `nav` element, and save this code in the `nav.less` file. You can use the following code to do this:

```less
nav {
  button {
    border: 1px solid: white;
    background-color: red;
    color: white;
  }
}
```

2. To apply the same style rules on another button element, you can use the following Less code:

```less
footer {
  button:extend(nav button) {}
}
```

After compiling the preceding Less code with the command-line `lessc` compiler, you will find that the compiled CSS code will look as follows:

```css
nav button,
footer button {
  border: 1px solid: white;
  background-color: red;
  color: white;
}
```

How it works...

The nested `button` selector will not differ from the `nav` button selector. Instead of the nested selector, you can also write the following Less code:

```
nav button {
  border: 1px solid: white;
  background-color: red;
  color: white;
}
```

Less does not enable you to mix the `nav` button selector.

6

Advanced Less Coding

In this chapter, you will learn:

- Giving your rules importance with the `!important` statement
- Using mixins with multiple parameters
- Using duplicate mixin names
- Building a switch to leverage argument matching
- Avoiding individual parameters to leverage the `@arguments` variable
- Using the `@rest...` variable to use mixins with a variable number of arguments
- Using mixins as functions
- Passing rulesets to mixins
- Using mixin guards (as an alternative for the `if...else` statements)
- Building loops leveraging mixin guards
- Applying guards to the CSS selectors
- Creating color contrasts with Less
- Changing the background color dynamically
- Aggregating values under a single property

Introduction

Less helps you to write a better and more readable CSS code. With Less, you will code faster and will be able to meet the **don't repeat yourself** (**DRY**) principle of software programming. In this chapter, you will see how to create a dynamic and reusable Less code by exploring the features of Less in more detail.

You will find out how to create a switch leveraging argument matching, how to build the if... else constructs with the Less guards, and how to dynamically create a list of CSS classes with recursion in Less by creating a loop.

Giving your rules importance with the !important statement

The !important statement in CSS can be used to get some style rules always applied no matter where that rules appears in the CSS code. In Less, the !important statement can be applied with mixins and variable declarations too.

Getting ready

You can write the Less code for this recipe with your favorite editor. After that, you can use the command-line lessc compiler, as described in the *Installing the lessc compiler with npm* recipe in *Chapter 1, Getting to Grips with the Basics of Less*, to compile the Less code. Finally, you can inspect the compiled CSS code to see where the !important statements appear. To see the real effect of the !important statements, you should compile the Less code client side, with the client-side compiler less.js, as described in the *Downloading, installing, and integrating less.js* recipe in *Chapter 1, Getting to Grips with the Basics of Less*, and watch the effect in your web browser.

How to do it...

1. Create an important.less file that contains the code like the following snippet:

```
.mixin() {
  color: red;
  font-size: 2em;
}
p {
  &.important {
    .mixin() !important;
  }
```

```less
  &.unimportant {
    .mixin();
  }
}
```

2. After compiling the preceding Less code with the command-line `lessc` compiler, you will find the following code output produced in the console:

```css
p.important {
  color: red !important;
  font-size: 2em !important;
}
p.unimportant {
  color: red;
  font-size: 2em;
}
```

3. You can, for instance, use the following snippet of the HTML code to see the effect of the `!important` statements in your browser:

```html
<p class="important"
  style="color:green;font-size:4em;">important</p>
<p class="unimportant"
  style="color:green;font-size:4em;">unimportant</p>
```

Your HTML document should also include the `important.less` and `less.js` files, as follows:

```html
<link rel="stylesheet/less" type="text/css"
  href="important.less">
<script src="less.js" type="text/javascript"></script>
```

4. Finally, the result will look like that shown in the following screenshot:

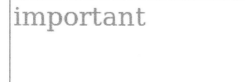

How it works...

In Less, you can use the `!important` statement not only for properties, but also with mixins. When `!important` is set for a certain mixin, all properties of this mixin will be declared with the `!important` statement. You can easily see this effect when inspecting the properties of the `p.important` selector, both the color and size property got the `!important` statement after compiling the code.

There's more...

You should use the `!important` statements with care as the only way to overrule an `!important` statement is to use another `!important` statement. The `!important` statement overrules the normal CSS cascading, specificity rules, and even the inline styles. Any incorrect or unnecessary use of the `!important` statements in your Less (or CCS) code will make your code messy and difficult to maintain.

In most cases where you try to overrule a style rule, you should give preference to selectors with a higher specificity and not use the `!important` statements at all.

With Less V2, you can also use the `!important` statement when declaring your variables. A declaration with the `!important` statement can look like the following code:

```
@main-color: darkblue !important;
```

See also

▸ You can read more about the cascade, specificity, and inheritance of style rules in CSS at http://reference.sitepoint.com/css/inheritancecascade

▸ Read the first chapter of my book, *Less Web Development Essentials*, *Bass Jobsen*, *Packt Publishing, April 2014*, available at http://www.packtpub.com/web-development/less-web-development-essentials

Using mixins with multiple parameters

As also seen in the *Setting the properties of CSS styles with mixins* recipe in *Chapter 1, Getting to Grips with the Basics of Less* and the *Using parametric mixins* recipe in *Chapter 3, Using Variables and Mixins*, mixins can take arguments, which are variables passed to the block of selectors when it is mixed in. The mixin in the recipe in *Chapter 1, Getting to Grips with the Basics of Less*, accepts a single parameter as argument only, but mixins can be built to accept more than one parameter. In this section, you will learn how to use mixins with more than one parameter.

Getting ready

For this recipe, you will have to create a Less file, for instance, `mixins.less`. You can compile this `mixins.less` file with the command-line `lessc` compiler, as described in the *Installing the lessc compiler with npm* recipe in *Chapter 1, Getting to Grips with the Basics of Less.*

How to do it...

1. Create the `mixins.less` file and write down the following Less code into it:

```
.mixin(@color; @background: black;) {
  background-color: @background;
  color: @color;
}
div {
    .mixin(red; white;);
}
```

2. Compile the `mixins.less` file by running the command shown in the console, as follows:

```
lessc mixins.less
```

3. Inspect the CSS code output on the console, and you will find that it looks like that shown, as follows:

```
div {
  background-color: #ffffff;
  color: #ff0000;
}
```

How it works...

In Less, parameters are either semicolon-separated or comma-separated. Using a semicolon as a separator will be preferred because the usage of the comma will be ambiguous. The comma separator is not used only to separate parameters, but is also used to define a `csv` list, which can be an argument itself.

The mixin in this recipe accepts two arguments. The first parameter sets the `@color` variable, while the second parameter sets the `@background` variable and has a default value that has been set to `black`. In the argument list, the default values are defined by writing a colon behind the variable's name, followed by the value. Parameters with a default value are optional when calling the mixins. So the `.color` mixin in this recipe can also be called with the following line of code:

```
.mixin(red);
```

Because the second argument has a default value set to `black`, the `.mixin(red);` call also matches the `.mixin(@color; @background:black){}` mixin, as described in the *Building a switch to leverage argument matching* recipe.

Only variables set as parameter of a mixin are set inside the scope of the mixin. You can see this when compiling the following Less code:

```
.mixin(@color:blue) {
  color2: @color;
}
@color: red;
div {
  color1: @color;
  .mixin;
}
```

The preceding Less code compiles into the following CSS code:

```
div {
  color1: #ff0000;
  color2: #0000ff;
}
```

As you can see in the preceding example, setting `@color` inside the mixin to its default value does not influence the value of `@color` assigned in the main scope. So lazy loading is applied on only variables inside the same scope; nevertheless, you will have to note that variables assigned in a mixin will leak into the caller. The leaking of variables can be used to use mixins as functions, as described in the *Using mixins as functions* recipe.

There's more...

Consider the mixin definition in the following Less code:

```
.mixin(@font-family: "Helvetica Neue", Helvetica, Arial,
  sans-serif;) {
  font-family: @font-family;
}
```

The semicolon added at the end of the list prevents the fonts after the `"Helvetica Neue"` font name in the `csv` list from being read as arguments for this mixin. If the argument list contains any semicolon, the Less compiler will use semicolons as a separator. In the CSS3 specification, among others, the border and background shorthand properties accepts `csv`.

Also, note that the Less compiler allows you to use the named parameters when calling mixins. This can be seen in the following Less code that uses the `@color` variable as a named parameter:

```
.mixin(@width:50px; @color: yellow) {
  width: @width;
  color: @color;
}
span {
  .mixin(@color: green);
}
```

The preceding Less code will compile into the following CSS code:

```
span {
  width: 50px;
  color: #008000;
}
```

Note that in the preceding code, `#008000` is the hexadecimal representation for the green color. When using the named parameters, their order does not matter.

See also

▶ You can look up the allowed values for a certain CSS property at `http://cssvalues.com/`

Using duplicate mixin names

When your Less code contains one or more mixins with the same name, the Less compiler compiles them all into the CSS code. If the mixin has parameters (see the *Building a switch to leverage argument matching* recipe) the number of parameters will also match.

Getting ready

You can compile the Less code in this recipe with the command-line `lessc` compiler, as described in the *Installing the lessc compiler with npm* recipe in *Chapter 1, Getting to Grips with the Basics of Less*. Use your favorite text editor to create and edit the Less files used in this recipe.

How to do it...

1. Create a file called `mixins.less` that contains the following Less code:

```less
.mixin(){
  height:50px;
}
.mixin(@color) {
  color: @color;
}

.mixin(@width) {
  color: green;
  width: @width;
}

.mixin(@color; @width) {
  color: @color;
  width: @width;
}

.selector-1 {
  .mixin(red);
}

.selector-2 {
  .mixin(red; 500px);
}
```

2. Compile the Less code from step 1 by running the following command in the console:

   `lessc mixins.less`

3. After running the command from the previous step, you will find the following Less code output on the console:

```less
.selector-1 {
  color: #ff0000;
  color: green;
  width: #ff0000;
}
.selector-2 {
  color: #ff0000;
  width: 500px;
}
```

How it works...

The `.selector-1` selector contains the `.mixin(red);` call. The `.mixin(red);` call does not match the `.mixin(){};` mixin as the number of arguments does not match. On the other hand, both `.mixin(@color){};` and `.mixin(@width){};` match the color. For this reason, these mixins will compile into the CSS code. The `.mixin(red; 500px);` call inside the `.selector-2` selector will match only the `.mixin(@color; @width){};` mixin, so all other mixins with the same `.mixin` name will be ignored by the compiler when building the `.selector-2` selector.

The compiled CSS code for the `.selector-1` selector also contains the `width: #ff0000;` property value as the `.mixin(@width){};` mixin matches the call too. Setting the width property to a color value makes no sense in CSS but the Less compiler does not check for this kind of errors. In this recipe, you can also rewrite the `.mixin(@width){};` mixin, as follows: `.mixin(@width) when (ispixel(@width)){};`.

There's more...

Maybe you have noted that the `.selector-1` selector contains two color properties. The Less compiler does not remove duplicate properties unless the value also is the same. The CSS code sometimes should contain duplicate properties in order to provide a fallback for older browsers.

In the case that you are using more than one library with prebuilt mixins, as described in *Chapter 7, Leveraging Libraries with Prebuilt Mixins*, duplicate mixin names could mess up your CSS code and will give you unexpected and unwanted results. Using namespaces, as described in the *Using namespaces to make your code reusable and portable* recipe in *Chapter 1, Getting to Grips with the Basics of Less*, prevent equal-named mixins of different libraries from touching each other.

Note that the `.mixin(@color; @width){};` mixin does not match the `.mixin(red);` caller in the example code of this recipe, but this mixin should indeed match and will be compiled into the CSS when the second argument sets a default value. So, the `.mixin(green);` call will match the `.mixin(@color; @width: 50px){};` mixin.

See also

- ► You can use CSSlint, as described in the *Analyzing your code with CSS Lint* recipe in *Chapter 11, Compiling Less Real Time for Development Using Grunt*, to check your code for errors

- ► Using guarded mixins, as described in the *Using mixin guards (as an alternative for the if...else statements)* recipe, can also help you to avoid the CSS syntax errors

- ► You can read more about the built-in function, such as the `ispixel()` function in the *Evaluating the type of a value* recipe in *Chapter 4, Leveraging the Less Built-in Functions*

Building a switch to leverage argument matching

The Less mixin will compile into the final CSS code only when the number of arguments of the caller and the mixins match. This feature of Less can be used to build switches. Switches enable you to change the behavior of a mixin conditionally. In this recipe, you will create a mixin, or better yet, three mixins with the same name.

Getting ready

Use the command-line `lessc` compiler, as described in the *Installing the lessc compiler with npm* recipe in *Chapter 1, Getting to Grips with the Basics of Less*, to evaluate the effect of this mixin. The compiler will output the final CSS to the console. You can use your favorite text editor to edit the Less code.

This recipe makes use of browser-vendor prefixes, such as the `-ms-transform` prefix. CSS3 introduced **vendor-specific rules**, which offer you the possibility to write some additional CSS, applicable for only one browser. These rules allow browsers to implement proprietary CSS properties that would otherwise have no working standard (and might never actually become the standard). To find out which prefixes should be used for a certain property, you can consult the **Can I use** database (available at `http://caniuse.com/`).

How to do it...

1. Create a `switch.less` Less file, and write down the following Less code into it:

```less
@browserversion: ie9;
.mixin(ie9; @degrees){
  transform:rotate(@degrees);
  -ms-transform:rotate(@degrees);
  -webkit-transform:rotate(@degrees);
}
.mixin(ie10; @degrees){
  transform:rotate(@degrees);
  -webkit-transform:rotate(@degrees);
}
.mixin(@_; @degrees){
  transform:rotate(@degrees);
}
div {
  .mixin(@browserversion; 70deg);
}
```

2. Compile the Less code from step 1 by running the following command in the console:

   `lessc switch.less`

3. Inspect the compiled CSS code that has been output to the console, and you will find that it looks like the following code:

```
div {
  -ms-transform: rotate(70deg);
  -webkit-transform: rotate(70deg);
  transform: rotate(70deg);
}
```

4. Finally, run the following command and you will find that the compiled CSS will indeed differ from that of step 2:

   `lessc --modify-var="browserversion=ie10" switch.less`

Now the compiled CSS code will look like the following code snippet:

```
div {
  -webkit-transform: rotate(70deg);
  transform: rotate(70deg);
}
```

How it works...

The switch in this recipe is the `@browserversion` variable that can easily be changed just before compiling your code. Instead of changing your code, you can also set the `--modify-var` option of the compiler.

Depending on the value of the `@browserversion` variable, the mixins that match will be compiled, and the other mixins will be ignored by the compiler. The `.mixin(ie10; @degrees){}` mixin matches the `.mixin(@browserversion; 70deg);` call only when the value of the `@browserversion` variable is equal to `ie10`. Note that the first `ie10` argument of the mixin will be used only for matching (`argument = ie10`) and does not assign any value.

You will note that the `.mixin(@_; @degrees){}` mixin will match each call no matter what the value of the `@browserversion` variable is. The `.mixin(ie9,70deg);` call also compiles the `.mixin(@_; @degrees){}` mixin. Although this should result in the `transform: rotate(70deg);` property output twice, you will find only one. Since the property got exactly the same value twice, the compiler outputs the property only once.

There's more...

Not only switches, but also mixin guards, as described in the *Using mixin guards (as an alternative for the if...else statements)* recipe, can be used to set some properties conditionally.

Note that the compiled CSS code will always be stateless. After compilation, the same CSS code will be loaded independently of the browser you use to interpret the CSS code. Of course, the results and the interpretation of the compiled style rules can differ depending on the browser used.

At compilation time, the compiler knows nothing about the browser environment, so setting `@browserversion` to `ie9` will compile code that can be read by Internet Explorer 9, but other browsers will interpret exactly the same code. When compiling browser-specific styles, you should only serve these styles to specific browsers. The client-side `less.js` compiler, as described in the *Downloading, installing, and integrating less.js* recipe in *Chapter 1, Getting to Grips with the Basics of Less*, compiles your Less code again for every browser request, which allows you to set some variables dynamically with the `modify-var` option of the compiler. The `--modify-var` option sets the value of a Less variable, the variable has been assigned at the end of the code, which means that it will override anything defined in your Less file. Note that you should not use the client-side compiler in production environments for performance reasons.

Note that mostly browser-specific styles are not compiled at all. Autoprefix postprocessors help you to create a single file with prefixes to support different browsers. Web browsers ignore properties that are not supported. Since Version 2 of Less, you can use the autoprefix plugin to add your vendor prefixes automatically.

Current versions of Less also support JavaScript evaluating; JavaScript code put between back quotes will be evaluated by the compiler, as can be seen in the following Less code example:

```less
@string: "example in lower case";
p {
  &:after { content: "`@{string}.toUpperCase()`"; 
  }
}
```

The preceding code will be compiled into CSS, as follows:

```css
p:after {
  content: "EXAMPLE IN LOWER CASE";
}
```

When using client-side compiling, JavaScript evaluating can also be used to get some information from the browser environment, such as the screen width (`screen.width`), but as mentioned already, you should not use client-side compiling for production environments.

Because you can't be sure that future versions of Less still support JavaScript evaluating, and alternative compilers not written in JavaScript cannot evaluate the JavaScript code, you should always try to write your Less code without JavaScript.

See also

- The Less autoprefix plugin can be found at `https://github.com/less/less-plugin-autoprefix`
- In *Chapter 11*, *Compiling Less Real Time for Development Using Grunt*, you can read how to add the vendor prefixes with Grunt
- The `-prefix-free` JavaScript script, which can be found at `http://leaverou.github.io/prefixfree/`, can be used as an alternative for the autoprefixed CSS code

Avoiding individual parameters to leverage the @arguments variable

In the Less code, the `@arguments` variable has a special meaning inside mixins. The `@arguments` variable contains all arguments passed to the mixin. In this recipe, you will use the `@arguments` variable together with the the CSS `url()` function to set a background image for a selector.

Getting ready

You can inspect the compiled CSS code in this recipe after compiling the Less code with the command-line `lessc` compiler. Alternatively, you can inspect the results in your browser using the client-side `less.js` compiler. When inspecting the result in your browser, you will also need an example image that can be used as a background image. Use your favorite text editor to create and edit the Less files used in this recipe.

How to do it...

1. Create a `background.less` file that contains the following Less code:

    ```less
    .background(@color; @image; @repeat: no-repeat; @position:
      top right;)
    {
      background: @arguments;
    }
    ```

```
div {
  .background(#000; url("./images/bg.png"));
  width:300px;
  height:300px;
}
```

2. Finally, inspect the compiled CSS code, and you will find that it will look like the following code snippet:

```
div {
  background: #000000 url("./images/bg.png") no-repeat top
    right;
  width: 300px;
  height: 300px;
}
```

How it works...

The four parameters of the `.background()` mixin are assigned as a space-separated list to the `@arguments` variable. After that, the `@arguments` variable can be used to set the background property. Also, other CSS properties accept space-separated lists, for example, the margin and padding properties.

Note that the `@arguments` variable does not contain only the parameters that have been set explicit by the caller, but also the parameters set by their default value. You can easily see this when inspecting the compiled CSS code of this recipe. The `.background(#000; url("./images/bg.png"));` caller doesn't set the `@repeat` or `@position` argument, but you will find their values in the compiled CSS code.

There's more...

In this recipe, the background image has been set with the CSS `url()` function. Less also enables you to embed your images with the data URIs, as described in the *Embedding images with data URIs* recipe in *Chapter 4, Leveraging the Less Built-in Functions*. In this recipe, you can do this by replacing `.background(#000; url(images/bg.png));` with the `.background(#000; data-uri(images/bg.png));` call.

See also

▶ In the *Installing the lessc compiler with npm* recipe in *Chapter 1, Getting to Grips with the Basics of Less*, you can read how to use the `lessc` compiler

▶ Also read the *Downloading, installing, and integrating less.js* recipe in *Chapter 1, Getting to Grips with the Basics of Less*

Using the @rest... variable to use mixins with a variable number of arguments

As you can also see in the *Using mixins with multiple parameters* and *Using duplicate mixin names* recipes, only matching mixins are compiled into the final CSS code. In some situations, you don't know the number of parameters or want to use mixins for some style rules no matter the number of parameters. In these situations, you can use the special . . . syntax or the @ rest . . . variable to create mixins that match independent of the number of parameters.

Getting ready

You will have to create a file called rest . less, and this file can be compiled with the command-line lessc compiler, as described in the *Installing the lessc compiler with npm* in *Chapter 1, Getting to Grips with the Basics of Less*. You can edit the Less code with your favorite editor.

How to do it...

1. Create a file called rest . less that contains the following Less code:

    ```
    .mixin(@a...)
    {
      .set(@a) when (iscolor(@a)) {
        color: @a;
      }
      .set(@a) when (length(@a) = 2) {
        margin: @a;
      }
      .set(@a);
    }
    p{
      .mixin(red);
    }
    p {
      .mixin(2px;4px);
    }
    ```

2. Compile the rest . less file from step 1 using the following command in the console:

    lessc rest.less

3. Inspect the CSS code output to the console that will look like the following code:

```
p {
  color: #ff0000;
}
p {
  margin: 2px 4px;
}
```

How it works...

The special `...` syntax (three dots) can be used as an argument for a mixin. Mixins with the `...` syntax in their argument list match any number of arguments. When you put a variable name starting with an `@` in front of the `...` syntax, all parameters are assigned to that variable.

You will find a list of examples of mixins that use the special `...` syntax as follows:

▶ `.mixin(@a; ...) {}`: This mixin matches 1-N arguments

▶ `.mixin(...) {}`: This mixin matches 0-N arguments; note that `mixin()` without any argument matches only 0 arguments

▶ `.mixin(@a: 1; @rest...) {}`: This mixin matches 0-N arguments; note that the first argument is assigned to the `@a` variable, and all other arguments are assigned as a space-separated list to `@rest`

Because the `@rest...` variable contains a space-separated list, you can use the Less built-in list function, as described in the *Working with lists* recipe in *Chapter 4, Leveraging the Less Built-in Functions*, to evaluate them.

There's more...

In this recipe, the `.set(@a);` caller is nested in the `.mixin(@a...)` mixin, this caller calls mixins with guards, as described in the *Using mixin guards (as an alternative for the if...else statements)* recipe, to compile the Less code conditional.

Using mixins as functions

People who are used to functional programming expect a mixin to change or return a value. In this recipe, you will learn to use mixins as a function that returns a value.

In this recipe, the value of the width property inside the `div.small` and `div.big` selectors will be set to the length of the longest side of a right-angled triangle based on the length of the two shortest sides of this triangle using the Pythagoras theorem.

Getting ready

The best and easiest way to inspect the results of this recipe will be compiling the Less code with the command-line `lessc` compiler, as described in the *Installing the lessc compiler with npm* in *Chapter 1, Getting to Grips with the Basics of Less*. You can edit the Less code with your favorite editor.

How to do it...

1. Create a file called `pythagoras.less` that contains the following Less code:

```less
.longestSide(@a,@b)
{
  @length: sqrt(pow(@a,2) + pow(@b,2));
}
div {
  &.small {
    .longestSide(3,4);
    width: @length;
  }
  &.big {
    .longestSide(6,7);
    width: @length;
  }
}
```

2. Compile the `pythagoras.less` file from step 1 using the following command in the console:

   `lessc pyhagoras.less`

3. Inspect the CSS code output on the console after compilation and you will see that it looks like the following code snippet:

```css
div.small {
  width: 5;
}
div.big {
  width: 9.21954446;
}
```

How it works...

Variables set inside a mixin become available inside the scope of the caller. This specific behavior of the Less compiler was used in this recipe to set the `@length` variable and to make it available in the scope of the `div.small` and `div.big` selectors and the caller.

As you can see, you can use the mixin in this recipe more than once. With every call, a new scope is created and both selectors get their own value of `@length`.

Also, note that variables set inside the mixin do not overwrite variables with the same name that are set in the caller itself. Take, for instance, the following code:

```
.mixin() {
  @variable: 1;
}
.selector {
  @variable: 2;
  .mixin;
  property: @variable;
}
```

The preceding code will compile into the CSS code, as follows:

```
.selector {
  property: 2;
}
```

There's more...

Note that variables won't leak from the mixins to the caller in the following two situations:

▶ Inside the scope of the caller, a variable with the same name already has been defined (lazy loading will be applied)

▶ The variable has been previously defined by another mixin call (lazy loading will not be applied)

When using mixins as functions, you can also call them in the global scope, which will make the variables available for the global scope too. Note that these global variables can also be used in other mixins, as can be seen when compiling the following Less code:

```
.mixin() {
  @v: 300;
}
```

```
.use-global-variable() {
  property: @v;
}
.mixin;
p {
  .use-global-variable;
}
```

The preceding Less code will compile into the following CSS code:

```
p {
  property: 300;
}
```

Nesting other rules inside the mixin used as a function will also be possible. When using guards, as described in the *Using mixin guards (as an alternative for the if...else statements)* recipe, with these nested rules, you are able to make these mixin functions conditional, as can been seen in the following example Less code:

```
.mixin(@a) {
  .test(@a) when (@a < 5) {
    @size: 5px;
  }
  .test(@a) when (@a >= 5) {
    @size: 50px;
  }
  .test(@a);
}
p {
  .mixin(6);
  size: @size;
}
```

The preceding Less code will compile into the following CSS code; also note the usage of the second `.test(@a);` caller nested inside the `.mixin(@a){}` mixin:

```
p {
  size: 50px;
}
```

You can find more examples of the usage of nested mixins as a function in the *Changing the background color dynamically* recipe.

When using mixins as a function, you cannot use nested media queries to set your variables conditionally based on those media queries. Media queries are evaluated when the CSS code loads in the browser; at compile time, media queries make no sense and cannot be evaluated. For this reason, consider the following Less code:

```less
.mixin() {
  @media (all) {
    @width: 50%;
  }
  @media (print) {
    @width: 100%;
  }
}
p {
  .mixin;
  width: @write;
}
```

The preceding code snippet should be rewritten to the Less code, as shown in the following code snippet:

```less
.mixin(all) {
  @width: 50%;
}
.mixin(print) {
  @width: 100%;
}


p {
  @media (all) {
    .mixin(all);
    width: @width;
  }
  @media (print) {
    .mixin(print);
    width: @width;
  }
}
```

The rewritten Less code will compile into the following CSS code, as follows:

```
@media (all) {
  p {
    width: 50%;
  }
}
@media (print) {
  p {
    width: 100%;
  }
}
```

See also

▶ Read more about the Pythagoras theorem at `http://www.mathcentre.ac.uk/resources/uploaded/mc-ty-pythagoras-2009-1.pdf`

Passing rulesets to mixins

Since Version 1.7, Less allows you to pass complete rulesets as an argument for mixins. Rulesets, including the Less code, can be assigned to variables and passed into mixins, which also allow you to wrap blocks of the CSS code defined inside mixins. In this recipe, you will learn how to do this.

Getting ready

For this recipe, you will have to create a Less file called `keyframes.less`, for instance. You can compile this `mixins.less` file with the command-line `lessc` compiler, as described in the *Installing the lessc compiler with npm* recipe in *Chapter 1, Getting to Grips with the Basics of Less*. Finally, inspect the Less code output to the console.

How to do it...

1. Create the `keyframes.less` file, and write down the following Less code into it:

```
// Keyframes
.keyframe(@name; @roules) {
  @-webkit-keyframes @name {
    @roules();
  }
  @-o-keyframes @name {
    @roules();
  }
  @keyframes @name {
    @roules();
  }
}
.keyframe(progress-bar-stripes; {
  from  { background-position: 40px 0; }
  to    { background-position: 0 0; }
});
```

2. Compile the `keyframes.less` file by running the following command shown in the console:

```
lessc  keyframes.less
```

3. Inspect the CSS code output on the console and you will find that it looks like the following code:

```
@-webkit-keyframes progress-bar-stripes {
  from {
    background-position: 40px 0;
  }
  to {
    background-position: 0 0;
  }
}
@-o-keyframes progress-bar-stripes {
  from {
    background-position: 40px 0;
  }
  to {
    background-position: 0 0;
  }
}
```

```
@keyframes progress-bar-stripes {
  from {
    background-position: 40px 0;
  }
  to {
    background-position: 0 0;
  }
}
```

How it works...

Rulesets wrapped between curly brackets are passed as an argument to the mixin. As you can read in the *Setting the properties of CSS styles with mixins* recipe in *Chapter 1, Getting to Grips with the Basics of Less*, a mixin's arguments are assigned to a (local) variable. When you assign the ruleset to the `@ruleset` variable, you are enabled to call `@ruleset()`; to "mixin" the ruleset.

Note that the passed rulesets can contain the Less code, such as built-in functions too. You can see this by compiling the following Less code:

```less
.mixin(@color; @rules)
{
  @othercolor: green;
  @media (print) {
    @rules();
  }
}

p {
  .mixin(red; {color: lighten(@othercolor,20%);
    background-color:darken(@color,20%);})
}
```

The preceding Less code will compile into the following CSS code:

```css
@media (print) {
  p {
    color: #00e600;
    background-color: #990000;
  }
}
```

A group of CSS properties, nested rulesets, or media declarations stored in a variable is called a detached ruleset. Less offers support for the detached rulesets since Version 1.7.

There's more...

As you could see in the last example in the previous section, rulesets passed as an argument can be wrapped in the `@media` declarations too. This enables you to create mixins that, for instance, wrap any passed ruleset into a `@media` declaration or class. Consider the example Less code shown here:

```
.smallscreens-and-olderbrowsers(@rules)
{
  .lt-ie9 & {
    @rules();
  }
  @media (min-width:768px) {
    @rules();
  }
}
nav {
  float: left;
  width: 20%;
  .smallscreens-and-olderbrowsers({
    float: none;
    width:100%;
  });
}
```

The preceding Less code will compile into the CSS code, as follows:

```
nav {
  float: left;
  width: 20%;
}
.lt-ie9 nav {
  float: none;
  width: 100%;
}
@media (min-width: 768px) {
  nav {
    float: none;
    width: 100%;
  }
}
```

The style rules wrapped in the `.lt-ie9` class can, for instance, be used with Paul Irish's `<html>` conditional classes' technique or Modernizr. Now you can call the `.smallscreens-and-olderbrowsers(){}` mixin anywhere in your code and pass any ruleset to it. All passed rulesets get wrapped in the `.lt-ie9` class or the `@media (min-width: 768px)` declaration now. When your requirements change, you possibly have to change only these wrappers once.

See also

▸ You can read more about Paul Irish's `<html>` conditional classes technique at `http://www.paulirish.com/2008/conditional-stylesheets-vs-css-hacks-answer-neither/`

▸ The Modernizr library can be found at `http://modernizr.com/`

Using mixin guards (as an alternative for the if...else statements)

Most programmers are used to and familiar with the `if...else` statements in their code. Less does not have these `if...else` statements. Less tries to follow the declarative nature of CSS when possible and for that reason uses guards for matching expressions. In Less, conditional execution has been implemented with guarded mixins. Guarded mixins use the same logical and comparison operators as the `@media` feature in CSS does.

Getting ready

You can compile the Less code in this recipe with the command-line `lessc` compiler, as described in the *Installing the lessc compiler with npm* recipe in *Chapter 1, Getting to Grips with the Basics of Less*. Also, check the compiler options; you can find them by running the `lessc` command in the console without any argument. In this recipe, you will have to use the `-modify-var` option.

How to do it...

1. Create a Less file named `guards.less`, which contains the following Less code:

```less
@color: white;
.mixin(@color) when (luma(@color) >= 50%) {
  color: black;
}
.mixin(@color) when (luma(@color) < 50%) {
```

```
    color: white;
  }

  p {
    .mixin(@color);
  }
```

2. Compile the Less code in the `guards.less` using the command-line `lessc` compiler with the following command entered in the console:

   `lessc guards.less`

3. Inspect the output written on the console, which will look like the following code:

```
p {
  color: black;
}
```

4. Compile the Less code with different values set for the `@color` variable and see how to output change. You can use the command as follows:

   `lessc --modify-var="color=green" guards.less`

   The preceding command will produce the following CSS code:

```
p {

  color: white;

}
```

5. Now, refer to the following command:

   `lessc --modify-var="color=lightgreen" guards.less`

   With the color set to light green, it will again produce the following CSS code:

```
p {

  color: black;

}
```

How it works...

The use of guards to build an `if...else` construct can easily be compared with the switch expression, which can be found in the programming languages, such as PHP, C#, and pretty much any other object-oriented programming language.

Guards are written with the `when` keyword followed by one or more conditions. When the condition(s) evaluates `true`, the code will be mixed in. Also note that the arguments should match, as described in the *Building a switch to leverage argument matching* recipe, before the mixin gets compiled.

The syntax and logic of guards is the same as that of the CSS `@media` feature.

> A condition can contain the following comparison operators:
>
> `>`, `>=`, `=`, `=<`, and `<`
>
> Additionally, the keyword `true` is the only value that evaluates as `true`.

Two or more conditionals can be combined with the `and` keyword, which is equivalent to the logical `and` operator or, on the other hand, with a comma as the logical `or` operator. The following code will show you an example of the combined conditionals:

```
.mixin(@a; @color) when (@a<10) and (luma(@color) >= 50%) { }
```

The following code contains the `not` keyword that can be used to negate conditions:

```
.mixin(@a; @color) when not (luma(@color) >= 50%) { }
```

There's more...

Inside the guard conditions, (global) variables can also be compared. The following Less code example shows you how to use variables inside guards:

```
@a: 10;
.mixin() when (@a >= 10) {}
```

The preceding code will also enable you to compile the different CSS versions with the same code base when using the `modify-var` option of the compiler. The effect of the guarded mixin described in the preceding code will be very similar with the mixins built in the *Building a switch to leverage argument matching* recipe.

Note that in the preceding example, variables in the mixin's scope overwrite variables from the global scope, as can be seen when compiling the following code:

```
@a: 10;
.mixin(@a) when (@a < 10) {property: @a;}
selector {
   .mixin(5);
}
```

The preceding Less code will compile into the following CSS code:

```
selector {
  property: 5;
}
```

When you compare guarded mixins with the `if...else` constructs or switch expressions in other programming languages, you will also need a manner to create a conditional for the default situations. The built-in Less `default()` function can be used to create such a default conditional that is functionally equal to the `else` statement in the `if...else` constructs or the `default` statement in the switch expressions. The `default()` function returns `true` when no other mixins match (matching also takes the guards into account) and can be evaluated as the guard condition.

See also

- You can find a detailed example of using the `default()` function with guarded mixins in the *Using the default() function* recipe in *Chapter 4, Leveraging the Less Built-in Functions*

- The so-called `is` functions, which are already described in the *Evaluating the type of a value* recipe in *Chapter 4, Leveraging the Less Built-in Functions*, are also suitable for evaluation in guard conditions; in this recipe, you will also find an example of using the `iscolor()` (and `default()`) function(s) with guarded mixins

- Since Version 1.5 of Less, you can also apply guards on the CSS selectors directly; you can read more about this in the *Applying guards to the CSS selectors* recipe

Building loops leveraging mixin guards

Mixin guards, as described besides others in the *Using mixin guards (as an alternative for the if...else statements)* recipe, can also be used to dynamically build a set of CSS classes. In this recipe, you will learn how to do this.

Getting ready

You can use your favorite editor to create the Less code in this recipe.

How to do it...

1. Create a `shadesofblue.less` Less file, and write down the following Less code into it:

```
.shadesofblue(@number; @blue:100%) when (@number > 0)
{

  .shadesofblue(@number - 1, @blue - 10%);

  @classname: e(%(".color-%a",@number));
  @{classname} {
    background-color: rgb(0, 0, @blue);
    height:30px;
  }
}
.shadesofblue(10);
```

2. You can, for instance, use the following snippet of the HTML code to see the effect of the compiled Less code from the preceding step:

```
<div class="color-1"></div>
<div class="color-2"></div>
<div class="color-3"></div>
<div class="color-4"></div>
<div class="color-5"></div>
<div class="color-6"></div>
<div class="color-7"></div>
<div class="color-8"></div>
<div class="color-9"></div>
<div class="color-10"></div>
```

Your HTML document should also include the `shadesofblue.less` and `less.js` files, as follows:

```
<link rel="stylesheet/less" type="text/css"
  href="shadesofblue.less">
<script src="less.js" type="text/javascript"></script>
```

3. Finally, the result will look like that shown in this screenshot:

How it works...

The CSS classes in this recipe are built with recursion. The recursion here has been done by the `.shadesofblue(){}` mixin calling itself with different parameters. The loop starts with the `.shadesofblue(10);` call. When the compiler reaches the `.shadesofblue(@number - 1, @blue - 10%);` line of code, it stops the current code and starts compiling the `.shadesofblue(){}` mixin again with `@number` decreased by one and `@blue` decreased by 10 percent. The process will be repeated till `@number < 1`. Finally, when the `@number` variable becomes equal to 0, the compiler tries to call the `.shadesofblue(0,0);` mixin, which does not match the `when (@number > 0)` guard. When no matching mixin is found, the compiler stops, compiles the rest of the code, and writes the first class into the CSS code, as follows:

```
.color-1 {
  background-color: #00001a;
  height: 30px;
}
```

Then, the compiler starts again where it stopped before, at the `.shadesofblue(2,20);` call, and writes the next class into the CSS code, as follows:

```
.color-2 {
  background-color: #000033;
  height: 30px;
}
```

The preceding code will be repeated until the tenth class.

There's more...

When inspecting the compiled CSS code, you will find that the `height` property has been repeated ten times, too. This kind of code repeating can be prevented using the `:extend` Less pseudo class, as described in the *Using extend to merge selectors recipe* in *Chapter 5, Extending and Referencing*. The following code will show you an example of the usage of the `:extend` Less pseudo class:

```less
.baseheight {
  height: 30px;
}
.mixin(@i: 2) when(@i > 0) {
  .mixin(@i - 1);
  .class@{i} {
    width: 10*@i;
    &:extend(.baseheight);
  }
}
.mixin();
```

Alternatively, in this situation, you can create a more generic selector, which sets the `height` property as follows:

```less
div[class^="color"-] {
  height: 30px;
}
```

Recursive loops are also useful when iterating over a list of values. Max Mikhailov, one of the members of the Less core team, wrote a wrapper mixin for recursive Less loops, which can be found at `https://github.com/seven-phases-max`. This wrapper contains the `.for` and `.-each` mixins that can be used to build loops. The following code will show you how to write a nested loop:

```less
@import "for";
#nested-loops {
  .for(3, 1); .-each(@i) {
    .for(0, 2); .-each(@j) {
      x: (10 * @i + @j);
    }
  }
}
```

The preceding Less code will produce the following CSS code:

```
#nested-loops {
  x: 30;
  x: 31;
  x: 32;
  x: 20;
  x: 21;
  x: 22;
  x: 10;
  x: 11;
  x: 12;
}
```

Finally, you can use a list of mixins as your data provider in some situations. The following Less code gives an example about using mixins to avoid recursion:

```
.data() {
  .-("dark"; black);
  .-("light"; white);
  .-("accent"; pink);
}

div {
  .data();
  .-(@class-name; @color){
    @class: e(@class-name);
    &.@{class} {
      color: @color;
    }
  }
}
```

The preceding Less code will compile into the CSS code, as follows:

```
div.dark {
  color: black;
}
div.light {
  color: white;
}

div.accent {
  color: pink;
}
```

See also

▸ A more complex variant of this recursive code can be found in the *Using mathematical functions* recipe in *Chapter 4, Leveraging the Less Built-in Functions*

▸ In the *There's more...* section of the *Using the built-in functions of Less* recipe in *Chapter 1, Getting to Grips with the Basics of Less*, you will find another example of this kind of recursion

▸ Recursive loops are also used in the *Building a grid with grid classes* recipe in *Chapter 8, Building a Layout with Less*

▸ Mikhailov's mixins that provide you a for (each) structure can be found at `https://github.com/seven-phases-max/less.curious/blob/master/articles/generic-for.md`

Applying guards to the CSS selectors

Since Version 1.5 of Less, guards can be applied not only on mixins, but also on the CSS selectors. This recipe will show you how to apply guards on the CSS selectors directly to create conditional rulesets for these selectors.

Getting ready

The easiest way to inspect the effect of the guarded selector in this recipe will be using the command-line `lessc` compiler. How to use the command-line `lessc` compiler has been described in the *Installing the lessc compiler with npm* recipe in *Chapter 1, Getting to Grips with the Basics of Less*.

How to do it...

1. Create a Less file named `darkbutton.less` that contains the following code:

```less
@dark: true;
button when (@dark){
  background-color: black;
  color: white;
}
```

2. Compile the `darkbutton.less` file with the command-line `lessc` compiler by entering the following command into the console:

```
lessc darkbutton.less
```

3. Inspect the CSS code output on the console, which will look like the following code:

```
button {
  background-color: black;
  color: white;
}
```

4. Now try the following command and you will find that the `button` selector is not compiled into the CSS code:

```
lessc --modify-var="dark=false" darkbutton.less
```

How it works...

The guarded CSS selectors are ignored by the compiler and so not compiled into the CSS code when the guard evaluates `false`. Guards for the CSS selectors and mixins leverage the same comparison and logical operators. You can read in more detail how to create guards with these operators in *Using mixin guards (as an alternative for the if...else statements)* recipe.

There's more...

Note that the `true` keyword will be the only value that evaluates `true`. So the following command, which sets `@dark` equal to `1`, will not generate the `button` selector as the guard evaluates `false`:

```
lessc --modify-var="dark=1" darkbutton.less
```

The following Less code will give you another example of applying a guard on a selector:

```
@width: 700px;
div when (@width >= 600px ){
  border: 1px solid black;
}
```

The preceding code will output the following CSS code:

```
div {

  border: 1px solid black;

}
```

On the other hand, nothing will be output when setting `@width` to a value smaller than 600 pixels.

You can also rewrite the preceding code with the & feature referencing the selector, as follows:

```
@width: 700px;
div {
  & when (@width >= 600px ){
    border: 1px solid black;
  }
}
```

Although the CSS code produced of the latest code does not differ from the first, it will enable you to add more properties without the need to repeat the selector. You can also add the code in a mixin, as follows:

```
.conditional-border(@width: 700px) {
    & when (@width >= 600px ){
    border: 1px solid black;
  }
  width: @width;
}
```

Creating color contrasts with Less

Color contrasts play an important role in the first impression of your website or web application. Color contrasts are also important for web accessibility. Using high contrasts between background and text will help the visually disabled, color blind, and even people with dyslexia to read your content more easily.

In *Chapter 4, Leveraging the Less Built-in Functions*, you can find some examples that use the built-in contrast() function of Less. This contrast() function returns a light (white by default) or dark (black by default) color depending on the input color. The contrast function can help you to write a dynamical Less code that always outputs the CSS styles that create enough contrast between the background and text colors. Setting your text color to white or black depending on the background color enables you to meet the highest accessibility guidelines for every color. A sample can be found at http://www.msfw.com/accessibility/tools/contrastratiocalculator.aspx, which shows you that either black or white always gives enough color contrast.

When you use Less to create a set of buttons, for instance, you don't want some buttons with white text while others have black text. In this recipe, you solve this situation by adding a stroke to the button text (text shadow) when the contrast ratio between the button background and button text color is too low to meet your requirements.

Getting ready

You can inspect the results of this recipe in your browser using the client-side `less.js` compiler, as described in the *Downloading, installing, and integrating less.js* recipe in *Chapter 1, Getting to Grips with the Basics of Less*. You will have to create some HTML and Less code, and you can use your favorite editor to do this. You will have to create the following file structure:

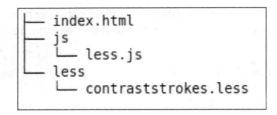

```
├── index.html
├── js
│   └── less.js
└── less
    └── contraststrokes.less
```

How to do it...

1. Create a Less file named `contraststrokes.less`, and write down the following Less code into it:

    ```less
    @safe: green;
    @danger: red;
    @warning: orange;
    @buttonTextColor: white;
    @ContrastRatio: 7; //AAA, small texts

    .setcontrast(@backgroundcolor) when (luma(@backgroundcolor)
      =< luma(@buttonTextColor)) and
        (((luma(@buttonTextColor)+5)/
          (luma(@backgroundcolor)+5)) < @ContrastRatio) {
      color:@buttonTextColor;
      text-shadow: 0 0 2px black;
    }
    .setcontrast(@backgroundcolor) when (luma(@backgroundcolor)
      =< luma(@buttonTextColor)) and
        (((luma(@buttonTextColor)+5)/
          (luma(@backgroundcolor)+5)) >= @ContrastRatio) {
      color:@buttonTextColor;
    }

    .setcontrast(@backgroundcolor) when (luma(@backgroundcolor)
      >= luma(@buttonTextColor)) and
        (((luma(@backgroundcolor)+5)/
          (luma(@buttonTextColor)+5)) < @ContrastRatio) {
    ```

```less
    color:@buttonTextColor;
    text-shadow: 0 0 2px white;
  }
  .setcontrast(@backgroundcolor) when (luma(@backgroundcolor)
    >= luma(@buttonTextColor)) and
      (((luma(@backgroundcolor)+5)/
        (luma(@buttonTextColor)+5)) >= @ContrastRatio) {
    color:@buttonTextColor;
  }

button {
  padding:10px;
  border-radius:10px;
  color: @buttonTextColor;
  width:200px;
}

.safe {
  .setcontrast(@safe);
  background-color: @safe;
}

.danger {
  .setcontrast(@danger);
  background-color: @danger;
}

.warning {
  .setcontrast(@warning);
  background-color: @warning;
}
```

2. Create an HTML file, and save this file as `index.html`. Write down the following HTML code into this `index.html` file:

```html
<!DOCTYPE html>
<html>
  <head>
    <meta charset="utf-8">
    <title>High contrast buttons</title>
    <link rel="stylesheet/less" type="text/css"
      href="contraststrokes.less">
    <script src="less.min.js"
      type="text/javascript"></script>
  </head>
```

```
<body>
  <button style="background-color:green;">safe</button>
  <button class="safe">safe</button><br>
  <button style="background-color:red;">danger</button>
  <button class="danger">danger</button><br>
  <button style="background-color:orange;">
    warning</button>
  <button class="warning">warning</button>
</body>
</html>
```

3. Now load the `index.html` file from step 2 in your browser. When all has gone well, you will see something like what's shown in the following screenshot:

On the left-hand side of the preceding screenshot, you will see the original colored buttons, and on the right-hand side, you will find the high-contrast buttons.

How it works...

The main purpose of this recipe is to show you how to write dynamical code based on the color contrast ratio.

Web Content Accessibility Guidelines (WCAG) 2.0 covers a wide range of recommendations to make web content more accessible. They have defined the following three conformance levels:

▶ **Conformance Level A**: In this level, all Level A success criteria are satisfied

▶ **Conformance Level AA**: In this level, all Level A and AA success criteria are satisfied

▶ **Conformance Level AAA**: In this level, all Level A, AA, and AAA success criteria are satisfied

If you focus only on the color contrast aspect, you will find the following paragraphs in the WCAG 2.0 guidelines. You can find a link to these guidelines in the *See also* section.

- ▶ **1.4.1 Use of Color**: Color is not used as the only visual means of conveying information, indicating an action, prompting a response, or distinguishing a visual element. (Level A)

- ▶ **1.4.3 Contrast (Minimum)**: The visual presentation of text and images of text has a contrast ratio of at least 4.5:1 (Level AA)

- ▶ **1.4.6 Contrast (Enhanced)**: The visual presentation of text and images of text has a contrast ratio of at least 7:1 (Level AAA)

The contrast ratio can be calculated with a formula that can be found at `http://www.w3.org/TR/WCAG20/#contrast-ratiodef`:

(L1 + 0.05) / (L2 + 0.05)

In the preceding formula, `L1` is the relative luminance of the lighter of the colors, and `L2` is the relative luminance of the darker of the colors.

In Less, the relative luminance of a color can be found with the built-in `luma()` function. In the Less code of this recipe are the four guarded `.setcontrast(){}` mixins. The guard conditions, such as `(luma(@backgroundcolor) =< luma(@buttonTextColor))` are used to find which of the `@backgroundcolor` and `@buttonTextColor` colors is the lighter one. Then the `(((luma({the lighter color})+5)/(luma({the darker color})+5)) < @ContrastRatio)` condition can, according to the preceding formula, be used to determine whether the contrast ratio between these colors meets the requirement (`@ContrastRatio`) or not. When the value of the calculated contrast ratio is lower than the value set by the `@ContrastRatio`, the `text-shadow: 0 0 2px {color};` ruleset will be mixed in, where `{color}` will be white or black depending on the relative luminance of the color set by the `@buttonTextColor` variable.

There's more...

In this recipe, you added a stroke to the web text to improve the accessibility. First, you will have to bear in mind that improving the accessibility by adding a stroke to your text is not a proven method. Also, automatic testing of the accessibility (by calculating the color contrast ratios) cannot be done.

Other options to solve this issue are to increase the font size or change the background color itself. You can read how to change the background color dynamically based on color contrast ratios in the *Changing the background color dynamically* recipe.

When you read the exceptions of the *1.4.6 Contrast (Enhanced)* paragraph of the WCAG 2.0 guidelines, you will find that large-scale text requires a color contrast ratio of 4.5 instead of 7.0 to meet the requirements of the AAA Level. Large-scaled text is defined as at least 18 point or 14 point bold or font size that would yield the equivalent size for **Chinese, Japanese, and Korean** (**CJK**) fonts. To try this, you could replace the text-shadow properties in the Less code of step 1 of this recipe with the font-size, 14pt, and font-weight, bold; declarations. After this, you can inspect the results in your browser again. Depending on, among others, the values you have chosen for the @buttonTextColor and @ContrastRatio variables, you will find something like the following screenshot:

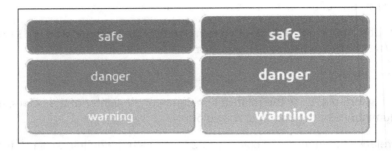

On the left-hand side of the preceding screenshot, you will see the original colored buttons, and on the right-hand side, you will find the high-contrast buttons. Note that when you set the @ContrastRatio variable to 7.0, the code does not check whether the larger font indeed meets the 4.5 contrast ratio requirement.

See also

> ► You can read more about adding strokes to the web text at http://css-tricks. com/adding-stroke-to-web-text/. The complete text of the Web Content Accessibility Guidelines (WCAG) 2.0, including a discussion on the techniques to meet this guidelines can be found at http://www.w3.org/TR/WCAG20/.

Changing the background color dynamically

When you define some basic colors to generate, for instance, a set of button elements, you can use the built-in contrast() function to set the font color. The built-in contrast() function provides the highest possible contrast, but does not guarantee that the contrast ratio is also high enough to meet your accessibility requirements. In this recipe, you will learn how to change your basic color automatically to meet the required contrast ratio.

Getting ready

You can inspect the results of this recipe in your browser using the client-side `less.js` compiler, as described in the *Downloading, installing, and integrating less.js* recipe in *Chapter 1, Getting to Grips with the Basics of Less*. Use your favorite editor to create the HTML and Less code in this recipe. You will have to create the following file structure:

```
├── index.html
├── js
│   └── less.js
└── less
    └── backgroundcolors.less
```

How to do it...

1. Create a Less file named `backgroundcolors.less`, and write down the following Less code into it:

```less
@safe: green;
@danger: red;
@warning: orange;
@ContrastRatio: 7.0; //AAA
@precision: 1%;
@buttonTextColor: black;
@threshold: 43;

.setcontrastcolor(@startcolor) when (luma(@buttonTextColor)
  < @threshold) {
  .contrastcolor(@startcolor) when (luma(@startcolor) < 100
    ) and (((luma(@startcolor)+5)/
      (luma(@buttonTextColor)+5)) < @ContrastRatio) {
    .contrastcolor(lighten(@startcolor,@precision));
  }
  .contrastcolor(@startcolor) when (@startcolor =
    color("white")),(((luma(@startcolor)+5)/
      (luma(@buttonTextColor)+5)) >= @ContrastRatio) {
    @contrastcolor: @startcolor;
  }
  .contrastcolor(@startcolor);
}
```

```less
.setcontrastcolor(@startcolor) when (default()) {
  .contrastcolor(@startcolor) when (luma(@startcolor) < 100
    ) and (((luma(@buttonTextColor)+5)/
      (luma(@startcolor)+5)) < @ContrastRatio) {
    .contrastcolor(darken(@startcolor,@precision));
  }
  .contrastcolor(@startcolor) when (luma(@startcolor) = 100
    ),(((luma(@buttonTextColor)+5)/(luma(@startcolor)+5))
      >= @ContrastRatio) {
    @contrastcolor: @startcolor;
  }
  .contrastcolor(@startcolor);
}

button {
  padding:10px;
  border-radius:10px;
  color:@buttonTextColor;
  width:200px;
}

.safe {
  .setcontrastcolor(@safe);
  background-color: @contrastcolor;
}

.danger {
  .setcontrastcolor(@danger);
  background-color: @contrastcolor;
}

.warning {
  .setcontrastcolor(@warning);
  background-color: @contrastcolor;
}
```

2. Create an HTML file and save this file as `index.html`. Write down the following HTML code into this `index.html` file:

```html
<!DOCTYPE html>
<html>
  <head>
    <meta charset="utf-8">
    <title>High contrast buttons</title>
```

```
    <link rel="stylesheet/less" type="text/css"
      href="backgroundcolors.less">
    <script src="less.min.js"
      type="text/javascript"></script>
  </head>
  <body>
    <button style="background-color:green;">safe</button>
    <button class="safe">safe</button><br>
    <button style="background-color:red;">danger</button>
    <button class="danger">danger</button><br>
    <button style="background-color:orange;">warning
      </button>
    <button class="warning">warning</button>
  </body>
</html>
```

3. Now load the `index.html` file from step 2 in your browser. When all has gone well, you will see something like the following screenshot:

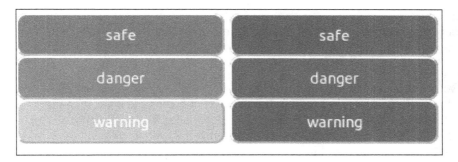

On the left-hand side of the preceding figure, you will see the original colored buttons, and on the right-hand side, you will find the high contrast buttons.

How it works...

The guarded `.setcontrastcolor() {}` mixins are used to determine the color set depending upon whether the `@buttonTextColor` variable is a dark color or not. When the color set by `@buttonTextColor` is a dark color, with a relative luminance below the threshold value set by the `@threshold` variable, the background colors should be made lighter. For light colors, the background colors should be made darker.

Inside each `.setcontrastcolor(){}` mixin, a second set of mixins has been defined. These guarded `.contrastcolor(){}` mixins construct a recursive loop, as described in the *Building loops leveraging mixin guards* recipe. In each step of the recursion, the guards test whether the contrast ratio that is set by the `@ContrastRatio` variable has been reached or not. When the contrast ratio does not meet the requirements, the `@startcolor` variable will darken or lighten by the number of percent set by the `@precision` variable with the built-in `darken()` and `lighten()` functions. You can read more about the `darken()` and `lighten()` functions in the *Creating color a variants with the darken() and lighten() functions* recipe in *Chapter 4, Leveraging the Less Built-in Functions*. When the required contrast ratio has been reached or the color defining the `@startcolor` variable has become white or black, the modified color value of `@startcolor` will be assigned to the `@contrastcolor` variable. The guarded `.contrastcolor(){}` mixins are used as functions, as described in the *Using mixins as functions* recipe to assign the `@contrastcolor` variable that will be used to set the `background-color` property of the `button` selectors.

There's more...

A small value of the `@precision` variable will increase the number of recursions (possible) needed to find the required colors as there will be more and smaller steps needed. With the number of recursions also, the compilation time will increase. When you choose a bigger value for `@precision`, the contrast color found might differ from the start color more than needed to meet the contrast ratio requirement.

When you choose, for instance, a dark button text color, which is not black, all or some base background colors will be set to white. The chances of finding the highest contrast for white increase for high values of the `@ContrastRatio` variable. The recursions will stop when white (or black) has been reached as you cannot make the white color lighter. When the recursion stops on reaching white or black, the colors set by the mixins in this recipe don't meet the required color contrast ratios.

See also

▶ You can read more about guarded mixins in *Using mixin guards (as an alternative for the if...else statements)* recipe

▶ In the *Creating color contrasts with Less* recipe, you can read more about the Web Content Accessibility Guidelines (WCAG) 2.0 and the formula used to calculate the color contrast ratios

Aggregating values under a single property

The merge feature of Less enables you to merge property values into a list under a single property. Each list can be either space-separated or comma-separated. The merge feature can be useful to define a property that accepts a list as a value. For instance, the background accepts a comma-separated list of backgrounds.

Getting ready

For this recipe, you will need a text editor and a Less compiler. In *Chapter 1, Getting to Grips with the Basics of Less*, you can read how to use and install the less.js client-side or command-line lessc compiler.

How to do it...

1. Create a file called defaultfonts.less that contains the following Less code:

```
.default-fonts() {
  font-family+:  Helvetica, Arial, sans-serif;
}
p {
  font-family+: "Helvetica Neue";
  .default-fonts();
}
```

2. Compile the defaultfonts.less file from step 1 using the following command in the console:

```
lessc defaultfonts.less
```

3. Inspect the CSS code output on the console after compilation and you will see that it looks like the following code:

```
p {
  font-family: "Helvetica Neue", Helvetica, Arial, sans-
    serif;
}
```

How it works...

When the compiler finds the plus sign (+) before the assignment sign (:), it will merge the values into a CSV list and will not create a new property into the CSS code.

There's more...

Since Version 1.7 of Less, you can also merge the property's values separated by a space instead of a comma. For space-separated values, you should use the +_ sign instead of a + sign, as can be seen in the following code:

```
.text-overflow(@text-overflow: ellipsis) {
  text-overflow+_ :  @text-overflow;
}
p, .text-overflow {
  .text-overflow();
  text-overflow+_ : ellipsis;
}
```

The preceding Less code will compile into the CSS code, as follows:

```
p,
.text-overflow {
  text-overlow: ellipsis ellipsis;
}
```

Note that the text-overflow property doesn't force an overflow to occur; you will have to explicitly set, for instance, the overflow property to hidden for the element.

See also

▶ The text-overflow property, especially the second value of the list, is not currently well-supported. You can check it's support at http://caniuse.com/text-overflow or read more at https://developer.mozilla.org/en-US/docs/Web/CSS/text-overflow.

7
Leveraging Libraries with Prebuilt Mixins

In this chapter, we will cover the following topics:

- ▶ Importing and downloading prebuilt mixin libraries
- ▶ Using namespacing with prebuilt libraries
- ▶ Creating background gradients
- ▶ Building unlimited gradients with Less Hat
- ▶ Building a layout with the CSS3 flexbox module
- ▶ Getting retina-ready with Preboot
- ▶ Generating font-face declarations with Clearless
- ▶ Improving your website's SEO with 3L mixins
- ▶ Leveraging sprite images with Pre
- ▶ Creating bidirectional styling without code duplication
- ▶ Creating animations with `animations.css`
- ▶ Creating animations with `More.less`
- ▶ Building semantic grids with `semantic.gs`
- ▶ Building an alternative for fluid grids with Frameless
- ▶ Building a fluid responsive grid system

Introduction

Less enables you to write your CSS code effectively with the DRY principle of software programming in mind, but Less does not dictate to you in regard to how to build your CSS code. CSS3 extends the old CSS with new selectors, text effects, background gradients, and animations. The power of CSS3, the new functionalities, and the high acceptance of mobile devices using HTML5 and CSS3 make them the standard for modern web design. On the other hand, CSS3 makes coding CSS more complex, and some properties are related to others or can be set to lists of values. To support the wide range of browsers, you can't ignore vendor-prefixes, as described in the *Using mixins to set properties* recipe in *Chapter 3, Using Variables and Mixins*. Less provides you with mixins to set these properties, but you will have to create these mixins yourself. Happily, you do not have to reinvent the wheel for every new project. Others already have written many mixins that you can reuse in your projects. In this chapter, you can read about libraries with prebuilt mixins and learn how to use them.

Not all libraries used in this chapter have been updated recently; you can still use them, and they are useful to understand how to use and create a set of reusable mixins for your project. All code in the recipes of this chapter has been tested and works with the latest version of Less available at the time of writing this book. If the mixins used in these recipes do not exactly compile into the desired style for your elements, you could probably try to write your own version than use the mixin and try to fix the problems.

You can find an overview of the mixin libraries at `http://lesscss.org/usage/#frameworks-using-less`. Please note that some of these libraries focus on creating single and concise declarations for cross-browser prefixes. In the *Automatically prefix your code with Grunt* recipe in *Chapter 11, Compiling Less Real Time for Development Using Grunt* you can learn how to autoprefix automatically after preproccessing.

Since Version 2 of Less, you can use the Less autoprefix plugin to prefix your compiled CSS code. Even when the autoprefixing has been built-in, there will be many use cases for the mixin libraries, and they will help you to meet the DRY principle of software programming. These libraries can provide you with mixins that can be used for code shortcuts in your code.

Most libraries described in this chapter can be installed with **Bower**, too. Bower is a package manager for the Web. Bower can be found at `http://bower.io/`. A Less plugin that tries first to resolve your imported Less files from `bower_components/directory` can be found at `https://github.com/Mercateo/less-plugin-bower-resolve/`.

Importing and downloading prebuilt mixin libraries

In this recipe, you will download and install Less Elements. Less Elements is a library with prebuilt mixins that focuses on consolidating cross-browser prefixes into single, concise declarations. In the *Using namespacing with prebuilt libraries* and *Creating background gradients* recipes, you will find some other use cases for this library.

Getting ready

First, download Less Elements from `http://lesselements.com/`; the file should be saved and unzipped into the same directory with your other Less files. You can use the steps that are shown after the following command:

```
mkdir less
cd less
wget "https://github.com/dmitryf/elements/archive/master.zip"
unzip master.zip
```

Now, create an `index.html` page and a `less/greyscalegradient.less` file. You can compile your Less code using the client-side `less.js` compiler, as described in the *Downloading, installing, and integrating less.js* recipe in *Chapter 1, Getting to Grips with the Basics of Less*, also, add a copy of `less.js` into the `js/` directory, which is your working directory. Finally, you should end up with the following file and directory structure:

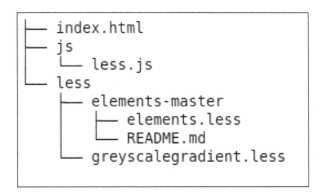

```
├── index.html
├── js
│   └── less.js
└── less
    ├── elements-master
    │   ├── elements.less
    │   └── README.md
    └── greyscalegradient.less
```

How to do it...

Perform the following steps:

1. Use your favorite editor to edit the `less/greyscalegradient.less` file, and write down the following code into this file:

```
@import "elements-master/elements.less";
div.gradient {
  .bw-gradient(#eee, 125, 255);
  line-height: 50px;
  color:black;
}
```

2. Create and edit the `index.html` file, and make sure you include `less/greyscalegradient.less` from step 1, and of course, the `less.js` compiler, as follows:

```
<link rel="stylesheet/less" type="text/css"
  href="less/greyscalegradient.less">
<script src="js/less.js" type="text/javascript"></script>
```

Note that you do not have to include the `elements.less` file in `index.html`. The `elements.less` has been imported already in the `less/greyscalegradient.less` file, which makes explicit including unnecessary.

3. Finally, inspect the results by loading the `index.html` file into your web browser. You will find that it looks like the following screenshot:

Greyscale gradient background

How it works...

The Less Element file provides the `.bw-gradient()` mixin, which can be used in your Less code. This `.bw-gradient()` mixin helps you to create a horizontal grayscale gradient and needs three parameters set. The first parameter defines the fallback color, and the second and third parameters are the start and end brightness parameters, which range from 0 to 255.

There's more...

When using prebuilt mixins, you don't have to rely on only one library. You can combine as many libraries as you need. In some situations, two or more libraries get mixins with the same name, which gives you unexpected results. You can use namespaces to prevent collisions of mixins with the same name.

Of course, you can also build your own library with mixins, which enables you to reuse your CSS over project boundaries. In this recipe, the vertical alignment of the text has been set with a 50 pixels declaration line-height. Although the vertical alignment of elements inside the div elements seems trivial at first, it is not in CSS. There are many solutions for this *problem*. When you define the vertical alignment inside a mixin, for instance, as shown in the following code, you only have to change that mixin when your insights or requirements change:

```
.verticalAlignment(@availableHeight:50px) {
  line-height: @availableHeight;
}
```

See also

- The *Using namespaces to make your code reusable and portable* recipe in *Chapter 1, Getting to Grips with the Basics of Less*

- The *Using namespacing with prebuilt libraries* recipe explains how to prevent collisions of mixins with the same name

- A full list of mixins provided by Less Elements can also be found at http://lesselements.com/

- Six methods for vertical centering with CSS can be found at http://www.vanseodesign.com/css/vertical-centering/

- In this recipe, the @import directive was used to import elements.less of Less Elements; you can read more about this directive in the *Importing files with the @import directive* recipe in *Chapter 8, Building a Layout with Less*

Using namespacing with prebuilt libraries

In this recipe, you will learn how to use different mixin libraries together and use namespaces to prevent collisions between mixins with the same name.

Getting ready

In this recipe, two mixin libraries are used: Less Elements, which can be downloaded from `https://github.com/dmitryf/elements/archive/master.zip`, and the Less Hat library, which can be downloaded from `https://github.com/madebysource/lesshat/archive/v3.0.2.zip`.

Unzip both the ZIP archives into your working directory, and use the command-line `lessc` compiler, as described in the *Installing the lessc compiler with npm* recipe in *Chapter 1, Getting to Grips with the Basics of Less*, to compile your Less code.

How to do it...

Write down the Less code shown here into a file, and compile the file with the command-line `lessc` compiler:

```
#lesselements {
  @import "elements-master/elements.less";
}
#lesshat {
  @import "lesshat-master/build/lesshat.less";
}
div.drop-shadow {
  #lesselements > .drop-shadow(0, 1px, 20px, 0.2);
}
img.drop-shadow {
  #lesshat > .drop-shadow(16 16 10 black);
}
```

Finally, you will find that the preceding Less code will compile into the CSS code, as follows:

```
div.drop-shadow {
  -webkit-box-shadow: 0 1px 2px rgba(0, 0, 0, 0.2);
  -moz-box-shadow: 0 1px 2px rgba(0, 0, 0, 0.2);
  box-shadow: 0 1px 2px rgba(0, 0, 0, 0.2);
}
img.drop-shadow {
  -webkit-filter: drop-shadow(16px 16px 10px #000000);
  -moz-filter: drop-shadow(16px 16px 10px #000000);
  -ms-filter: drop-shadow(16px 16px 10px #000000);
  filter: drop-shadow(16px 16px 10px #000000);
}
```

How it works...

Both the Less Elements and Less Hat libraries have a mixin named `drop-shadow`. Although the name of these mixins is the same and both can accept four arguments, they compile into quite different CSS code.

The `.drop-shadow()` mixin of the Less Elements library generates a CSS `box-shadow` property, while the `.drop-shadow()` mixin of the Less Hat library sets drop shadow with the `filter` property on. The `filter` property can only be applied on an image. The CSS filter with drop shadow is very similar to the CSS `drop-shadow` property except that some browsers can provide hardware acceleration for the CSS `filter` property for better performance.

In this recipe, both libraries are imported into their own namespaces. Mixins can now only be called with their namespace using the `#namespace > mixin` syntax, and therefore prevent you from using the wrong mixin or mix up two or more mixins with the same name.

With the `@import` directive, you can import the Less code from different files into your project file. The project file, including the imported code, can be compiled into the CSS code once.

The complete code of the imported file can be wrapped by placing the `@import` directive inside the namespace declaration. In contrast to the CSS `@import` directive, the Less directive is allowed anywhere in your code and not only at the beginning.

Consider the following Less code that does not use namespaces:

```
@import "elements-master/elements.less";
@import "lesshat-master/build/lesshat.less";
div.drop-shadow {
   .drop-shadow(0, 1px, 2px, 0.2);
}
```

In the preceding Less code, both `drop-shadow` mixins were compiled for the `drop-shadow(16 16 10 black)` call, which results in the following CSS code:

```
div.drop-shadow {
   -webkit-box-shadow: 0 1px 2px rgba(0, 0, 0, 0.2);
   -moz-box-shadow: 0 1px 2px rgba(0, 0, 0, 0.2);
   box-shadow: 0 1px 2px rgba(0, 0, 0, 0.2);
   -webkit-filter: drop-shadow(0 1px 2px 0.2px);
   -moz-filter: drop-shadow(0 1px 2px 0.2px);
   -ms-filter: drop-shadow(0 1px 2px 0.2px);
   filter: drop-shadow(0 1px 2px 0.2px);
}
```

As you can see in the preceding code, the `div-drop-shadow` selector put the properties from both mixins together, which makes no sense. You should not use both the `box-shadow` and the `filter` with the `drop-shadow` property for the same selector. Also, the effect of the input parameters becomes unexpected. In this recipe, you saw that namespaces prevent these problems.

There's more...

As you have seen, every library can easily be wrapped in a namespace. Some libraries, such as Twitter's Bootstrap, already have wrapped mixins with commonly used names in a namespace. The background gradient mixins of Twitter's Bootstrap are already wrapped in the `#gradient` namespace.

The Less Hat mixin library also comes with an alternative solution for conflicting mixin names. The Less Hat mixin library offers you a so-called prefixed version. In the prefixed version of the Less Hat library, all mixin names start with the `.rh-` prefix. As long as other libraries and your own code do not use the same prefix, all mixin names will be unique.

Note that namespaced mixins are called in the scope (the global scope, mostly) of the caller. This means that variables set inside the namespace are no longer available inside the mixin. Consider the following Less code. it will generate a `SyntaxError:` variable `@var`, which is an undefined error:

```less
#namespace-1 {
  @var: 1;
  .mixin() {
    selector {
      property: @var;
    }
  }
}
#namespace-1 > .mixin();
```

See also

► You can read more about the `@import` directive in the *Importing files with the @import directive* recipe in *Chapter 8, Building a Layout with Less*

► Namespaces are introduced in the *Using namespaces to make your code reusable and portable* recipe in *Chapter 1, Getting to Grips with the Basics of Less*

► You can read more about the CSS `filter` property with drop shadows at `https://developer.mozilla.org/en-US/docs/Web/CSS/filter#drop-shadow()`

Creating background gradients

In the *Importing and downloading prebuilt mixin libraries* recipe, you can read how to create a grayscale gradient with the Less Elements library. In this recipe, you will learn how to create a colored gradient with the Less Elements library.

Getting ready

For this recipe, you will have to create the `index.html` and `less/gradient.less` files. You can compile your Less code using the client-side `less.js` compiler, as described in the *Downloading, installing, and integrating less.js* recipe in *Chapter 1, Getting to Grips with the Basics of Less* also, add a copy of `less.js` into your working directory. Finally, you should end up with the following file and directory structure:

```
├── index.html
├── js
│   └── less.js
└── less
    ├── elements-master
    │   ├── elements.less
    │   └── README.md
    └── gradient.less
```

You will also have to download and unzip the Less Elements library into your working directory. The Less Elements library can be found at `http://www.lesselements.com/`. Read the *Importing and downloading prebuilt mixins libraries* recipe to find out how to install the Less Elements library.

How to do it...

1. Use your favorite editor to edit the `less/gradient.less` file, and write down the following code into this file:

```
@import "elements-master/elements.less";
div.gradient {
  .gradient(red, red, blue);
  line-height: 50px;
  color:white;
}
```

2. Create and edit the `index.html` file, making sure you include `less/gradient.less` from step 1 and of course, the `less.js` file, as follows:

```
<link rel="stylesheet/less" type="text/css"
  href="less/gradient.less">
<script src="js/less.js" type="text/javascript"></script>
```

3. Finally, inspect the results by loading the `index.html` file into your web browser. You will find that it looks like the following screenshot:

How it works...

The Less Elements file provides you with the `.gradient()` mixin that can be used in your Less code. This `.gradient()` mixin helps you to create a horizontal gradient and needs a three-parameter set. All parameters should be defined as colors; the first parameter defines the fallback color and the second parameter sets the top color, while the third and last parameter sets the bottom color of the gradient.

Whoever studies the compiled CSS code will find that there are a lot of style rules needed to support older browsers. Older browsers don't support the official W3C syntax. Also, the way of defining the angle of the gradient has changed over time. The official syntax will now be as follows:

```
background-image: linear-gradient(  [ <angle> | to <side-or-corner>
,]? <color-stop> [, <color-stop>]+ );
```

Note that gradients can be applied on both the `background-image` and `background` properties because the `background` property is only a shorthand notation to set the individual background values, including the `background-image` property, in a single place in the style sheet.

Because the `linear-gradient()` function returns an image, it can be used to set the `background-image` property. Instead of the `linear-gradient()` function, you can use the `repeating-linear-gradient()`, `radial-gradient()`, or `repeating-radial-gradient()` functions to set the `background-image` property.

Fallback for older browsers can be split into two parts.

The first part includes browsers that do not support the new angle definition. This can be solved by calculating the old angle from the new angle as follows: `old = (450 - new)% 360` degrees. The same is true for the keyword version of direction, for instance, `to right` should be written as `left` in the old degree system.

The second part includes browsers that do not support the gradient functions at all. Internet Explorer 9 and lower versions do not support the gradient functions; fallback for these browsers can be provided by adding an SVG gradient image. This SVG gradient image can be set by either `data-uri` or `filter`. Both Less Elements and Twitter's Bootstrap use the `filter` method, while the Less Hat mixin library uses the `data-uri` method. You can read more about the `data-uri` methods in the *Embedding images with data URIs* recipe in *Chapter 4, Leveraging the Less Built-in Functions*.

Filters are beyond the scope of this book, but you can read more about them at `http://msdn.microsoft.com/en-us/library/ie/ms530752(v=vs.85).aspx`. The `filter` property used by Windows Internet Explorer Version 4 through 9 should not be confused with the standard CSS `filter` property.

The standard CSS `filter` property is also mentioned in the *Using namespacing with prebuilt libraries* recipe, and more information can be found at `https://developer.mozilla.org/en-US/docs/Web/CSS/filter`.

If you are proficient at using gradients, you might have come across a third issue. Old versions of webkit browsers, such as Safari, only support the `webkit-gradient()` function. Note that the Safari 4 web browser was the first one that supported the CSS gradients; see also `https://www.webkit.org/blog/175/introducing-css-gradients/`.

When adding fallbacks for older browsers, and especially the `filter` variant, you also will have to note that the calculation of the gradient might cost some computation time. Older browsers mostly run on older hardware, too. Additional computation time may slow down your website for these older browsers.

Background gradients are, for the most part, not a part of the basic functionality of your website, and so are suitable for applying graceful degradation; see `http://www.w3.org/wiki/Graceful_degredation_versus_progressive_enhancement` for more information on this.

A simple solution that applies graceful degradation is to only declare a `background-color` property as a fallback. You could define, for instance, the following mixin:

```
.gradient(@color: #F5F5F5, @start: #EEE, @stop: #FFF) {
  background-color: @color;
  background-image: linear-gradient(to bottom, @start-color
    @start-percent, @end-color @end-percent);
  background-repeat: repeat-x;
}
```

It has already been made clear that you should only use the mixins from the libraries discussed in this chapter if the results fit your requirements. For a graceful degradation approach, it is better to write your own mixin.

There's more...

Also, other libraries provide you with mixins to create background gradients. Twitter's Bootstrap, as discussed in *Chapter 9, Using Bootstrap with Less*, comes with different mixins for different types of gradients; these mixins are already wrapped inside a `#gradient` namespace and include a `.striped()` mixin. The striped mixin will comprise the following code and show you some kind of alternative for the `repeating-linear-gradient()` function:

```
.striped(@color: rgba(255,255,255,.15); @angle: 45deg) {
  background-image: -webkit-linear-gradient(@angle, @color 25%,
    transparent 25%, transparent 50%, @color 50%, @color 75%,
      transparent 75%, transparent);
  background-image: linear-gradient(@angle, @color 25%,
    transparent 25%, transparent 50%, @color 50%, @color 75%,
      transparent 75%, transparent);
}
```

 Both the autoprefixing method discussed in the *Automatically prefix your code with Grunt* recipe in *Chapter 11, Compiling Less Real Time for Development Using Grunt*, and the Less `Autoprefix` plugin add only browsers prefixes, and none of the `fallback` methods discussed in this recipe are applied on the CSS code. Both methods are derived from the `PostCSS/ autoprefixer`, which only adds prefixes, not polyfills. `PostCSS/ autoprefixer` recommends that you use the graceful degradation strategy.

See also

▶ An article that gives insights into the change between the old and new syntax for the CSS gradients, including the new degree system, can be found at `http://www. codeproject.com/Articles/494653/Using-Unprefixed-CSS-Gradients- in-Modern-Browsers`

▶ Also, Chris Coyier of `css-trick.com` can tell you even more about gradients at `http://css-tricks.com/css3-gradients/`

▶ The following sources will provide more information on the `gradient` functions: `https://developer.mozilla.org/en-US/docs/Web/CSS/linear- gradient` and `https://developer.mozilla.org/en-US/docs/Web/CSS/ repeating-linear-gradient`

▶ The Less `Autoprefix` plugin can be found at `https://github.com/less/ less-plugin-autoprefix`

▶ Finally, you can read more about the `PostCSS/autoprefixer` plugin at `https://github.com/postcss/autoprefixer/`

Building unlimited gradients with Less Hat

In the *Creating background gradients* recipe, you can read how to create a background gradient with the Less Elements library. In this recipe, you will create a background gradient with the Less Hat mixin library. The Less Hat library advertises on its website the ability to create unlimited gradients.

Getting ready

For this recipe, you will have to download the Less Hat mixin library, which can be done at `http://lesshat.madebysource.com/`. Use your favorite text editor to edit the Less code. The Less code can be compiled with the client-side `less.js` compiler and be inspected in your browser. You should include the `less.js` compiler in your HTML document, as described in the *Downloading, installing, and integrating less.js* recipe in *Chapter 1, Getting to Grips with the Basics of Less.*

How to do it...

1. First, download and unzip the Less Hat mixin library from `http://lesshat.madebysource.com/` into your working directory.

2. Secondly, create a `gradient.less` file, and write out the following Less code into it:

```
@import "lesshat-master/build/lesshat.less";
div.gradient {
  .background-image(linear-gradient(to right, #1e5799
    0%,#2989d8 50%,#207cca 78%,#7db9e8 100%));
  line-height: 50px;
  color:white;
}
```

3. Then, create an HTML file named `index.html` and include the client-side `less.js` compiler and the `gradient.less` file by adding the following lines of the HTML code into the `head` section:

```
<link rel="stylesheet/less" type="text/css"
  href="less/gradient.less">
<script src="js/less.js" type="text/javascript"></script>
```

Write down the following snippet of HTML code into the `body` section of `index.html` to display the gradient:

```
<div class="gradient">Example Gradient</div>
```

4. Finally, load `index.html` in your browser, and you will find that it looks like the following screenshot:

Example Gradient

5. Visit the Ultimate CSS Gradient Generator from ColorZilla at `http://www.colorzilla.com/gradient-editor/` and generate some splendid gradients. Copy the W3C syntax of the generated gradients into the `.background-image()` mixin in the `index.html` file. Reload the file in your browser.

How it works...

With the Less Hat `.background-image()` mixin, you can create prefixed linear or radial gradients. The input parameter for this mixin should be the official W3C syntax for linear or radial gradients. See also the *How it works...* section in the *Creating background gradients* recipe for more information about this syntax. Keeping this in mind, the Less code of your caller can look like the following code:

```
.background-image(linear-gradient(to bottom, #fb83fa 0%,#e93cec
    100%));
```

Note that you do not need to have to escape or interpolate the value (see also the *Value escaping with the ~"value" syntax* recipe in *Chapter 3, Using Variables and Mixins*) to set the argument. The mixin has no support for the `repeating-linear-gradient` and `repeating-radial-gradient` CSS functions.

Instead of a single gradient function, the input can also be a comma-separated list of the gradient functions. That's why they mention the ability to create unlimited gradients. If possible, the `.background-image()` mixin also generates an SVG fallback for older browsers.

Finally, the preceding example's caller will compile into the following CSS code:

```
background-image: url(data:image/svg+xml;
   base64,PD94b
   ...z4=);
background-image: -webkit-linear-gradient(top, #fb83fa 0%, #e93cec
   100%);
background-image: -moz-linear-gradient(top, #fb83fa 0%, #e93cec
   100%);
background-image: -o-linear-gradient(top, #fb83fa 0%, #e93cec
   100%);
background-image: linear-gradient(to bottom, #fb83fa 0%, #e93cec
   100%);
```

There's more...

In this recipe, you saw that the `background-image` mixin of Less Hat is very robust because it accepts the complete W3C syntaxes. Now, you may wonder how to write such a robust mixin in Less yourself.

Most of the mixins of Less Hat are written in JavaScript. The `less.js` compiler itself is written in JavaScript and evaluates the native JavaScript calls, placed between back quotes, in your Less code. For more details about using active JavaScript in Less, see the *There's more...* section in the *Replacing a text within a string* recipe in *Chapter 4, Leveraging the Less Built-in Functions*.

Coding JavaScript is beyond the scope of this book. Also, note that using native JavaScript in your Less code depreciates it. The JavaScript calls make your code less compatible with future versions of Less, and also less portable for alternative compilers not written in JavaScript.

See also

▸ If you want to learn more about JavaScript, you can read *Object-Oriented JavaScript, Stoyan Stefanov, Packt Publishing, July 2008,* see `https://www.packtpub.com/web-development/object-oriented-javascript`.

▸ If you are already familiar with JavaScript, you can study the source code of Less Hat to find out how to deploy Less mixins leveraging JavaScript. The source code of the Less Hat library can be found at `https://github.com/madebysource/lesshat`.

Building a layout with the CSS3 flexbox module

The CSS Flexible box module level 3, called **flexbox** for short, enables you to arrange elements inside a container based on the available space. The flexbox module gives you the power to build dynamic and responsive layouts easily, without the need to use floats. The flexbox layouts will likely play an important role in modern web design in the future, but currently, the support for different browsers varies. The module has only a recommendation status now, and the flexbox syntax has been changed globally three times over the last few years. As an impact of these changes, you should adapt your Less code to support older browsers, too. More information of this change can be found at `http://css-tricks.com/old-flexbox-and-new-flexbox/`.

In this recipe, you will learn how to build the flexbox layouts with the Less Hat library. The Less Hat flexbox mixins offer cross-browser support, but do not support older syntaxes. Leveraging the Less Hat library, you will build a responsive navigation menu with flexboxes.

Getting ready

Use a modern browser with full support for flexible boxes to test the code of this recipe. You will find more about browser support of the CSS Flexible box module level 3 at `http://caniuse.com/#feat=flexbox`. Because you will inspect the results in the browser, you should use the client-side `less.js` compiler to compile the Less code into the CSS code. In the *Downloading, installing, and integrating less.js* recipe in *Chapter 1, Getting to Grips with the Basics of Less*, you can read how to use and install the client-side `less.js` compiler. Use your favorite editor to edit the Less code of this recipe.

If you are not familiar with the CSS Flexible box module already, it's strongly recommended that you read more about it before starting this recipe. An excellent article, titled *A Complete Guide to Flexbox,* can be found at `http://css-tricks.com/snippets/css/a-guide-to-flexbox/`.

How to do it...

1. First, download and unzip the Less Hat mixin library from `http://lesshat.madebysource.com/` into your working directory.

2. Secondly, create a `navigation.less` file, and write out the following Less code into it:

```less
@import "lesshat-master/build/lesshat.less";
nav > ul {
  list-style: none;
  margin: 0;
  background: black;
  .display(flex);
  .flex-direction(column);

  @media all and (min-width: 768px) {
    .justify-content(space-around);
    .flex-direction(row);
  }
  @media all and (min-width: 970px) {
    .justify-content(flex-end);
  }
  li {
    padding: 20px;
    a {
      color: white;
      &:hover{
        color: red;
      }
    }
  }
}
```

3. Then, create an HTML file named `index.html` and include the client-side `less.js` compiler and the `navigation.less` file into it by adding the following lines of the HTML code into the `head` section:

```html
<link rel="stylesheet/less" type="text/css"
  href="less/navigation.less">
<script src="js/less.js" type="text/javascript"></script>
```

Write down the following snippet of the HTML code into the `body` section of `index.html` to display the navigation:

```
<nav role="navigation">
  <ul>
    <li><a href="">Menu item 1</a></li>
    <li><a href="">Menu item 2 (long text)</a></li>
    <li><a href="">Three</a></li>
  </ul>
</nav>
```

4. Finally, load the `index.html` file in your browser, and you will find that, depending on your screen width, it looks like what's shown in the following screenshot:

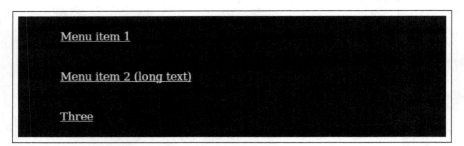

5. Finally, resize your browser window to see the effect of the media queries. On screen widths smaller than 768 pixels, the navigation should look like what's shown in the following screenshot:

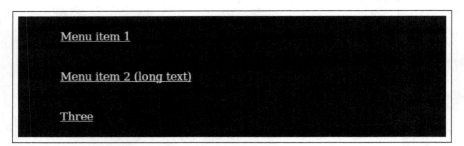

How it works...

The Less Hat mixins for flexible boxes enable you to build your flexbox designs without taking care of browser prefixing. You can code your Less code using the newest W3C standard syntax for flexboxes. More information about the syntax can be found at `http://www.w3.org/TR/css3-flexbox/`.

The navigation menu built in this recipe has three states.

The first step is declaring the display property of the `nav > ul` selector as a flexbox. This had been done with the following call in the Less code:

```
nav > ul {
  .display(flex);
}
```

Because the coding is mobile first, in the first state, the navigation items should stack under each other. The items stack `flex-direction` has been set to the `column` value using the following Less code:

```
nav > ul {
  .flex-direction(column);
}
```

In the second state, for screens wider than 768 pixels, the navigation should start floating. In Less, `flex-direction` has been set to the `row` value, as can be seen in the following Less code:

```
@media all and (min-width: 768px) {
  .justify-content(space-around);
  .flex-direction(row);
}
```

In the preceding code, the `.justify-content(space-around);` call centers the navigation. For wider screens, the navigation will be moved to the right-hand side (assuming **left-to-right** (**ltr**) text direction, see also the *Creating bidirectional styling without code duplication* recipe) by deploying the following Less code, which includes the second media query:

```
@media all and (min-width: 970px) {
  .justify-content(flex-end);
}
```

Although some people claim that the CSS Flexible box module is only intended for small blocks and not for the overall website layout, it's possible to set up your page layout with (nested) flexboxes. You could try the following Less code:

```
@import "lesshat-master/build/lesshat.less";
nav > ul {
  list-style: none;
  margin: 0;
  background: black;
  .display(flex);
  .flex-direction(column);
  @media all and (min-width: 768px) {
    .justify-content(space-around);
```

```less
      .flex-direction(row);
    }
    @media all and (min-width: 970px) {
      .justify-content(flex-end);
    }
    li {
      padding: 20px;
      a {
        color: white;
        &:hover{
          color: red;
        }
      }
    }
  }
}

.main {
  .display(flex);
  .flex-direction(column);
  section {
    background-color:blue;
  }
@media all and (min-width: 768px) {
    .flex-direction(row);
    section {
      .flex-grow(3);
    }
    aside {
      .flex-grow(1);
    }
  }
}
```

The compiled CSS code of the preceding Less code can be used with the following snippet of HTML code:

```html
<nav role="navigation">
  <ul>
    <li><a href="">Menu item 1</a></li>
    <li><a href="">Menu item 2 (long text)</a></li>
    <li><a href="">Three</a></li>
  </ul>
</nav>
```

```
<div class="main" role="content">
  <section>
    <nav role="navigation">
      <ul>
        <li><a href="">Menu item 1</a></li>
        <li><a href="">Menu item 2 (long text)</a></li>
        <li><a href="">Three</a></li>
      </ul>
    </nav>
    Content</section>
    <aside>Subcontent</aside>
</div>
```

Loaded in your browser, the result of the preceding code should look like the following screenshot:

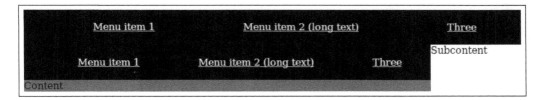

There's more...

Although the CSS Flexible box module level 3 is very powerful, syntax changes over time make its deployment complicated when you have to support older browsers. The mixin libraries, such as the Less Hat library, can be used to set the right browser prefixes for the Flexible box module.

Modernizr is a JavaScript library that detects which HTML5 and CSS3 features a browser supports. Modernizr can also be used to detect which version of the flexbox syntax is supported. Modernizr adds a class named `flexbox` to the `html` tag on browsers that support flexbox or, otherwise, a `no-flexbox` class. Modernizr is also able to detect the syntax version by adding the `flexboxlegancy` class for the old syntax and the `flexboxtweener` class for the syntax used by the Internet Explorer 10 browser. With Modernizr, you can write fallbacks for browsers that do not support flexboxes or just support an older flexbox syntax.

Alternatively, you can create an `inline-block` fallback by defining the `display` property, as follows:

```
.flexbox {
  display: inline-block;
  display: -webkit-flex;
  display: -moz-flex;
  display: -ms-flex;
  display: flex;
}
```

Older browsers will ignore the nonsupported flex values and fall back on the `display: inline-block;` declaration. In *Chapter 8, Building a Layout with Less*, you will learn how to build a web page layout using this technique.

See also

▶ A complete guide to code flexboxes in CSS can be found at `http://css-tricks.com/snippets/css/a-guide-to-flexbox/`

▶ You can read more about cross-browser support at `http://dev.opera.com/articles/advanced-cross-browser-flexbox/`

▶ The Modernizr JavaScript library can be found at `http://modernizr.com/`

Getting retina ready with Preboot

The Preboot library of the Less variables and mixins has been created by Mark Otto (@ mdo), and can be seen as the precursor of Twitter's Bootstrap. In this recipe, you will use the Preboot library to create retina-ready images.

Although many improvements of the mixins and code are brought back from Bootstrap to the second version of Preboot, Bootstrap is more powerful to start a project in most situations. You can read more about Bootstrap in *Chapter 9, Using Bootstrap with Less*.

Getting ready

You can download the Preboot library from `http://getpreboot.com/`. Unzip the ZIP archive into your working directory, and use the command-line `lessc` compiler, as described in the *Installing the lessc compiler with npm* recipe in *Chapter 1, Getting to Grips with the Basics of Less* to compile your Less code.

How to do it...

Create a Less file that contains the following Less code, and use the command-line `lessc` compiler to compile this file into the CSS code:

```less
@import "preboot-master/less/preboot.less";
.selector{
  .retina-image("/img/bg.png", "/img/bg@2x.png", 100px, 100px);
}
```

Then, you will find that the preceding Less code will compile into the following CSS code:

```css
.selector {
  background-image: url("/img/bg.png");
}
@media only screen and (-webkit-min-device-pixel-ratio: 2), only
  screen and (min--moz-device-pixel-ratio: 2), only screen and
    (-o-min-device-pixel-ratio: 2/1), only screen and
      (min-device-pixel-ratio: 2), only screen and
        (min-resolution: 192dpi), only screen and (min-resolution:
          2dppx) {
  .selector {
    background-image: url("/img/bg@2x.png");
    background-size: 100px 100px;
  }
}
```

How it works...

High-density devices have more pixels per inch or centimeter than normal displays. Apple introduced the term **Retina** for its double-density displays. If you zoom-in on an image (or scale it up), it will become blurred. This is the problem web designers have to solve when designing for high-density devices. You might be wondering, "what has this to do with Less?" CSS, in combination with media queries, can help you to prevent your images blur on high-density display.

To understand what happens, you have to realize that the CSS pixels are, in fact, device-independent. The CSS pixels are used to give elements in the browser psychical dimensions. On normal screens, a CSS pixel matches a device pixel. High-density displays have more device pixels in a CSS pixel—in the case of retina, four times the number of pixels. More and smaller pixels make it impossible to see the individual pixels with the human eye.

So, on a retina display, an image of a 300 CSS pixels width requires 600 device pixels in order to keep the same physical size. Now, you can prevent your images from blurring so as to use a with a higher bitmap resolution (CSS pixels) and scale it with HTML or CSS.

On normal displays, your HTML code will look like the following code:

```
<img src="photo300x300.png" width="300px" height="300px">
```

On a retina display, you will show the same image with the following code:

```
<img src="photo600x600.png" width="300px" height="300px">
```

Currently, there is a convention to give the high-density images @2x in their name, for example, `example@2x.png`.

The mixin in this recipe does not set an `img` tag, but sets the image as a `background-image` property. Note that setting all your images as `background` is not a good idea with respect to usability. Website usability guidelines require that all images that are not part of the design and have a contextual meaning be placed inside an `img` tag and have a proper `alt` attribute that describes them.

The media queries check among others for `min-device-pixel-ratio > 2`. The pixel ratio may vary depending on the device type and brand. Visit `http://www.devicepixelratio.com/` to get an impression of the different pixel ratios used.

There's more...

When using the `.retina-image()` mixin of this recipe, you should also realize that Less does not merge or group media queries. The number of bytes of the compiled CSS grows with the length of the media queries times the number of retina images you have added with the `.retina-image()` mixin. If you want to add many retina images, you should consider grouping them all inside the retina media queries. This can be archived by creating a CSS file with retina images and import this CSS file into your Less project file.

See also

The recipe does not wrap the images in `data-uri` (see also the *Embedding images with data URIs* recipe in *Chapter 4, Leveraging the Less Built-in Functions*). You do not need `data-uri` here because, according to the tests at `http://timkadlec.com/2012/04/media-query-asset-downloading-results/`, media queries also prevent the images from loading if the media query does not match. For this reason, loading the retina images does not require an additional HTTP request.

Generating font-face declarations with Clearless

The `@font-face` CSS rule allows authors to specify fonts that are not installed on the user's system to display text on their web pages.

Getting ready

For this recipe, you will need to generate the EOT, WOFF, and TTF formats of a font. You can use, for instance, the Webfont generator at `http://www.fontsquirrel.com/tools/webfont-generator` to get the different formats of a TTF font file. You should save the generated font files with the same name and different extension in your working directory. Make sure you do not choose any copyrighted fonts unless you are willing to pay for it.

You can inspect the fonts in your browser, so use the client-side `less.js` compiler, as described in the *Downloading, installing, and integrating less.js* recipe in *Chapter 1, Getting to Grips with the Basics of Less*, to compile the Less code of this recipe in your browser. The Less code will use mixins from the Clearless library.

How to do it...

1. Start with downloading and unzipping the Clearless library into your working directory. You can find the Clearless files at `http://clearleft.github.io/clearless/`.

2. Secondly, download a (free) font from `http://www.fontsquirrel.com/` or use their Webfont generator, as described in the *Getting ready* section of this recipe. Save the font files in a `fonts` directory in your working directory.

> In this recipe, the 3Dumb font will be used. You can find this font at `http://www.fontsquirrel.com/fonts/3Dumb`. Use the `download @font-face kit` button on this page to download the files. Unzip these file into the `font` directory.

3. Then, create a `fontface.less` file, and write out the following Less code into it:

```
@import "clearleft-clearless-63e2363/mixins/all.less";
.font-face( '3Dumb', '../fonts/web
  fonts/3dumb_regular_macroman/3Dumbwebfont');
h1 {
  font-family: "3Dumb";
}
```

4. Now, create an HTML file named `index.html` and include the client-side `less.js` compiler and the `fontface.less` file into it by adding the following lines of the HTML code into the `head` section:

```
<link rel="stylesheet/less" type="text/css"
  href="less/fontface.less">
<script src="js/less.js" type="text/javascript"></script>
```

Write down the following snippet of the HTML code into the `body` section of the `index.html` file to display the gradient:

```
<h1>A heading in the 3Dumb font</h1>
```

5. After the first four steps, you should end up with a file and directory structure:

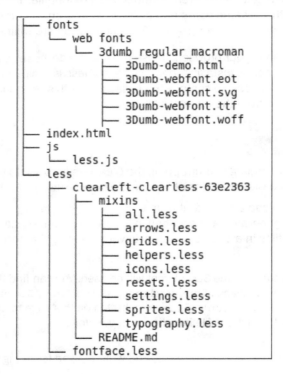

```
── fonts
│   └── web fonts
│       └── 3dumb_regular_macroman
│           ├── 3Dumb-demo.html
│           ├── 3Dumb-webfont.eot
│           ├── 3Dumb-webfont.svg
│           ├── 3Dumb-webfont.ttf
│           └── 3Dumb-webfont.woff
├── index.html
├── js
│   └── less.js
└── less
    ├── clearleft-clearless-63e2363
    │   ├── mixins
    │   │   ├── all.less
    │   │   ├── arrows.less
    │   │   ├── grids.less
    │   │   ├── helpers.less
    │   │   ├── icons.less
    │   │   ├── resets.less
    │   │   ├── settings.less
    │   │   ├── sprites.less
    │   │   └── typography.less
    │   └── README.md
    └── fontface.less
```

6. Finally, load the `index.html` file in your browser; it should look like the following screenshot:

How it works...

The `.font-face()` mixin should be called once for each font you want to include. The caller should not be called inside a selector because the `@font-face` rule defines a font available for the document. The selector can use the defined fonts with the `font-family` property. To use the declared font inside a selector, you can use the name of the font, set as the first parameter of the `.font-face()` call, as a value for the `font-family` property.

The `.font-face()` mixin accepts five parameters, the last three of which are optional and used to set the font weights and styles. The optional last parameter is set to normal by default. The first parameter, as already mentioned, sets the name for the font, and the second parameter should be set to the path/URL of the font, including the font name without the file extensions.

Finally, the `.font-face( '3Dumb', '../fonts/web fonts/3dumb_regular_macroman/3Dumbwebfont');` call used in this recipe will compile into the following CSS code:

```
@font-face {
  font-family: '3Dumb';
  src: url('../fonts/web fonts/3dumb_regular_macroman/3Dumb-
    webfont.eot');
  src: url('../fonts/web fonts/3dumb_regular_macroman/3Dumb-
    webfont.eot?#iefix') format('embedded-opentype'),
    url('../fonts/web fonts/3dumb_regular_macroman/3Dumb-
    webfont.woff') format('woff'), url('../fonts/web
    fonts/3dumb_regular_macroman/3Dumb-webfont.ttf')
    format('truetype');
  font-weight: normal;
  font-style: normal;
}
```

There's more...

The `@font-face` rule declarations can also be used to integrate iconized fonts into your project. Using iconized fonts instead of images for icons will reduce the number of HTTP requests. Just like image sprites, as described in the *Leveraging sprite images with Pre* recipe, there is only a single file that has to be downloaded. Another advantage of iconized fonts is that they are scalable with CSS. Also, coloring the icons or even adding drop-shadows can be done by leveraging CSS.

An example of iconized fonts is the Glyphicons library, which is also used by Twitter's Bootstrap, and another example is the **Font Awesome** font. You can find these fonts at `http://glyphicons.com/` and `http://fortawesome.github.io/Font-Awesome/`.

Most iconized fonts include some CSS code to integrate them into your web projects. To integrate an iconized font in your Less code, you will have to perform the following steps:

1. Firstly, create rules, as described in this recipe:

```
@import "clearleft-clearless-63e2363/mixins/all.less";
.font-face( 'MyFont', '../fonts/MyFont -webfont');
```

2. Then, create a base class using, for instance, the following code:

```
.icon {
  font-family: 'MyFont';
  speak: none;
  font-style: normal;
  font-weight: normal;
  font-variant: normal;
  text-transform: none;
  line-height: 1;
  -webkit-font-smoothing: antialiased;
  -moz-osx-font-smoothing: grayscale;
}
```

Note that using a base class in this situation should be preferred over using the :extend() pseudo class, as described in the *Using extend to reduce the compiled CSS size* recipe in *Chapter 5, Extending and Referencing*, because the list of sectors grows with the number of classes in step 3. Alternatively, you could use the CSS attribute selectors to avoid the base class in your HTML code. Depending on the class prefix in step 3, you can use the [class^="icon-"], [class*=" icon-"] selector instead of the .icon selector.

3. Finally, create a class for each icon, as can been seen in the following lines of the example Less code:

```
.icon-euro     { &:before { content: "\20ac"; } }
.icon-minus    { &:before { content: "\2212"; } }
.icon-cloud    { &:before { content: "\2601"; } }
```

Note that the icons are added to the content with the :before pseudo class. You can read more about the :before and :after pseudo classes in the *There's more...* section of the *Improving your website's SEO with 3L mixins* recipe.

See also

▸ You can read more about custom web fonts and the `@font-face` rule at `http://css-tricks.com/snippets/css/using-font-face/`.

▸ Use the Icomoon app to build your own iconized fonts. You can find the Icomoon app at `https://icomoon.io/app/`.

Improving your website's SEO with 3L mixins

In modern web design, **search engine optimization** (**SEO**) cannot be ignored. The **Lots of Love for Less**, or, in short, **3L**, mixins library provides you with a lot of mixins for single-line declarations that can also be found in other libraries. 3L also contains a mixin called `SEO helper`. This `.seo-helper()` mixin generates the CSS code that makes common mistakes about SEO in your web pages visible.

Getting ready

First, download the latest version of the 3L library from `http://mateuszkocz.github.io/3l/`. The compiled CSS code of this recipe can be loaded into an existing web page to make common SEO issues visible. Use a modern browser to load the Less code together with the client-side `less.js` compiler in a web page. In the *Downloading, installing, and integrating less.js* recipe in *Chapter 1, Getting to Grips with the Basics of Less*, you can read about how to use and install the client-side `less.js` compiler.

How to do it...

1. First, download and unzip the 3L library into your working directory. You can find the 3L files at `http://mateuszkocz.github.io/3l/`.

2. Then, create an `seo.less` file and write out the following Less code into it:
   ```less
   @import "3l-master/3L/3L.less";
   .seo-helper();
   ```

3. Thirdly, create an HTML file named `index.html` and include the client-side `less.js` compiler and the `seo.less` file into it. The `index.html` file should look like the following code:
   ```html
   <!DOCTYPE html>
   <html>
     <head>
       <meta name="description" content="">
   ```

```
        <meta name="viewport" content="width=device-width,
          initial-scale=1.0">
        <link rel="stylesheet/less" type="text/css"
          href="less/seo.less">
        <script src="js/less.js"
          type="text/javascript"></script>
      </head>
      <body>
        <div>
          <p></p>
          <img src="image.png">
        </div>
      </body>
    </html>
```

Note that this HTML document has no title and an empty `meta` description (content attribute), and contains an empty `<p>` tag and an `<img>` tag without an `alt` attribute.

4. Finally, load the `index.html` file in your browser, and you will see that it looks like the following screenshot:

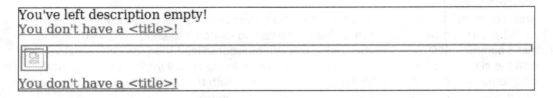

How it works...

This recipe will show you that you can add the following lines of code to the HTML files of your projects to make some common errors visible:

```
<link rel="stylesheet/less" type="text/css" href="less/seo.less">
<script src="js/less.js" type="text/javascript"></script>
```

The compiled CSS code of the `seo.less` file will be as follows:

```
img:not([alt]),
img[alt=""],
img[alt^=" "],
a[href=""],
a[href^=" "],
a[href="#"],
a[rel*="nofollow"],
```

```
div:empty,
span:empty,
li:empty,
p:empty,
td:empty,
th:empty,
*[title=""],
*[class=""],
*[id=""] {
  outline: 2px solid red !important;
  outline-offset: 3px !important;
}
head,
title:empty,
link,
meta {
  display: block;
}
title:empty:before {
  content: "You've left the <title> empty!";
}
link:before {
  content: "You don't have a <title>!";
}
title ~ link {
  display: none;
}
meta[name="description"][content=""]:before,
meta[name="description"][content=" "]:before {
  content: "You've left description empty!";
}
```

Of course, you can study the source files of the 3L library to find out how to code this in Less. Further interesting parts of the CSS code are the :empty pseudo class and code that results in the "You don't have a <title>!" message, because there is no title selector to attach this message. The "You don't have a <title>!" message is always declared and attached to the link:before selector, but the message will be hidden when there is a title selector due to the following lines of the CSS code:

```
title ~ link {
  display: none;
}
```

Note that the ~ combinator in the title ~ link selector is a general sibling combinator; here, it selects all the link selectors proceeded by a title selector. A link selector will always be available; otherwise, you would be unable to include the seo.less file.

There's more...

You should judge yourself if the `.seo-helper()` mixin is really useful for your projects. Useful or not, however, this recipe will show you another use case for Less (and CSS) other than styling. The compiled CSS displays warnings such as `no title` in the HTML code. CSS cannot manipulate or change the HTML DOM structure, but the `:before` and `:after` pseudo classes make it possible to add some content leveraging to the `content` property. You can use the same technique to make the URLs of hyperlinks visible in the printed version of your HTML document using the following Less code:

```
@media (print) {
  a[href]:after {
    content: " (" attr(href) ")";
  }
}
```

See also

▶   Read more about the basics of search engine friendly design and development at `http://moz.com/beginners-guide-to-seo/basics-of-search-engine-friendly-design-and-development`

▶   Additional information about child and sibling selectors can be found at `http://css-tricks.com/child-and-sibling-selectors/`

▶   A more extended description of the `:empty pseudo` class, including some examples, can be found at `https://developer.mozilla.org/en-US/docs/Web/CSS/:empty`

Leveraging sprite images with Pre

Sprite images can help to reduce the number of the HTTP requests needed to load your website. In this recipe, you will use the `Pre.less` mixin library. `Pre.less` is a CSS framework that provides useful mixins. The `util` module of `Pre.less` contains mixins for sprite images that will be used in this recipe.

Getting ready

In this recipe, you will create some social media buttons with a mouse-over effect. You can download the example sprite images with a social media button at `http://crunchify.com/social-media-css-sprite-example-for-your-wordpress-blog/`, or create a sprite image yourself.

The image should look like the following screenshot:

When you create the sprite image yourself, you will have to use a square grid for your images. Each square should contain one image; a bigger image might overlap more than one grid square, but make sure the overlapping grid squares form a square of squares, too. Evaluate the result of your sprite image in your browser, and use the client-side less.js, as described in the *Downloading, installing, and integrating less.js* recipe in *Chapter 1, Getting to Grips with the Basics of Less*, to compile your CSS code into the Less code.

 In this recipe, you will make use of the Pre.less mixin library that can be downloaded from https://github.com/yuanyan/pre.

How to do it...

1. Create/download a sprite image, as described in the *Getting ready* section of this recipe.

2. Download and unzip the Pre.less mixin library into your working directory.

3. Create a project.less file that contains the following Less code:

```less
@import "pre-master/dist/pre.less";
@sprite-default-size: 23px;
@sprite-default-margin: 0px;
@sprite-image-base-path: "../images";
@sprite-image: "social-icons1.png";

a{
  display:inline-block;
  &.twitter {
    .sprite-img(@sprite-image, 1,2);
    &:hover {
      .sprite-img(@sprite-image, 1,1);
    }
  }
  &.facebook {
    .sprite-img(@sprite-image, 2,2);
    &:hover {
      .sprite-img(@sprite-image, 2,1);
```

```
        }
      }
      display:inline-block;
      &.rss {
        .sprite-img(@sprite-image, 3,2);
        &:hover {
          .sprite-img(@sprite-image, 3,1);
        }
      }
      &.google {
        .sprite-img(@sprite-image, 4,2);
        &:hover {
          .sprite-img(@sprite-image, 4,1);
        }
      }
    }
  }
```

4. You can, for instance, use the following snippet of the HTML code to see how the compiled CSS code styles your social media buttons in your browser:

```
<p class="important"
   style="color:green;font-size:4em;">important</p>
<p class="unimportant"
   style="color:green;font-size:4em;">unimportant</p>
```

Your HTML document should also include the `project.less` and `less.js` files, as follows:

```
<link rel="stylesheet/less" type="text/css"
  href="project.less">
<script src="less.js" type="text/javascript"></script>
```

5. Finally, load the HTML file into your browser, and you will find that it looks like the following screenshot:

How it works...

The compiled CSS code sets the sprite image as the value of a `background-image` property of the selector. After this, with the starting point of the background image set by the `background-image` property, due to the square grid, it is easy to calculate the position of a certain image. For the Google icon in the example sprite image, you will have to set the starting point to three times the size of a square of the grid to the right-hand side, and one time the size of a square of the down grid.

As you have probably noted, the same `@sprite-image` variable had been used repeatedly as an argument for the `.sprite-img()` mixins. The `Pre.less` mixin library provides you with an alternative syntax that allows you to set the sprite image only once. The following Less code will show you an example of this alternative syntax for sprite images:

```
a{
  .sprite-background("icons-32.png")
  .twitter{
    .sprite-position(1,1);
  }
}
```

There's more...

The mixins in this recipe use an equal dimensioned square grid. The Spritebox tool at `http://www.spritebox.net/` allows you to create a Less mixin for any sprite image.

A `spritebox` mixin, including retina support, will look like the following code:

```
.spritebox(@left, @top, @height, @width) {
  background-image: url(spritebox-sprite@2x.png);
  background-repeat: no-repeat;
  background-position: @left @top;
  height: @height;
  width: @width;
  @media only screen and (-webkit-min-device-pixel-ratio: 1.5),
  only screen and (-moz-min-device-pixel-ratio: 1.5),
  only screen and (-o-min-device-pixel-ratio: 3/2),
  only screen and (min-device-pixel-ratio: 1.5) {
    background-image: url(spritebox-sprite@2x.png);
    background-size: 476px 748px;
  }
}
```

The main proposal of using images sprite is to reduce the number of HTTP requests when loading your website. Instead of loading many images, the browser will have to load only one single sprite image. In the *Embedding images with data URIs* recipe in *Chapter 4, Leveraging the Less Built-in Functions*, you can read how to embed your images in your CSS with data URIs and base 64 encoding.

At first sight, leveraging data URIs to embed your inline images in your CSS seems a better alternative for sprite images because these embedded images no longer require any extra HTTP request. Nevertheless, this theoretical assumption should be read with care. For instance, the blog post at `http://www.mobify.com/blog/css-sprites-vs-data-uris-which-is-faster-on-mobile/` prescribes that image sprites, which load faster on mobile devices, are still should preferred for larger images.

In this recipe, you create icons using a sprite image. Iconized fonts, as described in the *Generating font-face declarations with Clearless* recipe can be a good alternative to creating a list of icons. Iconized font can be easily styled with CSS.

See also

> ▸ A more detailed explanation of using square grids for your sprites can be found at `http://www.smashingmagazine.com/2012/04/11/css-sprites-revisited/`

Creating bidirectional styling without code duplication

Some languages, including Arabic, Farsi, Hebrew, and Urdu, are written from **right-to-left** (`rtl`). In this recipe, you will learn how to write Less code that can be compiled for `rtl` and `ltr` languages by leveraging the Less-bidi mixin library.

Getting ready

For this recipe, you will have to download the Less-bidi mixin library from `https://github.com/danielkatz/less-bidi`. The Less code will be compiled in the browser by using the client-side `less.js` compiler, as described in the *Downloading, installing, and integrating less.js* recipe in *Chapter 1, Getting to Grips with the Basics of Less*.

How to do it...

In this recipe, you will create the Less and HTML code for the example shown at `https://github.com/danielkatz/less-bidi`, as follows:

1. Download and unzip the Less-bidi mixin library into your working directory.

2. Then, create a `bidi.less` file that contains the following Less code:

```less
@import "less-bidi-master/src/bidi.less";

.ltr {
  .style(ltr);
}
.rtl {
  .style(rtl);
}
.style(@bidi) {
  .bidi-direction();
  .bidi-text-shadow(2px,2px,1px,silver);
  font-size:1em;
  h1 {
    .bidi-margin-start(20px);
    margin-bottom: 10px;
  }
  .two-col article {
    .bidi-float(start);
    width: 70%;
  }
  .two-col nav {
    .bidi-float(end);
  }
}
```

3. In this step, you will have to create an `index.html` file that includes the `bidi.less` and `less.js` files, as follows:

```html
<link rel="stylesheet/less" type="text/css"
  href="bidi.less">
<script src="less.js" type="text/javascript"></script>
```

After this, write down the following HTML structure into the `body` section of the `index.html` file.

4. Finally, load the HTML file into your browser, and you will find that it looks like the following screenshot:

How it works

When you change the text direction of your website from `ltr` to `rtl` or vice versa, you will have to make, at the very least, the following changes to the properties in your Less code:

- text direction
- float
- clear

These attributes should change the value from right to left and vice versa. So, for instance, `float:left` becomes `float:right`.

Alternatively, you can use the Less-bidi mixin library, which enables you to compile the CSS code for different text directions without the need to change your code. To accomplish this, you can use a switch, as described in *Building a switch to leverage argument matching* recipe of *Chapter 6, Advanced Less Coding*.

The Less-bidi mixin library provides you with solutions for more than only the preceding three properties mentioned. The library, for instance, has also a mixin to change `text-shadow` when the text direction changes.

The text direction is set to `rtl` or `ltr` with the `direction` property, which can be seen when you inspect the compiled source of the code from this recipe. The compiled CSS code of the `.ltr` selector will look like the following code:

```
.ltr {
  direction: ltr;
  text-shadow: 2px 2px 1px #c0c0c0;
  font-size: 1em;
}
```

There's more...

As you saw, you will also have to change the floating direction of the elements. Changing the floating direction will be of special interest for layouts based on floats, such as the grid system of Twitter's Bootstrap. The CSS layouts based on the inline-block declaration and layouts build with flexbox, as described in the *Building a layout with the CSS3 flexbox module* recipe, will not require any adaptation when changing the text direction.

When using flexible boxes, the `justify-content` property defines how to arrange items in the current row. Instead of `left` or `right`, this property accepts the `flex-start` and `flex-end` values. Depending on the text direction, the end is on the left or right-hand side of the available space. Less-bidi uses the same strategy for the `.bidi-text-align()` and `.bidi-float()` mixins, which accepts an argument that should be set to `start` or `end`, too.

See also

▶ In the situation that a block of text contains both left-to-right and right-to-left text, you should use the `direction` property, together with the `unicode-bidi` property. You can read more about the `unicode-bidi` property at `https://developer.mozilla.org/en-US/docs/Web/CSS/unicode-bidi`.

▶ HTML itself also contains a `bdi` element; see `http://www.w3.org/TR/HTML-markup/bdi.html`, and there is a `dir` attribute that can be used to set the text direction. More information about the `dir` attribute can be found at `http://www.w3.org/TR/html401/struct/dirlang.html`. The `bdi` element and `dir` attribute are used together with the CSS style rules often.

▶ A clear summary about the CSS `direction` property can be found at `http://css-tricks.com/almanac/properties/d/direction/`.

▶ When working on international projects, it can be useful to keep bidirectional styling in mind from the start. At `http://blog.dictionary.com/righttoleft/`, you can read how and when Twitter supports right-to-left languages and why some language are written from right to left, or even from bottom to top.

▶ The Less `css-flip` plugin generates **left-to-right** (**LTR**) or **right-to-left** (**RTL**) CSS from your Less code. This plugin can be found at: `https://github.com/bassjobsen/less-plugin-css-flip`

Creating animations with animations.css

CSS3 makes it possible to animate transitions from one CSS style configuration to another. CSS animation can even replace Flash animations, animated images, and JavaScript in your projects. In this recipe, you will learn how to integrate `animate.css` in your Less code.

Getting ready

A cross-browser library of the CSS animations is `animate.css`. Download the uncompressed version of `animate.css` from `https://github.com/daneden/animate.css`. You can use your favorite text editor to create a Less version of `animate.css`. Test the CSS animation in your browsers using the client-side `less.js` compiler, as described in the *Downloading, installing, and integrating less.js* recipe in *Chapter 1, Getting to Grips with the Basics of Less*.

How to do it...

CSS animation have brought about many new things for web designers using CSS. On the other hand make vendor-prefixes coding them complex. Mixins help you to build animations fast and efficiently, as follows:

1. Open the `animate.css` file with a text editor. Firstly, remove the .animated, `.animated.infinite`, and `animated.hinge` classes at the beginning of the file. Then, add the following Less code into this file:

```less
// The Animation
.animation(@name) {
  -webkit-animation-name: @name;
  -moz-animation-name: @name;
  -o-animation-name: @name;
  animation-name: @name;
}
// Duration and mode
.animated(@duration: 1s; @mode: both;) {
  -webkit-animation-duration: @duration;
    -moz-animation-duration: @duration;
      -o-animation-duration: @duration;
        animation-duration: @duration;

  -webkit-animation-fill-mode: @mode;
    -moz-animation-fill-mode: @mode;
      -o-animation-fill-mode: @mode;
        animation-fill-mode: @mode;
}
```

```
.animation-iteration-count(@count: 1)
{
    -webkit-animation-duration: @count;
      -moz-animation-iteration-count: @count;
        -o-animation-iteration-count: @count;
            animation-iteration-count: @count;
}
```

2. Then save this file as `animate.less`.

   Notice that the mixins used in the preceding code come from `https://github.com/jonschlinkert/animate.less`, which is a fork of the original `animate.css` project. Unfortunately, the code is not up to data at the time of writing this book.

3. Secondly, create `animation.less`, which imports the `animate.less` file from the previous step that should contain the following Less code:

```
@import "animate.css/animate.less";
body > header {
color:red;
.animation(flip); // animation
.animated(10s); // duration
.animation-iteration-count(infinite); // number of iterations
}
```

4. Then, you will have to create an `index.html` file, which contains the following lines of HTML code in the head section:

```
<link rel="stylesheet/less" type="text/css" href="less/animation.less>
<script src="js/less.js" type="text/javascript"></script>
```

5. Now, write down the following HTML snippet into the `body` section:

```
<header>Site header</header>
```

6. Finally, you can load this `index.html` file in your browser to see the header "flipping". Also try to replace `.animation(flip)` with one of the other animations that `animate.css` does provide you. You can also test and find these animations at `http://daneden.github.io/animate.css/`.

How it works...

A CSS animation has two parts. The first part sets the name of the animation, the duration, and some other properties. The name of the animation refers to the name of the `@keyframes` at-rule. The `@keyframes` at-rules describe the different states of the animation. A `@keyframes` at-rule should contain at least a start state and an end state, but it is also possible to add other states between the start and end of the animation.

A simple animation, written without any prefix, can look as follows:

```
h1 {
  animation-duration: 10s;
  animation-name: trafficlight;
}
@keyframes trafficlight{
  from {
   color: red;
  }
  to {
    color: green;
  }
}
```

To add a third color to this animation, you can rewrite the `@keyframes` declaration as shown in the following code:

```
@keyframes trafficlight{
  0 {
   color: red;
  }
  50% {
   color: orange;
  }
  100% {
    color: green;
  }
}
```

Inside the `@keyframes` at-rule, you can use the CSS `transform` property. The `transform` property applies transformation, such as move, scale, turn, spin, or stretch to an element.

After reading the preceding text, you should inspect the source of the `animate.less` file again. Now, you should realize that `animate.css` provides you with a list of predefined and prefixed `@keyframes` at-rules that you can use to build your animations in Less (or CSS).

There's more...

Both the animation and the transformation enable you to set a timing function using the CSS animation-timing-function or transition-timing-function property. Both timing functions accepts keywords, such as linear, ease or ease-in, as input. The timing function can also be set using the CSS `cubic-bezier()` function.

- ▸ CSS tricks has created a screencast video about using CSS animations, which can be watched at `http://css-tricks.com/video-screencasts/97-intro-to-css-animations/`

- ▸ A guide about using CSS transitions can be found at `https://developer.mozilla.org/en-US/docs/Web/Guide/CSS/Using_CSS_transitions`

- ▸ You can create your own `cubic-bezier()` functions at `http://cubic-bezier.com/`

Creating animations with More.less

`More.less` is a mixin library that can help you to create cross-browser CSS animations. `More.less` includes all `animate.css` animations, see the *Creating animations with animations.css* recipe of this chapter for more information about `animate.css`.

Getting ready

Download and unzip the `More.less` mixin library into the `less` subdirectory of your working directory. You can download the ZIP file at `https://github.com/weinitz/More.less/archive/master.zip`. In this recipe you will build some CSS animation. You should watch these animations in your browser. The Less code in this recipe can be compiled into client-side CSS code, leveraging the `less.js` compiler. In *Chapter 1, Getting to Grips with the Basics of Less*, of this book, you can read how to download and install this compiler.

How to do it...

1. The bundled animations of `More.less` are saved as `more/animation/{name}/(in|out)/name.less`. Create a new file `more/animation/orbit.less`, and write down the following Less code into it:

```
@keyframes orbit {
    25% {
        transform: scale(0.75,0.75) translateY(-50px)
translateX(100px);
    }

    50% {
        transform:  scale(1,1) translateX(200px);
    }
    75% {
```

```
        transform: scale(1.5,1.5) translateY(100px)translateX(100px);
      }
  }

  #animation {
      .orbit() {
          #animation > .name(orbit);
      }
  }
```

 Notice that you will have to add the prefix @keyframes at-rules yourself; see also the *There's more...* section of this recipe.

2. Secondly create a animation.less file that contains the following Less code:

```
@import "More.less-master/more.less";
@import "More.less-master/more/animation/orbit.less";
@import "More.less-master/more/animation/special.less";

body {
background-color: black;
}

.earth {
position: absolute;
top:150px;
left:150px;
#shape > .circle(180px);
#gradient > .horizontal(blue,silver);
.box-shadow(-2px 3px 54px darkblue);
#animation .rotate();
            #animation > .init(10s);
#animation > .infinite;
}

.moon {
position: absolute;
top:100px;
left:100px;
            #shape > .circle(80px);
#gradient > .horizontal(yellow,silver);
.box-shadow(-2px 3px 54px gold);
#animation > .init(2s);
#animation > .infinite;
```

```
#animation > .orbit();
}
```

3. Then create an `index.html` file that includes the `animation.less` file from the previous step. This `index.html` file should contain the following HTML code:

```
<!DOCTYPE html>
<html>
  <head>
    <title>Gradients with Less Elements</title>
    <meta name="viewport" content="width=device-width,
initialscale=1.0">
    <link rel="stylesheet/less" type="text/css" href="animation.
less">
    <script src="js/less.js" type="text/javascript"></script>
  </head>
  <body>
    <div class="earth"></div>
    <div class="moon"></div>
  </body>
</html>
```

4. Finally, load `index.html` in your browser, and find that the animation will look like what's shown in the following figure:

How it works...

The `More.less` mixins are already namespaced. See the *Using namespacing with prebuilt libraries* recipe of this chapter to read more about namespace. The orbit `@keyframes` declaration can be easily called with the `#animation > .orbit();` caller. Also, other animation properties can be set in the same way.

Also, creating the circles and gradients can be done by calling respectively the namespaced `#shape > .circle()` and `#gradient > .horizontal()` mixins inside the `.moon` and `.earth` selectors.

Finally, you should notice that the transform property accepts a space separated list of values as can be seen in the following declaration:

```
transform: scale(0.75,0.75) translateY(-50px) translateX(100px);
```

The preceding code enables you to apply different translations on the same element for a state described in a `@keyframes` at-rule.

There's more...

In this recipe, you have added some `@keyframes` rules to create the rotate animation. Adding new animation in this manner is not an example of Don't Repeat Yourself (DRY). The `@keyframes` rules requires many vendor-prefixes that generate many code duplications. The More or Less library, which can be found at `https://github.com/pixelass/more-or-less`, provides you with a special mixin for keyframes. This `.keyframes()` mixin should be wrapped inside a selector and will look like the following code:

```
& {
    .keyframes(testanimation);.-frames(@-...){
        0% {
            left: 0;
            @{-}transform: translate(10px, 20px);
        }

        100% {
            left: 100%;
            @{-}transform: translate(100px, 200px);
        }
    }
}
```

Building semantic grids with semantic.gs

HTML5 introduced many new semantic HTML tags, such as footer, header, section, among others; nevertheless, many modern CSS grid systems are build with non-semantic `div` tags and CSS classes. Critics even say that building your grids with `div` tags does not differ from the old-school table layouts. The `semantic.gs` mixins library provides you with a simple manner to build a twelve-column semantic grid. Grids can be used as the skeleton of a responsive website.

Using grids in web design will help both the web designer and the web developer to prevent inconsistencies from occurring between the original design and the final implementation in HTML.

Getting ready

For this recipe, you have to download the latest version of the `semantic.gs` mixins, which can be found at `https://github.com/tylertate/semantic.gs/zipball/master`. After editing the Less files with a text editor, you can test the result in your browser. The client-side `less.js` compiler is used to compile the Less code, as described in *Chapter 1, Getting to Grips with the Basics of Less*.

How to do it...

In this recipe, you will rebuild the example that is also shown on the home page of the `semantic.gs` website. The media queries in the example code are changed so that the compiled CSS code will follow the mobile-first approach.

1. Use your favorite editor to create a `semantic.less` file, and write down the following code into this file:

```
@import "tylertate-semantic.gs-22e0e79/stylesheets/less/grid.less";
@column-width: 60;
@gutter-width: 20;
@columns: 12;
@total-width: 100%;

header { .column(12); }
article { .column(12); }
aside { .column(12); }

@media (min-width: 960px) {
    article { .column(9); }
    aside { .column(3); }
}
```

2. Create and edit the `index.html` file, which should contain the following HTML code:

```
<!DOCTYPE html>
<html>
<head>
<title>Semantic Grid</title>
<meta name="viewport" content="width=device-width, initial
scale=1.0">
<link rel="stylesheet/less" type="text/css" href="semantic.less">
<script src="js/less.min.js" type="text/javascript"></script>
</head>
<body>
<header>This is a header</header>
<article>This is an article</article>
<aside>This is an aside</aside>
</body>
</html>
```

3. Finally, load the `index.html` file in your browser. You will find that the `aside` tags float on the left-hand side of the article as expected.

How it works...

The `semantic.gs` mixins provide you an easy way to build a responsive grid without classes, and that is it. It is good to realize that using a grid does not have to break the semantic structure of your website.

Creating a responsive layout with the `semantic.gs` mixins is easy and straightforward. You can set the number of columns with the `@columns` variable; also, the column width and the gutter size are set by variables.

You will also have to notice that the grid had some limitations. In the recipe, the column size of the compiled CSS is fixed although the columns stack for screen width below 960 pixel, their width will be set to 960 (*12 x(@column-width + @gutter-width)*). The gutter is set with the margin property. This issue can be partly solved by setting the `@total-width` variable to `100%` after that the column widths (and margin) are also calculated as a percentage of the total available width and the grid had become fluid.

There's more

Twitter's Bootstrap as discussed in *Chapter 9, Using Twitter Bootstrap with Less* also builds its grid with `div` elements and classes. But Bootstrap also includes Less variables and mixins to quickly generate semantic layouts.

You can download Bootstrap's Less files at. After that, you can import `bootstrap.less` into your project file and write down the following Less code into it:

```
import (reference) "bootstrap.less";
@grid-columns:              12;
@grid-gutter-width:         30px;
@grid-float-breakpoint:     768px;

// Reset the box-sizing
*,
*:before,
*:after {
   .box-sizing(border-box);
}

.wrapper {
.make-row();
header {
.make-xs-column(12);
}
article {
.make-sm-column(8);
}
aside {
.make-sm-column(4);
}
}
```

The compiled CSS code of the preceding Less code can be used with the `index.html` file you have created in this recipe. Notice that you will have to wrap the layout in `<div class="wrapper">` to use the CSS code. Also, the `.box-sizing(border-box);` call is required. As you will see, the result will be a layout similar to that you already had created with the semantic.gs mixins.

See also

▶   On the `semantic.gs` website at `http://semantic.gs/`, you can find other examples of how to build the fluid, nested, and responsive layout with the `semantic.gs` mixins

▶   More information about Twitter's Bootstrap can be found at `http://www.getbootstrap.com/`

Building an alternative for fluid grids with Frameless

The Frameless grid offers you an alternative to fluid grids. The grid does not add more pixels when the screen width increases, but adds additional columns for wider screens. In this recipe, you will build a site navigation that stacks into two columns on small screens with centers floated on wider screens and moves to the right-hand side of the layout for wide screens.

Getting ready

You will need to download the Less template for the Frameless grid for this recipe. You can download this Less template at `https://github.com/jonikorpi/Frameless/blob/master/frameless.less`. To see how the navigation acts for different screen widths and browser zoom levels, you should load the HTML code into your browser and compile the Less code with the client-side `less.js` compiler.

You can read how to use the client-side `less.js` compiler in the *Downloading, installing and integrating less.js* recipe of *Chapter 1, Getting to Grips with the Basics of Less*. For client-side compiling, you will have to create an `index.html` file that loads the `frameless-example.less` file and the `less.js` compiler with the following code in the head section:

```
<link rel="stylesheet/less" type="text/css" href="frameless-example.less">
<script src="less.js" type="text/javascript"></script>
```

How to do it...

1. First save the Less template as described in the *Getting ready* section into your working directory.

2. Then create the `frameless-example.less` file, and write down the following Less code into it:

```
@import "frameless.less";
body {
font-size: (@font-size - 2)/16*1em;
}

#container
{
margin: auto;
width: @4cols;
}
```

```
nav {
ul {
list-style:none;
}

li {
padding:5px;
background-color:darkred;
color:white;
float:left;
width: @2cols;
}
}
//wide phone
@media screen and (min-width: 40em) {
#container
{
width: @8cols;
}
nav {
width: @8cols;
}
}
// > tablet
@media screen and (min-width: 60em) {
body {
background-color: red;
font-size: (@font-size + 2)/16*1em;
}

#container {
width: @12cols;
}
nav {
float:right;
}
}
```

3. Create the index.html file as described in the *Getting ready* section, and write down the following snippet of HTML code in the body part of this file:

```
<div id="container">
<nav>
  <ul>
    <li>item1</li>
```

```
            <li>item2</li>
            <li>item3</li>
            <li>item4</li>
        </ul>
    </nav>
    </div>
```

4. Now, you can load the `index.html` file from step 3 into your browser; when all goes well, you should see something like what's shown in the following figure:

5. Resize your browser window, and see what happens with the navigation.
6. Finally try the zoom function of your browser with your window size fixed.

How it works...

Apart from the fact that the Frameless grid does not have a fixed number of columns in the grid, the code also differs from other solutions by defining sizes, dimensions, and widths in **ems** instead of pixels (or points).

An em is a font-relative length, officially defined as" being equal to the computed value of the `font-size` property of the element on which it is used." Only when used to set the `font-size` property, it refers to the computed value of the `font-size` property of the parent element.

So using ems as the unit allows the media queries to respond appropriately when people zoom the web page. Most modern browsers also scale pixel-based units on zooming by the user, so it is not easy to see the difference at first sight.

Consider the media query that is shown here:

```
@media(min width:500px) { //your styles}
```

When increasing your base font size from 16 to 32 pixels, the preceding media query still only reacts when the screen width becomes greater than 500 pixels. In the preceding media query, there is no relation between the increased font size and the break point of 500 pixels defined by the media query. Now, consider using ems as follows:

```
@media(min width:31.25em) { //your styles}
```

Setting the base size font to 16 pixels means that 1 em also is approximating 16 pixels, and the preceding media query responds at 31.25*16 = 500 pixels. After zooming in to a font size of 32 pixels, the value of 1 em also changes to 32 pixels, and the media query will respond now at a screen width of 32.25*32 = 1,000 pixels, which is properly related to the zoomed font size.

The Frameless grid code defines the base font size set `font-size` property on the body selector as follows:

```
@font-size: 16;
@em: @font-size*1em;   // Shorthand for outputting ems, e.g.
   "12/@em"
body {
font-size: (@font-size - 2)/16*1em;
}
```

Notice that relative units, including em units, in media queries are based on the initial value, which means that units are never based on the results of declarations. The initial value is that set by the user in the browser settings.

Column sizes in the Frameless grid are also defined in the em unit as follows:

```
@1cols: ( 1 * (@column + @gutter) - @gutter) / @em; @1col:
   @1cols;
@2cols: ( 2 * (@column + @gutter) - @gutter) / @em;
@3cols: ( 3 * (@column + @gutter) - @gutter) / @em;
```

The number of columns that can be defined this way will be endless, but sizes larger than the largest possible container width make no sense.

See also

> ▸ Mark Nugent wrote a excellent introduction and guide to the Frameless grid. You can find his article at `http://marknugent.tumblr.com/post/47212935858/a-guide-tutorial-to-the-frameless-grid-how-to`.
>
> ▸ In 2012, Lyza Gardner wrote an article about proportional media queries. You can find this article at `http://blog.cloudfour.com/the-ems-have-it-proportional-media-queries-ftw/`.
>
> ▸ Another well-written blog post about pixels versus em or rem in media queries can be found at `http://codeboxers.com/em-vs-px-vs-rem-in-media-queries/`.

Building a fluid responsive grid system

When building website layouts, especially fluid layouts with float, you will have to round some widths up or down. Unfortunately, not all browsers round numbers in the same way. Different rounding of width can break your layout. This problem has also been described as the sub-pixel rounding issue. The Zen Grid system solves this sub-pixel rounding issue.

Getting ready

The Zen Grid has no original Less version, but porting it to Less is possible. You can download some example code at `https://github.com/bassjobsen/LESS-Zen-Grid`. After downloading the example code, you can edit the files with your favorite text editor.

With the client-side `less.js` compiler, you can inspect the result of this recipe in your browser. To get more insight into the idea behind the Zen grid, compiling the Less code with command-line `lessc` will be recommended too. In the *Installing the lessc compiler with npm* recipe in *Chapter 1, Getting to Grips with the Basics of Less*, you can read how to install and use the command-line compiler.

How to do it...

In this recipe, you will build a simple layout that has got a main area with a side bar and a three-column footer.

1. Firstly, download and unzip the required files, which can be found at `https://github.com/bassjobsen/LESS-Zen-Grid/archive/master.zip`, into your working directory.

2. Then, open the `less/zen.less` file and replace its content with the following Less code:

```less
@import "variables.less";
@import "boxsizing.less";
@import "mixins.less";

@zen-columns: 12; // Set the total number of columns in the grid.
@zen-gutters: 40px; // Set the gutter size. A half-gutter is used
on each side of each column.

.container {
 .zen-grid-container;
  > article {
  .zen-grid-item(9, 1);
  }
  > aside {
   .zen-grid-item(3, 10);
  }
  > footer {
  .zen-new-row();
  > section {
  &:nth-child(1){.zen-grid-item(4, 1);}
  &:nth-child(2){.zen-grid-item(4, 5);}
  &:nth-child(3){.zen-grid-item(4, 9);}
  }
 }
}
```

3. Change the body section of the `index.html` file so that it contains the following HTML code:

```html
<div class="container">
  <article>
    Tha main content. We like semantic HTML ordering.
  </article>
  <aside>
    An aside.
  </aside>
  <footer>
    <section>First column</section>
    <section> The main content. We like semantic HTML
      ordering.</section>
    <section>Third column</section>
  </footer>
</div>
```

4. Finally, load the `index.html` file from the previous step into your browser and find that your layout should look like that shown in the following figure:

Tha main content. We like semantic HTML ordering.		An aside.
First column	Second column	Third column

How it works...

The Less code in this recipe has been spread over different files. There's a file for mixins and a file for variables. The organization of your code over different files seems good practice in most cases; you can find examples of it in *Chapter 8, Building a Layout with Less,* of this book or when inspecting the source of the Twitter's Bootstrap project.

The Zen grid solves this by positioning every float relative to its container, rather than the float before it. The preceding can easily been seen when inspecting the compiled CSS code of the `.container > article` selector; this CSS code will look as shown in the following code:

```
.container > article {
  float: left;
  width: 75%;
  margin-left: 0%;
  margin-right: -100%;
  padding: 0 20px;
}
```

The `margin-right: -100%;` declaration creates space for overflow and prevents wrapping. The space due to the negative right margin is also visible in the layout model that is shown in the following figure:

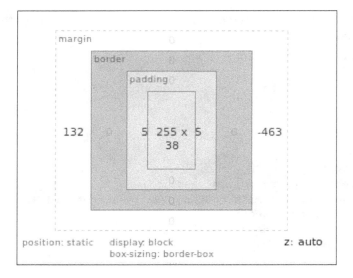

The project file also imports the `boxzing.less` file. This file contains a `.box-sizing()` mixin and the following Less code that calls this mixin:

```
// Reset the box-sizing
*,
*:before,
*:after {
  .box-sizing(border-box);
}
```

Declaring the `box-sizing` property as `border-box` will make using the grid easier. In the `border-box` model, the calculation of the width of an element includes the width of the border and the padding, so assigning some padding or a border to an element will not break your grid calculations.

There's more...

In this chapter, many grid systems are discussed, and it is not easy to say one is better than the other. Your choice can depend on personal favors and project requirement. The Zen Grid is used in many projects, but its Less implementation is not used regularly. This recipe shows you in the first place that it is possible and is not necessarily a recommendation to use it for your projects.

Also notice that construction of the grid changes the flow of your content.

Also the grid mixins of the `semantic.gs` project, as described in the *Building semantic grids with semantic.gs* recipe of this chapter have got a solution to solve the sub-pixel rounding problem.

See also

- ▶ More information about the sub-pixel rounding issue can be found at `http://tylertate.com/blog/2012/01/05/subpixel-rounding.html`

8
Building a Layout with Less

In this chapter, you will learn to do the following:

- ▶ Using CSS Reset with Less
- ▶ Importing and organizing your Less files
- ▶ Importing files with the `@import` directive
- ▶ Building a grid with grid classes
- ▶ Creating responsive grids
- ▶ Building a semantic grid with mixins
- ▶ Applying the flexbox grid on your design
- ▶ Integrating a navigation menu into the layout
- ▶ Repositioning your content

Introduction

In the recipes of this chapter, you will learn how to create a layout for your website or web application with Less. The grid forms the base of the layout. Grids help web designers and developers to work together and make deploying responsive layouts easier.

In the course of time, different ways to deploy layouts on the Web saw the light. For years, tables have been used (rather, misused) to build HTML layouts. Newer techniques leverage the CSS `float` property to arrange elements. The CSS `float` property is a positioning property that keeps HTML elements in the flow of the document instead of applying the `text-wrap` property to it. Other layouts are built with the `display: inline-block` property. HTML elements with the `display: inline-block` property are positioned like lines of text. Twitter's **Bootstrap**, as we will see in *Chapter 9, Using Bootstrap with Less*, uses the `float` technique, while `<bold>Cardinal</bold>` gives an example of the `inline-block` technique. Cardinal can be found at `http://cardinalcss.com`.

Even the CSS `display: table` declaration can be used to build a responsive layout, as can be seen at `https://github.com/mdo/table-grid`, but in this chapter, you will build a grid layout with the CSS3 flexbox module.

A short introduction on the CSS Flexible box module level 3 can also be found in the *Building a layout with the CSS3 flexbox module* recipe of *Chapter 7, Leveraging Libraries with Prebuilt Mixins*.

Every technique mentioned just now has its pros and cons. Saying you should prefer one over the other is not easy. Some people predict the CSS Flexible box module to be the most modern, and so the preferred technique is to build your layouts. The recipes in this chapter will show you how to build a grid layout with flexboxes, but I do not necessarily advise you to do so. The CSS Flexible box module is intended to describe the spatial position of child elements in relation to their parent, but flexboxes also intend to position only a single UI element and not the entire page layout. When using flexboxes for page layout, the browser has to do a lot of repainting of what can result in bad, slow, or unexpected rending of elements, which has also been described at `http://jakearchibald.com/2014/dont-use-flexbox-for-page-layout/`. On the other hand, others such as Paul Irish claim the opposite. You can read more about this at `http://updates.html5rocks.com/2013/10/Flexbox-layout-isn-t-slow`. The cons of the flexbox layouts are that it dramatically reduces the complexity of fluid grids. When you choose a technique, you should always carefully consider the pros and cons and make sure you are optimizing for the real bottlenecks.

Finally, you will notice that the Flexbox module has been intended to lay out major regions of an application. The **CSS3 Grid Layout** module, in contrast to the Flexbox module, can be applied to high-level HTML elements such as header, footer, and main. At the moment of writing this book, only a few browsers support the Grid Layout module.

Besides the flexbox layout, this chapter pays attention to CSS Resets, organizing your Less code and files, importing files in Less, and building a navigation menu for your site.

Using CSS Reset with Less

HTML elements without styles are styled with the default browser styles. Different browsers style HTML elements differently, by default, which is one of the most important reasons of having cross-browser issues. CSS Reset sets the default style of HTML elements to the same value (or output) for all browsers.

Getting ready

When you start a project, you should also think about the CSS Reset that you will have to use. Writing CSS Reset yourself seems like reinventing the wheel again. On the other hand, using a random CSS Reset code without any research may cause unwanted effects or unnecessary process time for your project. Your choice should depend on using HTML5 or not, the browsers that you will have to support, and so on. At http://www.cssreset.com/, you can find and download the most popular CSS Resets. To make a motivated choice, you can read the *Which CSS Reset Should I Use?* section on that website, too.

Download the CSS file (with the .css extension) of the CSS Reset of your choice and save this file into your working directory. You can use the command-line lessc compiler to see how CSS Reset compiles into your final CSS code.

How to do it...

Now, perform the following steps:

1. Download the CSS Reset, and rename this file so that it gets the .less extension. For instance, reset.css should be renamed to reset.less.

2. Create a main project file for your project and save this file as project.less. Write the following Less code at the beginning of this file:

```
@import "reset.less";
```

How it works...

Files with the .css extensions are imported as usual CSS. Renaming the file to the .less extension will guarantee that the code is processed by the compiler. Remember that a valid CSS code is also a valid Less code. You can read more about importing files in the Importing files with the @import directive recipe of this chapter. Instead of renaming the file to the .less extension, you can also use the less keyword as follows:

```
@import (less) "reset.css";
```

Importing the code as CSS without any keyword or using the inline keyword does not invoke the compiler, and it means that your code is not reusable. Importing regular CSS also means that the compiled CSS code contains a regular CSS `@import` statement, which requires an additional and unnecessary HTTP request.

If the CSS Reset code does not exactly meet your requirements after it is imported, you will have two choices. You can adopt the CSS Reset code itself (and maintain your own version) or override the defaults later in your CSS, if necessary.

Although CSS Resets are very useful, they should be used with care. For instance, resetting the form elements of a project without forms makes no sense. One should also consider the difference between resetting and normalizing into an account. Resets mostly set the default styles for all the elements, while normalizers only try to fix problems and retain other useful default browser styles.

There's more...

In this section, we'll discuss using the `box-sizing` property of the CSS Box model, and also about importing files with the `@import` directive.

Using the box-sizing property with Less

When building grids and layouts, it is useful to pay some attention to the `box-sizing` property. The `box-sizing` property sets the CSS Box model and is used to calculate the width and height of an element. The default value of the `box-sizing` property is `content-box`; this model does not take borders and padding into account when calculating dimensions. On the other hand, the `border-box` model calculates dimensions that include border and padding. The difference between these two models can be easily made clear with a simple example. Consider the following Less code:

```
// Box sizing
.box-sizing(@boxmodel) {
  -webkit-box-sizing: @boxmodel;
     -moz-box-sizing: @boxmodel;
          box-sizing: @boxmodel;
}
.container {
&.fit {
.box-sizing(border-box);
}
> div {
background-color: black;
border: 5px red solid;
width:50%;
float:left;
color:white;
padding:10px;
```

```
.box-sizing(inherit);
  }
}
```

The compiled CSS code of the preceding Less code can be applied to the following HTML snippet:

```
<div class="container">
  <div>col 1</div>
  <div>col 2</div>
</div>
<div class="container fit">
  <div>col 3</div>
  <div>col 4</div>
</div>
```

When you load the preceding code into your browser, it will look like what is shown in the following screenshot:

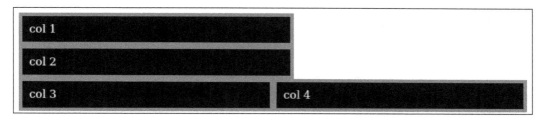

The `reference` keyword used in this recipe in the `@import (reference) "mixins. less";` line of code lets the compiler process the file without any output. As you can see in the compiled CSS code, the `.color()` mixin was processed (called from `forms.less`), but the `.thisClassShouldNOTOutput` class was not compiled into the final CSS code.

The last line of code in the `project.less` file uses the `inline` keyword as `@import (inline) "not-less-compatible.css";`. The `inline` keyword lets the compiler include external files, but not process them. Some CSS code contains code that may not be compatible with Less. In such cases, you can use the `inline` keyword to put all your CSS code into one single file; this will reduce the number of HTTP requests that appear when you load your page. Less compatible code can contain nonstandard CSS such as comments on unusual or other CSS hacks. The `not-less-compatible.css` file in this recipe contains an example of such a hack.

See also

▶ An overview of CSS hacks can be found at `http://browserhacks.com/`; most of these hacks can be useful but are not compatible with Less.

Importing and organizing your Less files

When starting a new project, it is important to think about how to organize your code. The best thing about Less is it provides the ability to reuse your code and deploy the DRY 'principle. Your file structure should also be optimized to take full advantage of these benefits.

Getting ready

In this recipe, you will set up a flexible file and directory structure that will enable you to easily extend and reuse your code.

Before setting up your own project, you can study the file structure of some other projects. You can look at the Less files of the following projects:'

- *Twitter' Bootstrap* at GitHub at `https://github.com/twbs/bootstrap`
- *Cardinal* at GitHub at `https://github.com/cbracco/cardinal`

How to do it...

1. First, create the file in your directory structure, as shown in the following figure:

```
├── boxmodel.less
├── buttons.less
├── main.less
├── mixins
│       ├── buttons.less
│       ├── gradients.less
│       └── vendor-prefixes.less
├── mixins.less
├── project.less
├── reset.less
└── variables.less
```

2. The `project.less` file includes all the Less code, including your custom code in `main.less`, as follows:

```less
@import "variables.less";
@import "mixins.less";
@import "reset.less";
@import "boxmodel.less";
@import "buttons.less";
@import "main.less";
```

3. The `variables.less` file will contain your project' variables and allow you to edit them in a single place. This file can contain, for instance, the following Less code:

```
@boxmodel: border-box;
```

4. The `mixins.less` files import other files with mixins, which are grouped by the element type or functionality. An example of the contents of this file can be found in the following code:

```
@import "gradients.less";
@import "vendor-prefixes.less";
```

5. The `vendor-prefixes.less` file should contain the box-sizing mixin, as shown here:

```
// Box sizing
.box-sizing(@boxmodel) {
    -webkit-box-sizing: @boxmodel;
        -moz-box-sizing: @boxmodel;
                box-sizing: @boxmodel;
}
```

How it works...

You can use the file and directory structure in this recipe for more than one project. Every project has its own `main.less` file. Be careful not to overwrite your customized `main.less` file when updating your project (see the *There's more* section of this recipe).

When you choose a CSS Reset, as discussed in the *Using a CSS Reset with Less* recipe of this chapter, you will only have to replace the `reset.less` file. The project variables can be set in the `variables.less` file or redeclared in the `main.less` file.

In files such as `buttons.less`, you can define the CSS classes for your buttons and mixins to build these button classes, and they can be stored in `mixins/buttons.less` so that you are able to reuse them.

You should pay some special attention for the vendor prefixes mixins in the `vendor-prefixes.less` file. When using mixins to add vendor prefixes, such as the `.box-sizing()` mixin in this recipe, you will only have to change the mixins when your requirements or insights change. Instead of these mixins, you can also use the autoprefixer, as described in the *Automatically prefix your code with Grunt* recipe in *Chapter 11, Compiling Less Real Time for Development using Grunt*. When you replace the vendor prefixes mixins with the autoprefixer, you also have to change the mixin calls everywhere in your code. The future version of Less may consist of built-in prefixing.

Gradient mixins are placed in a separate file called `gradient.less`. This file can contain Less code, such as the one shown in the following code:

```
.horizontal(@start-color: #555; @end-color: #333;
  @start-percent: 0%; @end-percent: 100%) {
background-image: linear-gradient(to right,
  @start-color @start-percent, @end-color @end-percent);
background-repeat: repeat-x;
filter: e(%("progid:DXImageTransform.Microsoft.gradient
  (startColorstr='%d', endColorstr='%d', GradientType=1)",
  argb(@start-color),argb(@end-color)));
}
```

The CSS filter function used in the preceding mixin to support horizontal gradients for older versions of the IE browser cannot be set with the autoprefixer. The autoprefixer only provides prefixes and doesn't add alternative syntaxes. As can be seen in the *Creating background gradients* recipe of *Chapter 7*, *Leveraging Libraries with Prebuilt Mixins*, mixin libraries can provide mixins for single line declarations of such properties.

There's more...

You have already seen that you libraries with prebuilt mixins can be easily imported. When the library changes, you will have nothing to change in your project code, unless the changes are not backward-compatible. In the situation where you are building or using frameworks such as Bootstrap or Cardinal, you should also account for the possibility to update the framework code. A project file with variables that can be edited in a single place is useful, but when this file is part of your framework, your customizations are easily overwritten when you update the framework. You can prevent yourself from overwriting your customization by creating a separate file structure for customizations, which includes redeclaration of customized project variables.

Just like CSS in Less for variables, the last declaration wins can be applied. Less also uses lazy loading of variable, which means that variables do not have to be declared before being used.

Consider the situation when the main project file of your framework (`famework.less`) looks as follows:

```
@import "variables.less";
//other imports
```

In this case, you can create a main file (`project.less`), which will look as shown here:

```
@import "framework.less";
@import "customvariables.less";
```

Inside the preceding structure, variables should only be redeclared in the `customvariables.less` file.

Importing files with the @import directive

You will know already that the `@import` directive in CSS can be used to import other CSS files into your CSS code. In Less, you can use the `@import` directive to import the Less code from other files. The `@import` directive enables you to spread your Less code over more than one file, which gives you the opportunity to build a logical and easy-to-maintain structure of Less files.

Getting ready

In this recipe, you will create a main project file that will import your other project files. You need to create the following files and directories:

```
├── forms.less
├── mixins.less
├── not-less-compatible.css
├── project.less
└── variables.less
```

You can edit the Less files with your favorite text editor and use the command-line lessc compiler, as described in the *Installing the lessc compiler with npm* recipe in *Chapter 1, Getting to Grips with the Basics of Less*, to compile the `project.less` file.

How to do it...

1. Start with editing the `project.less` file and write the following content into it:

```
@import "variables.less";
@import (reference) "mixins.less";
@import "forms.less";
@import (inline) "not-less-compatible.css";
```

2. Create the `variables.less` file imported in the `project.less` file with the following code:

```
@labelBackgroundColor:blue;
            mixins.less:
.color(@backgroundColor) {
    background-color: @backgroundColor;
```

```
        color: contrast(@backgroundColor);
    }
    .thisClassShouldNOTOutput {
    property: notvisible;
    }
```

3. Create the `forms.less` file imported in the `project.less` file with the following code:

```
label {
.color(@labelBackgroundColor);
}
not-less-compatible.css:
/* Modern browsers only (not IE 7) */
html>/**/body {
background-color:red;
}
```

4. Finally, compile the `project.less` file with the command-line compiler as follows:

```
lessc project.less
```

5. After running the compiler, you will find the following CSS code will be returned as output on the console:

```
/* Modern browsers only (not IE 7) */
html>/**/body {background-color:red;}

label {
  background-color: #0000ff;
  color: #ffffff;
}
```

How it works...

In the `project.less` file of this recipe, you see the `@import` directives with and without keywords. Keywords used in this recipe are the reference and line keywords. Keywords change the way the compiler imports the file. The meaning of keywords is discussed later on. By default, which means without a keyword, the imported file will be processed by the Less compiler into the CSS code. The `@import` directive can be anywhere in your Less code. Because Less uses lazy loading, you can call a mixin before you import it, but Less also applies the last declaration wins rule, which means that variables can be reassigned after you import them. When you import a mixin with the same name (and the same matching parameters) twice, both mixins are processed by the compiler. See the *Using namespacing with prebuilt libraries* recipe of *Chapter 7, Leveraging Libraries with Prebuilt Mixins*. Using namespaces, also described in the *Using namespaces to make your code reusable and portable* recipe of *Chapter 1, Getting to Grips with the Basic of Less*, prevents the equally named mixins of different imported files from touching each other.

The Less `@import` directive differs from the CSS `@import` directive, which only puts a reference to the file in the code. You can use the `css` keyword to add the CSS `@import` directive to your code. When using the `@import (css) "file.css";` code, `file.css` is not processed by the Less compiler and is written out at the beginning of the CSS code, as follows:

```
@import "file.css";
```

Note that the Less compiler also takes the file extensions into account. The preceding code means that `@import (css) "file.css";` and `@import "file.css";` of the Less code will have the same effect. In both cases, the compiler ignores the code and adds a `@import` directive to the compiled CSS code. There is also a `less` keyword that forces the compiler to process the file contents as Less code. Files without an extension, or an extension other than `.css`, are treated as Less files by the compiler. Keywords overrule the file extension, so `@import (less) "file.css";` will be processed as Less, while `@import (css) "file.less";` will be treated as CSS.

The reference keyword used in this recipe in the `@import (reference) "mixins.less";` line of code allows the compiler to process the file without any output. As you can see in the compiled CSS code, the `.color()` mixin has been processed (called from `forms.less`), but the `.thisClassShouldNOTOutput` class was not compiled into the final CSS code.

The last line of code in the `project.less` file uses the `@import (inline) "not-less-compatible.css";` keyword. The inline keyword allows the compiler to include external files, but does not process them. Some CSS code contains code that may not be Less-compatible. In such cases, you can use the `inline` keyword to put all your CSS code into one single file, which will reduce the number of HTTP requests when loading your page. Less-compatible code can contain nonstandard CSS, such as comments on unusual or other CSS hacks. The `not-less-compatible.css` file in this recipe contains an example of such a hack.

There's more...

Beside the keywords already mentioned in the previous section, two other keywords exist. The `once` keyword imports a file only once—other imports of the same file are ignored by the compiler—in contrast to the `multiple` keyword, which allows importing the same file more than once. Note that importing with the `multiple` keyword could generate duplicate selectors and properties. Importing a file only once is the default behavior of the Less compiler.

According the official documentation, which can be found at `http://lesscss.org/features/#import-options`, you can summarize the list of keywords for the `@import` directive as follows:

- ▶ `reference`: This use a Less file but does not output it
- ▶ `inline`: This includes the source file in the output but does not process it

- `less`: This treats the file as a Less file, no matter what the file extension is
- `css`: This treats the file as a CSS file, no matter what the file extension is
- `once`: This only includes the file once (this is the default behavior)
- `multiple`: This includes the file multiple times

You can use file paths with the `@import` directive. By default, the path should be relative to the current working directory. The `--include-path` option can be used to set the paths where the compiler should look for files to import. The `--include-path` option accepts a list of path separated by colons (or semicolons on Windows). When importing Less files, the `.less` extension is not required since `@import "bootstrap";` will have the same meaning as `@import "bootstrap.less";`.

See also

- An overview of CSS hacks can be found at `http://browserhacks.com/`. Most of these hacks can be useful but are not compatible with Less.

Building a grid with grid classes

Grids are formed by rows and columns. A grid with 12 columns can be easily adopted for different screen sizes. In this recipe, CSS classes are used to set the width of the grid items. There are 12 classes for a grid of 12 columns, where each class has a width that spans a number of columns. The total items that span the columns in a row should be equal to the total number of columns in the grid. So, when your grid has 12 columns, a row can contain, for instance, three items that span four columns, or one item that spans one column and one item that spans 11 columns.

Getting ready

The code used in this recipe is based on the Flexbox library, which can be found at `http://flexboxgrid.com`. The Flexbox library builds a grid, leveraging the CSS3 Flexible box module and using the same naming conventions as Twitter's Bootstrap.

Though it will be interesting to inspect the compiled code, the best way to test the grid you will construct in this recipe will be to use it in your browser. Notice that the code in this recipe uses the official W3C syntax for flexboxes, so you should use a browser that supports this syntax (refer to `http://caniuse.com/#feat=flexbox`). Also, the `box-sizing` property, as described in the *There's more...* section of the *Using CSS Reset with Less* recipe of this chapter, should be supported by your browser. In the *There's more...* section of this recipe, you can read how to add support for older browsers, too. The Less code can be compiled with the client-side `less.js` compiler, as described in the *Downloading, installing, and integrating less.js* recipe in *Chapter 1, Getting to Grips with the Basic of Less*, when using the browser to inspect the result.

If you are not familiar with the CSS Flexible box module already, it's strongly recommended that you read more about it before you start this recipe. An excellent article titled *A Complete Guide to Flexbox* can be found at `http://css-tricks.com/snippets/css/a-guide-to-flexbox/`.

How to do it...

Now, perform the following steps:

1. Firstly, create a Less file called `grid.less` and write the Less code shown here into this file:

```less
/* variables */

@half-gutter-width: 0.5rem;
@gutter-compensation: -0.5rem;
@outer-margin: 2rem;
@grid-columns: 12;

/* mixins */

.grid () {
  padding-right: @outer-margin;
  padding-left: @outer-margin;
}

.row() {
  box-sizing: border-box;
  display: flex;
  flex-direction: row;
  flex-wrap: wrap;
  margin-right: @gutter-compensation;
  margin-left: @gutter-compensation;
}

.make-column(@col-number)
{
.col-@{col-number} {
  flex-basis: ((100% / @grid-columns) * @col-number);
  max-width: ((100% / @grid-columns) * @col-number);
}
```

```
}

.make-cols(@col-number: @grid-columns) when (@col-number > 0) {
.make-cols((@col-number - 1));
.make-column(@col-number);
}

/* the grid */

.grid {
.grid();
}

.row {
.row();
}

[class^="col-"], [class*=" col-"] {
  box-sizing: border-box;
  display: flex;
  flex-direction: column;
  flex-grow: 0;
  flex-shrink: 0;
  padding-right: @half-gutter-width;
  padding-left: @half-gutter-width;
  border: 2px solid tomato;
}

.make-cols();
```

2. Then, create an HTML file named index.html and include the client-side less.js compiler and the grid.less file into it by adding the following lines of HTML code to the head section:

```
<link rel="stylesheet/less" type="text/css"
href="less/grid.less">
<script src="js/less.js" type="text/javascript"></script>
```

Write the following snippet of HTML code into the body of the index.html file to make the grid visible in your browser:

```
<div class="grid">
<div class="row">
  <div class="col-12"> </div>
</div>
<div class="row">
```

```
        <div class="col-6"> </div>
        <div class="col-6"> </div>
      </div>
      <div class="row">
        <div class="col-4"> </div>
        <div class="col-4"> </div>
        <div class="col-4"> </div>
      </div>
      </div>
```

3. Finally, load the `index.html` file in your browser and you will find that it will look as shown in the following screenshot:

How it works...

Firstly, notice that the Less code in the first step of this recipe could better be split up over different files, as described in the *Importing and organizing your Less files* recipe of this chapter. You can create separate files for variables, mixins, and even the grid code.

As already mentioned, the code used in this recipe is inspired by the flexbox grid library. The code has been simplified to keep the recipe clear and understandable. The flexbox grid library is not built with Less at the time of writing this book; hopefully, it has been done by the time you are reading this book. If no official Less version for the flexbox library is available yet, you can find one at `https://github.com/bassjobsen/flexboxgrid`.

The .make-cols() mixin is probably the most interesting part of the code in this recipe. This mixin calls itself recursively; finally, each recursion step calls the `.make-column()` mixin that creates a CSS class for a grid item. You can read more about recursions in Less in the *Building loops leveraging mixins guards* recipe of *Chapter 6, Advanced Less Coding*.

The general properties for the col-* classes are set with the `[class^="col-"]`, `[class*=" col-"]` selectors. These attribute selectors reduce the size of the CSS or make an additional base class unnecessary. Some developers avoid attribute selectors because they have a negative influence on the performance. Bottlenecks in CSS performance are tested and described at `http://benfrain.com/css-performance-revisited-selectors-bloat-expensive-styles/`. The partial attribute selector performance is indeed worse for Microsoft's Internet Explorer web browser. Also note that the overall performance of the CSS code never depends on a single selector, and calculations are complex. When optimizing your CSS code, removing unused selectors will have a more significant effect on the performance.

If you resize the browser window when looking at the results of this recipe, you will find that the flexbox grid already acts in a fluid manner. When the size of the grid changes, the grid items resize too and the aspect ratios are kept intact. To create a responsive design, you probably also want to change the size of your grid items depending on the screen size. In the *Creating responsive grids* recipe of this chapter, you will learn how to use CSS media queries to create a responsive grid.

There's more...

The Less code in this recipe does not add browser prefixes for properties to support older browsers. Of course, you can write your own set of mixins to add these vendor prefixes to your flexbox and `content-box` properties, but a better alternative in this situation seems to use a mixin library with support for the CSS3 flexbox module. In the *Building a layout with the CSS3 flexbox module* recipe of *Chapter 7, Leveraging Libraries with Prebuilt Mixins*, you can read how to create cross-browser flexbox layout leveraging the Less Hat library.

Alternatively, you can use the autoprefixer, which can be found at `https://github.com/postcss/autoprefixer/`. In contrast to Less, autoprefixer is a postprocessor for your CSS.

You can use the Less autoprefix plugin or read how to integrate the autoprefixer into your grunt build process in the *Automatic prefixing your code with Grunt* recipe in *Chapter 1, Getting to Grips with the Basics of Less*. The autoprefixer checks the *Can I Use* database.

The **-prefix-free** project, which can be found at `http://leaverou.github.io/prefixfree/`, enables you to use unprefixed CSS properties. Because the -prefix-free project code runs at the client side, just like the `less.js` compiler, some people claim that you should use it for production. Client-side code has a negative effect on end-user performance in many cases.

On the other hand, Lea Vera, the author of the -prefix-free project says, "-prefix-free detects which features need a prefix and only adds it if needed". With the -prefix-free library, you can use smaller CSS files without any prefix and you don't have to update your code when some new browser becomes available.

There are also prefix plugins available for some text editors.

See also

> ▶ An online service that prefixes your CSS code can be found at `http://prefixr.com/`.

> ▶ You can read an interview of Lea Vera, the author of the -prefix-free project, by Chris Coyier of CSS-tricks.com at `http://css-tricks.com/five-questions-with-lea-verou/`.

> ▶ The *Can I Use* database can be found at `http://caniuse.com/`.

Creating responsive grids

CSS media queries make it possible to only apply style rules when a certain condition is true. For responsive designs, the screen width can be used as a condition to evaluate the media queries. A typical media query looks like the following:

```
@media (min-width: 768px) {
//style rules
}
```

The style rules inside the preceding media query will be only applied when the screen's width is equal to or greater than 768 pixels.

Getting ready

In this recipe, you will have to use the code from the *Building a grid with grid classes* recipe of this chapter. You will use the command-line `lessc` compiler to create the CSS grid classes for a mobile-first responsive grid.

How to do it...

Perform the following steps:

1. Copy the `grid.less` file from the first step of the *Building a grid with grid classes* recipe of this chapter into a new `.less` file. Set the `@grid-columns` variable to 4 and change the `.make-cols()` and `.make-column()` mixins by adding a `@grid` parameter. Finally, the `.make-cols()` and `.make-column()` mixins should look like the following:

```
.make-column(@grid; @col-number)
{
.col-@{grid}-@{col-number} {
  flex-basis: ((100% / @grid-columns) * @col-number);
  max-width: ((100% / @grid-columns) * @col-number);
}
}

.make-cols(@grid; @col-number: @grid-columns) when (@col-number >
0) {
.make-cols(@grid; (@col-number - 1));
.make-column(@grid; @col-number);
}
```

2. Secondly, create a `project.less` file that will contain the following Less code:

```less
@import "grid.less";
@basefontsize: 16;
@sm-breakpoint: unit((768px / @basefontsize), em);
.make-cols(xs);
@media (min-width: @sm-breakpoint) {
.make-cols(sm);
}
```

3. Then, compile the `project.less` file by running the following command in the console:

```
lessc project.less
```

4. In the next code, you will find the part of the compiled CSS code that contains the styles for the columns of the grid. The other styles for the grid, including flexbox properties, are not shown:

```css
.col-xs-1 {
  flex-basis: 25%;
  max-width: 25%;
}
.col-xs-2 {
  flex-basis: 50%;
  max-width: 50%;
}
.col-xs-3 {
  flex-basis: 75%;
  max-width: 75%;
}
.col-xs-4 {
  flex-basis: 100%;
  max-width: 100%;
}
@media (min-width: 48em) {
  .col-sm-1 {
    flex-basis: 25%;
    max-width: 25%;
  }
  .col-sm-2 {
    flex-basis: 50%;
    max-width: 50%;
  }
  .col-sm-3 {
    flex-basis: 75%;
```

```
      max-width: 75%;
  }
  .col-sm-4 {
    flex-basis: 100%;
    max-width: 100%;
  }
}
```

How it works...

In this recipe, you created two grids — the xs (extra small) grid with the col-xs-* classes and the sm (small) grid with the col-sm-* classes for screen sizes wider than 40 em. Notice that the breakpoint has been set in the em unit instead of pixels. The em units let the media queries appropriately respond to a change in font size such as when the user magnifies the page.

You can read more about using the em unit in media queries in the *Building an alternative for fluid grids with Frameless* recipe of *Chapter 7, Leveraging Libraries with Prebuilt Mixins*.

There's more...

To make the code act in a mobile-first manner, the .make-cols(xs); is not wrapped in any media query. You can also use this strategy for other style rules. Start with the default style rules without media queries and add more or other style rules for wider screen sizes with media queries. The mobile-first strategy refers to earlier times when mobile browsers did not support JavaScript or the full range of CSS (or CSS3) rules. This strategy is still true, and the browser loads the default style rules first. Other style rules are loaded and applied if the browser supports them. The mobile-first strategy also prevents the browser from loading features and style rules that are never used in the situation where bandwidth and processing power are limited.

See also

- ▶ An insight into responsive design fundamentals can be found at https://developers.google.com/web/fundamentals/layouts/.

- ▶ Read more about the mobile-first strategy at http://www.uxmatters.com/mt/archives/2012/03/mobile-first-what-does-it-mean.php.

Building a semantic grid with mixins

In the *Building a grid with grid classes* recipe of this chapter, you can read how to build a grid with CSS grid classes. Using these grid classes on the `div` elements breaks the semantic nature of HTML5. In this recipe, you will learn how to keep the HTML5 semantic tags intact when deploying a grid.

Getting ready

In this recipe, you will have to use the code from the *Building a grid with grid classes* and *Creating responsive grids* recipes of this chapter. You will use the command-line `lessc` compiler.

How to do it...

You need to perform the following steps:

1. Leveraging the Less code from the *Building a grid with grid classes* and *Creating responsive grids* recipes, you can create a file called `grid.less` that will contain the following Less code:

```
@grid-columns: 4;
@basefontsize: 16px;
@sm-breakpoint: unit((768px / @basefontsize), em);

.set-span(@col-number) {
  flex-basis: ((100% / @grid-columns) * @col-number);
  max-width: ((100% / @grid-columns) * @col-number);
}

.griditem(@span; xs){
  .set-span(@span);
}
.griditem(@span; sm){
  @media (min-width: @sm-breakpoint) {
  .set-span(@span);
  }
}
article {
.griditem(4,xs);
.griditem(2,sm);
}
```

2. Then, compile the Less code from the first step using the command-line `lessc` compiler. Run the following command in your console:

    `lessc grid.less`

3. Find that the compiled CSS output in the console will look like the following:

```
article {
 flex-basis: 100%;
 max-width: 100%;
}
@media (min-width: 48em) {
  article {
    flex-basis: 50%;
    max-width: 50%;
  }
}
```

How it works...

The Less compiler does not group equal media queries; this is why the loop in the *Building a grid with grid classes* recipe was called inside a media query. When each iteration of the loop creates a class that includes the corresponding media query, the compiled CSS will become inefficient and contain many unnecessary media queries. The result of the preceding code is that the mixins of the flexbox grid library do not define media queries. Moreover, the original `.make-column()` mixin always creates a class.

To solve the issue in the preceding code, the `.make-column()` mixin has been split up into two new mixins as follows:

```
.set-span(@col-number) {
  flex-basis: ((100% / @grid-columns) * @col-number);
  max-width: ((100% / @grid-columns) * @col-number);
}
.make-column(@class; @col-number)
{
.col-@{class}-@{col-number} {
  .set-span(@col-number);
  }
}
```

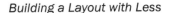

Now you can call the `.set-span()` mixin to set the flexbox properties without defining a class. To solve the media query issue, a `.griditem()` helper mixin has been created. The `.griditem()` helper mixin sets the required media query based on the `@span` input parameter and the already defined `@*-breakpoint` variables. Notice that media queries are still not grouped, but the number of media queries will be limited when you have to generate all the grid classes.

There's more...

Building your grid with responsive mixins instead of CSS classes helps you to write more semantic HTML code. Also notice that grid items still should be wrapped in a row, and a row in turn should have a grid as its parent. The need for these wrappers to set the flexbox properties will mean you can't build a pure semantic layout.

The `semantic.gs` grid system enables you to build pure semantic grids. You can read more about `semantic.gs` in the *Building semantic grids with semantic.gs* recipe of *Chapter 7, Leveraging Libraries with Prebuilt Mixins*.

See also

▶ More information on the Semantic Grid System can also be found at `http://semantic.gs/`.

▶ On the HTML5 doctor website at `http://html5doctor.com/`, you will find an easy-to-understand HTML5 sectioning element flowchart to help you get to grips with some of the semantic elements in HTML5.

Applying the flexbox grid on your design

In this recipe, you will learn how to build a layout using the flexbox library.

Getting ready

The flexbox grid library can be found at `http://www.flexboxgrid.com/`. The Less files for this library are not yet available at the time of writing this book, but you can download the Less code to build the grid from `https://github.com/bassjobsen/flexboxgrid`. You can see how the layout is built in this recipe in your browser, and the Less code can be compiled in your browser too, leveraging the client-side `less.js` compiler.

How to do it...

You need to perform the following steps:

1. Download the flexbox grid library from `https://github.com/bassjobsen/flexboxgrid` and unzip this file into your working directory.

2. Create an `index.html` file and write the following HTML code into it:

```
<!DOCTYPE html>
<html>
  <head>
    <title>Gradients with Less Elements</title>
    <meta name="viewport" content="width=device-width,
initial-scale=1.0">
    <link rel="stylesheet/less" type="text/css"
href="nested.less">
    <script src="js/less.min.js"
type="text/javascript"></script>
  </head>
  <body>
    <div class="grid">
      <header class="row">
        <h1 class="col-xs-12">Flexbox Grid System</h1>
      </header>
    <div class="row">
<!-- Main Body -->
      <section class="col-xs-12 col-sm-9">
        <ul class="row blocks">
          <li class="col-xs-12 col-sm-6 col-md-4">1</li>
          <li class="col-xs-12 col-sm-6 col-md-4">2</li>
          <li class="col-xs-12 col-sm-6 col-md-4">3</li>
          <li class="col-xs-12 col-sm-6 col-md-4">4</li>
          <li class="col-xs-12 col-sm-6 col-md-4">5</li>
          <li class="col-xs-12 col-sm-6 col-md-4">6</li>
          <li class="col-xs-12 col-sm-6 col-md-4">7</li>
          <li class="col-xs-12 col-sm-6 col-md-4">8</li>
          <li class="col-xs-12 col-sm-6 col-md-4">9</li>
        </ul>
      </section>
      <aside class="col-xs-12 col-sm-3">
        <h2>Sidebar</h2>
        <nav>
          <ul class="row">
            <li class="col-xs-12">Item 1</li>
```

```
        <li class="col-xs-12">Item 2</li>
        <li class="col-xs-12">Item 3</li>
      </ul>
    </nav>
  </aside>
</div>
</body>
</html>
```

3. Then, create the `nested.less` file that should be included in the `index.html` file created in the first step. The `nested.less` file should contain the following Less code:

```
@import "flexboxgrid/less/flexboxgrid.less";
header {
background-color: black;
color:white;
}

ul.blocks {
padding: 0;
li {
background-color: darkgreen;
color: white;
height: 100px;
padding: 10px;
font-size: 3em;
border: 2px solid;
}
}
```

4. Finally, load the `index.html` file in your browser and ensure that your layout looks like what is shown in the following screenshot:

Also, resize your browser window to see the effect of the media queries.

How it works...

The flexbox grid library defines different grids for different screen sizes. For each grid, there are a set of classes that set the column span for the grid items. The naming of the grid classes is equal to that of Twitter's Bootstrap 3 (see *Chapter 9, Using Twitter Bootstrap with Less* of this book).

This recipe also shows you that a grid row can be easily nested. The `<ul class="row blocks">` element defines a nested row. In the small (sm), medium (md), and large (lg) grids, this nested row has a 9 divided by 12 equals 75 percent of the screen width due to the `col-sm-9` class of its parent.

In the *Building a semantic grid with mixins* recipe of this chapter, you can read how to use mixins to set the properties of a grid item. Leveraging the mixins from this recipe, which are not included in the Less code you have downloaded, you could also use the following Less code to style the block structure:

```
.row.blocks li {
.griditem(12,xs);
.griditem(6,sm);
.griditem(4,md);
}
```

The compiled CSS of the preceding Less code will make the repeatedly usage of the `col-xs-12 col-sm-6` and `col-md-4` classes in the navigation list unnecessary, which will help you to keep your HTML clean and readable.

There's more...

As already mentioned, the Less code imported using the `@import "flexboxgrid/less/flexboxgrid.less";` declaration only contains the official and unprefixed W3C syntax for the flexbox properties. You should use the autoprefixer as described in the *Automatically prefix your code with Grunt* recipe of *Chapter 11, Compiling Less Real Time for Development Using Grunt*, to prefix your code; you can do this by performing the following steps, which run the Grunt build process of the flexbox grid library:

1. Copy the `nested.less` file to the `flexboxgrid/less/` folder.

2. Delete the first `@import "flexboxgrid/less/flexboxgrid.less";` line of code from the copied `nested.less` file.

3. Write the following line of code at the end of the `flexboxgrid.less` file:

    `@import "flexboxgrid/less/nested.less";`

4. Run the following command in your console:

    grunt

5. Finally, use the generated `css/flexboxgrid.min.css` file in the `index.html` file instead of including the `nested.less` file and the `less.js` compiler.

Adding the browser prefixes, as described in the preceding steps, do not add flexbox support for older browsers, such as Internet Explorer below version 9. For older browsers that don't support flexbox, you can create a fallback. Tools such as **Modernizr**, which can be found at `http://modernizr.com/`, can be used to check for flexbox support. In the *Reusing Bootstrap's grid* recipe of *Chapter 9, Using Bootstrap with Less*, you can read how to compile Bootstrap's grid into a single file. Because the flexbox grid library uses the same naming conventions for grid classes as that of Bootstrap, you could also consider using Bootstrap's grid as a fallback for Internet Explorer 8.

See also

▶ Read more about conditional style sheets by Paul Irish at `http://www.paulirish.com/2008/conditional-stylesheets-vs-css-hacks-answer-neither/`.

Integrating a navigation menu in the layout

In this recipe, you will learn how to integrate a menu into a layout. Both the menu and the layout are built with the CSS3 Flexible box module.

Getting ready

In the *Building a layout with the CSS3 flexbox module* recipe of *Chapter 7, Leveraging Libraries with Prebuilt Mixins*, you can read how to build a responsive navigation menu with the CSS3 Flexible box module. In this recipe, you will integrate this navigation menu in the example layout created in the *Applying the flexbox grid on your design* recipe of this chapter. Reading the preceding recipes mentioned in this chapter before you start is recommended.

Use a flex-box-ready browser to inspect the results of this recipe. You can check for support for the flexbox module of your browser at `http://caniuse.com/#feat=flexbox`. The Less code of this recipe can be compiled on the client side in your browser, leveraging the `less.js` compiler.

How to do it...

You need to perform the following steps:

1. Start with copying the files of the *Applying the flexbox grid on your design* recipe of this chapter.

2. Then create a `navigation.less` file and write the following Less code into it:

```
nav#mainmenu > ul {
  list-style: none;
  margin: 0;
  padding: 0;
  background: purple;
  display: flex;
  flex-direction: column;
  @media all and (min-width: 48em) {
  justify-content: space-around;
  flex-direction: row;
  }
  @media all and (min-width: 62em) {
  justify-content: flex-end;
  }
  li {
  padding: 20px;
  a {
  color: white;
  &:hover{
  color: red;
  }
  }
  }
}
```

3. Thirdly, you have to create another Less file called `project.less`. This `project.less` file should contain the following Less code:

```
@import "nested.less";
//from the Applying the Flexbox grid on your design recipe
@import  "navigation.less"; //from step 2
```

4. Open the `index.html` file you copied from the *Applying the flexbox grid on your design* recipe. Write the following HTML code between the `<header>` and `<div class="row">` tags:

```
<nav id="mainmenu" class="row" role="navigation">
  <ul class="col-xs-12">
  <li><a href="">Menu item 1</a></li>
  <li><a href="">Menu item 2 (long text)</a></li>
  <li><a href="">Three</a></li>
  </ul>
</nav>
```

5. Don't forget to link the `less.js` compiler and the `project.less` file from the third step in the `head` section of the `index.html` file, as follows:

```
<link rel="stylesheet/less" type="text/css"
href="project.less">
<script src="js/less.js" type="text/javascript"></script>
```

6. Finally, save the modified `index.html` file and load it into your browser. The result should look similar to what is shown in the following screenshot:

How it works...

The navigation menu from the *Building a layout with the CSS3 flexbox module* recipe of *Chapter 7, Leveraging Libraries with Prebuilt Mixins*, was rewritten to fit the flexbox grid layout. The `.row` and `.col-xs-12` classes were added to the HTML code.

Besides the flexbox syntax, as described in the following section, the Less code for the navigation menu in second step has undergone a number of small changes. Of course, the main selector has been changed as well. Also, see the em values inside the media query condition. Notice that both the navigation menu's and the layout's Less code now define the same values. For a better integration, these breakpoints should be declared as variables, too.

There's more...

Notice that the Less code to construct the navigation menu in the second step of this recipe differs from the Less code used in the *Building a layout with the CSS3 flexbox module* recipe. Instead of Less's Hat flexbox mixins, the official W3C syntax was used.

The flexbox grid library uses the autoprefixer to prefix the compiled CSS code.

In *Chapter 7, Leveraging Libraries with Prebuilt Mixins*, of this book, you can read more about using mixin libraries. If you're using Less Hat already, rewrite this code instead of using the autoprefixer. If you try to use both, you may get some odd results and code prefixed in two different ways.

Alternatively, you can compile the Less code with the command-line compiler and the Less autoprefix plugin, too.

See also

- ▶ You can read more about flexbox in the CSS specifications at `http://www.w3.org/TR/css3-flexbox/`.
- ▶ The Less autoprefix plugin can be found at `https://github.com/less/less-plugin-autoprefix`.

Repositioning your content

The CSS3 flexbox module enables you to reposition your content with the `position` property. This means that you can reorder the visual position of a child item of flexbox without the need to change you source's HTML code. Besides the `position` property, the `flex-direction` property can also be set to `column-reverse` or `row-reverse` to reverse the position of all child items.

In this recipe, you will learn how to do this repositioning by leveraging the flexbox grid library.

Getting ready

You can download the Less code to build the flexbox grid library from `https://github.com/bassjobsen/flexboxgrid`. In this recipe, you will reuse the Less and HTML code from the *Integrating a navigation menu in the layout* recipe of this chapter. The result can be easily seen in your browser, so use the client-side `less.js` compiler to compile the Less code.

How to do it...

Now, perform the following steps:

1. Copy the HTML and Less files from the *Integrating a navigation menu in the layout* recipe of this chapter.

2. Open the copied `project.less` file and write the following Less code at the end of this file:

```
@media all and (min-width: 62em) {
.row.blocks {
  .row-reverse();
  }
}
```

3. Then, open the `index.html` file in your text editor and add the `first-lg` class to the adjacent element that represents the sidebar of the layout. The adjacent element should now look like the following:

```
<aside class="col-xs-12 col-sm-3 first-lg">
```

4. Finally, open the modified and saved `index.html` file in your browser and ensure that it looks like the following:

Resize your browser's window or use the zoom function on your browser to see what happens on smaller screen sizes.

How it works...

On screens wider than 62 em (approximately 992 pixels), the sidebar moves to the left side of the layout. The `.row-reverse()` mixin sets the CSS3 `flex-direction` property to the `row-reverse` value. The `row-reverse` value does what its name says; it reverts all the items in a flexbox. Besides the `row-reverse` and `col-reverse` values for the `flex-direction` property, you can also set the position of an item in the flexbox with the `order` property.

The `order` property accepts integers as values; by default, `order` is set to `0`. When the text direction has been set to left to right (ltr), the items with the lowest order values are positioned on the left-hand side of items with a higher order value. When the `order` value of two items are equal, the items are positioned as declared in the HTML. The `.first-*` classes have an `order` property with the value `-1` assigned. As all the other items have their `order` property set to `0`, by default, items with `.first-*` class become the first item in the flexbox. So, the `.last-*` classes set the `order` to `1`, with all the other items possessing an `order` of `0`; this will move the items to the end of the flexbox.

There's more...

Besides the position classes for items in flexbox, the flexbox grid library also offers classes to set the position of the content inside a flexbox item itself. These classes include classes to center the content or align it.

The `.center-*` classes of course centers the content. You should replace `*` with the shorthand of the grid. You can test it by adding the `.center-lg` class to the `li` elements in the list of blocks, as follows:

```
<li class="col-xs-12 col-sm-6 col-md-4 center-lg">1</li>
<li class="col-xs-12 col-sm-6 col-md-4 center-lg">2</li>
```

Notice that if you add the `.center-xs` class instead of the `.center-lg` class, this will center the content for all the grids, and so the `.center-md` class will center the content on medium (md) or large (lg) grids. On the other hand, if you want to center the content only on the medium grid, you will have to add both the `.center-md` and `.start-lg` classes. You don't explicitly need to set the `.start-xs` class because `flex-start` is the default value for the `justify-content` property.

The `.start-*` and `.end-*` classes also set the `text-align` property to start and end, respectively. The start and end values for the `text-align` property are part of the **Working Draft** (**WD**) W3C syntax for CSS3 at the time of writing this book (more information can be found at `http://dev.w3.org/csswg/css-text/#text-align-property`). These new property values make bidirectional text support easier; you can read more about bidirectional text support in the *Creating bidirectional styling without code duplication* recipe of *Chapter 7, Leveraging Libraries with Prebuilt Mixins*.

See also

- The official website of the flexbox grid library can be found at `http://www.flexboxgrid.com/`.

- The unofficial Less version of the flexbox grid library can be found at `https://github.com/bassjobsen/flexboxgrid`.

- Read more about the renewed CSS3 `text-align` property at `https://developer.mozilla.org/en-US/docs/Web/CSS/text-align`.

9

Using Bootstrap with Less

In this chapter, you will learn the following topics:

- ▶ Downloading and installing Bootstrap
- ▶ Customizing Bootstrap with variables
- ▶ Making custom buttons
- ▶ Making custom panels
- ▶ Making custom navigation bars
- ▶ Extending components using :extend
- ▶ Reusing Bootstrap's grid
- ▶ Using Bootstrap classes and mixins
- ▶ Extending Bootstrap with your own mixins
- ▶ Making custom color schemes with 1pxdeep
- ▶ Autoprefixing Bootstrap's CSS

Introduction

Twitter's Bootstrap, or Bootstrap for short, is the most popular HTML, CSS, and JavaScript framework to develop responsive, mobile-first projects on the Web.

You can use Bootstrap to build responsive websites and applications. This framework helps you to develop faster and more efficient applications using proven CSS code and components. Bootstrap uses a responsive grid with 12 columns and many other reusable components.

In this chapter, you will learn more about Bootstrap's CSS. It is built with the Less preprocessor and Grunt. Using Less as a preprocessor makes Bootstrap's code reusable and extendable. In this chapter, you will learn how to customize and extend Bootstrap by leveraging Less.

Some of Bootstrap's components require JavaScript; Bootstrap ships with jQuery plugins for these components. Configuring and extending these plugins is out of the scope of this book.

The code used for the recipes in this chapter is based on version 3 of Bootstrap. Version 4 of Bootstrap was expected to be released during 2015. Of course, version 4 will differ from version 3, but many new features and changes, such as splitting up Less files and using the autoprefixer, are already present since version 3.2, too. Learning and understanding how to customize Bootstrap by leveraging Less will also help you to do the same with version 4.

Downloading and installing Bootstrap

In this recipe, you will learn how to install Bootstrap and start your first project.

Getting ready

You can download the required files from `http://getbootstrap.com/getting-started/#download`. Choose the source version at this page, which includes the Less source files, too.

For this recipe, you should have Node.js and Grunt installed on your system. You can read how to install Node.js and the Node.js Package Manager in the *Installing Node and Grunt* recipe in *Chapter 11, Compiling Less Real Time for Development Using Grunt*.

How to do it...

You need to perform the following steps:

1. Download the ZIP archive that contains the Bootstrap source files and unzip this file into your working directory. Alternatively, run the following command in your console:

   ```
   npm install bootstrap
   ```

2. Then, run this command in your console:

   ```
   npm install
   ```

3. Now, you can compile Bootstrap by running this command:

   ```
   grunt dist
   ```

4. The compiled CSS code can be used in your HTML by adding the following line of code:

```
<link rel="stylesheet" type="text/css" href="dist/bootstrap.css">
```

How it works...

The `grunt dist` command invokes the `grunt-contrib-less` task, among others. The `grunt-contrib-less` task compiles the Less files from the `less` directory into CSS. The compiled CSS code will be saved in the `dist/bootstrap.css` file, and a minified copy of this code will be saved in the `dist/bootstrap.min.css` file.

Since version 3.2 of Bootstrap, the build process also runs the autoprefixer postprocessor.

There's more...

You can also install Bootstrap with **Bower** by running the following command:

```
bower install bootstrap
```

Bower is a package manager that is optimized for frontend development.

The Grunt task not only compiles the Less code, but also bundles the required JavaScript plugins. Bootstrap components such as the navigation bar will not work without these plugins. Also, notice that JavaScript plugins depend on jQuery.

See also

▶ The official Bootstrap website can be found at `http://getbootstrap.com`

▶ More information on Node.js can be found at `http://nodejs.org/`

▶ Read more about Bower at `http://bower.io/`

▶ Read more about Grunt tasks in *Chapter 11*, *Compiling Less Real Time for Development Using Grunt*.

Customizing Bootstrap with variables

In the `less` directory of your Bootstrap installation, you will find the `variables.less` file. The `variables.less` file is the sole place to edit and customize Bootstrap.

Getting ready

Download and install Bootstrap as described in the *Downloading and installing Bootstrap* recipe of this chapter. The Less files are compiled by leveraging Grunt.

How to do it...

You need to do the following:

1. Create an `index.html` file that loads the `dist/css/bootstrap.css` file from your Bootstrap installation and contains the HTML code similar to what is shown here:

```
<!DOCTYPE html>
<html>
<head>
<title>Bootstrap's Buttons</title>
<link rel="stylesheet" type="text/css"
href="bootstrap-master/dist/css/bootstrap.css">
</head>
<body>

<!-- Standard button -->
<button type="button"
class="btn btn-default">Default</button>

<!-- Provides extra visual weight and identifies the primary
action in a set of buttons -->
<button type="button"
class="btn btn-primary">Primary</button>

<!-- Indicates a successful or positive action -->
<button type="button"
class="btn btn-success">Success</button>

<!-- Contextual button for informational alert messages -->
<button type="button" class="btn btn-info">Info</button>
```

```
<!-- Indicates caution should be taken with this action -->
<button type="button"
class="btn btn-warning">Warning</button>

<!-- Indicates a dangerous or potentially negative action -->
<button type="button"
class="btn btn-danger">Danger</button>

<!-- Deemphasize a button by making it look like a link while
maintaining button behavior -->
<button type="button"
class="btn btn-link">Link</button>

</body>
</html>
```

2. Load the `index.html` file from the first step in your browser, and it will look like what is shown in the following screenshot:

3. Then, open the `less/variables.less` file with a text editor. Now, change the brand color variables. After you make the changes, these variables should have the following values assigned to them:

```
@brand-primary:    orchid;
@brand-success:    palegoldenrod;
@brand-info:       olive;
@brand-warning:    turquoise;
@brand-danger:     thistle;
```

4. Run the following command in your console:

   grunt dist

5. Finally, reload the `index.html` file in your browser and you will find that the button now looks like what is shown in the following screenshot:

How it works...

All the colors that define Bootstrap's look and feel are declared in the `variables.less` file. Other Bootstrap Less code uses these variables. As you By changing the default color values, you will influence all the code, including the buttons, as you can see in this recipe.

There's more...

When you directly edit the original `variables.less file`, your customizations can be overwritten when upgrading Bootstrap.

One way to solve the problem shown in the preceding code is to create a separated file that will contain your customized variables. This file should be loaded after the original `variables.less` file. Because of the last declaration wins rule used by Less, all the variables in the code will use the value you assigned in the custom file instead of the value assigned in the original code. You can read more about Less variables in the *Declaring variables with Less for commonly used values* recipe in *Chapter 1, Getting to Grips with the Basic of Less*.

In a situation where you need to create a new file for your custom variables, your main project can look like the following code:

```
@import "bootstrap.less";
@import "customvariables.less"
```

Note that since Bootstrap 3.2, the autoprefixer postprocessor has been added to the default build process of Bootstrap. The autoprefixer postprocessor was added to automatically add vendor prefixes to the CSS properties. Although some kind of backward compatibility for Bootstrap 3 was guaranteed, there is a risk that not all your properties will be prefixed well when you do not run the autoprefixer postprocessor. Compiling Bootstrap or the project file we just discussed with the command-line `lessc` compiler does not run the autoprefixer postprocessor.

The autoprefixing problem can be solved by using the default build process for your modified code. Add the `@import "customvariables.less"` line of code to the original `bootstrap.less` file after the `@import "variables.less"` line of code. Alternatively, change the `Grunt.js` file so that it compiles your new project file instead of the original `bootstrap.less` file. You should repeat both these solutions each time you update your Bootstrap source code. You can run the following command in your console to compile Bootstrap after the preceding changes take place:

grunt dist

Running the autoprefixer postprocessor with Grunt is described in the *Automatically prefix your code with Grunt* recipe in *Chapter 11, Compiling Less Real Time for Development Using Grunt*, and you can read more about vendor prefixes in the *Using mixins to set properties* recipe in *Chapter 3, Using Variables and Mixins*.

- On the Bootstrap website, you can also find a customizer. This customizer allows you to set Bootstrap's variables and download a customized copy of Bootstrap. Notice that the copies are built with this customizer to only include the CSS and JavaScript files; Less files are not included. You can find Bootstrap's customizer at `http://getbootstrap.com/customize/`.

Making custom buttons

In the *Customizing Bootstrap with variables* recipe in this chapter, you can read how to change Bootstrap's buttons by setting the brand color variables. In this recipe, you will learn how to extend Bootstrap with one or more custom buttons by leveraging Less.

Getting ready

This recipe requires Bootstrap's source files. You can download these from `http://getbootstrap.com/getting-started/#download`. To recompile Bootstrap, your system should have Grunt up and running. Read more about Grunt in *Chapter 11, Compiling Less Real time for Development Using Grunt*. You can edit the source files with a text editor.

How to do it...

You need to perform the following steps:

1. Download and unzip the source files into your working directory from `http://getbootstrap.com/getting-started/#download`.

2. Open the `less/bootstrap.less` file and write the following lines of Less code at the end of this file:

```
.btn-custom {
.button-variant(white; darkblue; green);
}
```

3. Then, recompile Bootstrap's CSS by running the following command in your console:

   grunt dist

4. Now, you can include the newly generated CSS code into an HTML file with the following line of code:

```
<link rel="stylesheet" type="text/css"
href="bootstrap-master/dist/css/bootstrap.css">
```

The HTML file should also contain the following snippet of HTML code:

```
<button class="btn btn-custom">Custom button</button>
```

5. Finally, load the HTML file from the fourth step into your browser and you will find that it looks like what is shown in the following screenshot:

How it works...

Bootstrap's buttons have two CSS classes—a base class that sets the default button properties and a second class that provides buttons' styles, such as colors.

To add a custom button, you can generate a new style class with the `.button-variant()` mixin and reuse the base class. The `.button-variant()` mixin has three arguments. The first argument defines the font color, the second argument defines the background color, and the third argument defines the border color.

Bootstrap prefers the usage of base classes over the `[class^="btn-"]`, `[class*="btn-"]` attribute selectors because of performance issues in some browsers.

There's more...

In addition, to the already mentioned base and style classes, Bootstrap provides size classes for the button. You can add the `.btn-lg`, `.btn-sm` or `.btn-xs` classes to your HTML code to give your button the desired size. To use the Bootstrap button in your non-Bootstrap projects, you can use the following Less code:

```
@import "bootstrap-master/less/variables.less";
@import "bootstrap-master/less/mixins/vendor-prefixes.less";
@import "bootstrap-master/less/mixins/tab-focus.less";
@import "bootstrap-master/less/mixins/opacity.less";
@import (reference) "bootstrap-master/less/buttons.less";
@import (reference) "bootstrap-master/less/mixins/buttons.less";

.btn-custom {
.btn;
.btn-lg;
.button-variant(white; darkblue; green);
}
```

See also

With **Twitter's Bootstrap 3 Button Generator**, which can be found at `http://twitterbootstrap3buttons.w3masters.nl/`, you can see how the different states of a button look for a chosen input color. Note that this generator only generates CSS code.

Making custom panels

Bootstrap provides you with many CSS components to build your design. In the *Making custom buttons* recipe, you can read about the button component. In this recipe, you will learn how to use and reuse the panel component.

Getting ready

The steps here are similar to the *Getting ready* section of the *Making custom buttons* recipe.

How to do it...

You need to perform the following steps:

1. Download and unzip the source files into your working directory from `http://getbootstrap.com/getting-started/#download`.

2. Open the `less/bootstrap.less` file and write the following lines of Less code at the end of this file:

    ```
    .panel-custom {
      .panel-variant(black; white; purple; white);
    }
    ```

3. Then, recompile Bootstrap's CSS by running the following command in your console:

    `grunt dist`

4. Now, you can include the newly generated CSS code into an HTML file with the following line of code:

    ```
    <link rel="stylesheet" type="text/css" href="bootstrap-master/
    dist/css/bootstrap.css">
    ```

    The HTML file should also contain the following snippet of HTML code:

    ```
    <div class="panel panel-custom">
      <div class="panel-heading">
        <h3 class="panel-title">Panel title</h3>
      </div>
    ```

```
      <div class="panel-body">
        Panel content
      </div>
      <div class="panel-footer">Footer</div>
   </div>
```

5. Finally, load the HTML file from the fourth step into your browser and you will find that your custom panel looks like what is shown in the following screenshot:

Bootstrap's panels have different contextual states. States can be set with an additional CSS class. Each panel contains the panel's base class and a class that sets the styles that present the state. The state classes available by default are `panel-primary`, `panel-success`, `panel-info`, `panel-warning`, and `panel-danger`.

In this recipe, you extended the panel states with a new `panel-custom` state, leveraging the `.panel-variant()` mixin. The `.panel-variant()` mixin accepts four parameters; parameters define the colors to style the panels. The first parameter sets the general border color, the second parameter sets the font color of the header, the third parameter sets the background color of the header, and finally, the fourth and last parameter sets the border color for the header of the panels.

There's more...

The `.panel-variant()` mixin cannot be used to change the panel's footer. The footers of the different panel contextual states have a gray background color. The default background color of the footers has been defined by `@panel-footer-bg: #f5f5f5;` in the `variables.less` file. To change the footer background color of the custom panel to red, for instance, you can use the following Less code:

```
.panel-custom {
.panel-variant(black; white; purple; white);
.panel-footer {
background-color: red;
}
}
```

In the *Customizing Bootstrap with variables* recipe of this chapter, you can read how to change Bootstrap's default brand colors. These brand colors also influence the panel's look. In the `variables.less` file, you will find that the panel colors are declared as shown in the following code:

```
@panel-success-text:        @state-success-text;
@panel-success-border:      @state-success-border;
@panel-success-heading-bg:  @state-success-bg;
```

See also

▶ A complete list of Bootstrap's components can be found at
  `http://getbootstrap.com/components/`

Making custom navigation bars

The navigation bar, or navbar for short, is an important component used in many Bootstrap projects. In this recipe, you will learn how to modify the inverse navbar by leveraging Less. By default, Bootstrap contains two navbar styles, the default and inverse styles.

Getting ready

The steps here are similar to the *Getting ready* section of the *Making custom buttons* recipe.

How to do it...

1. Download and unzip the source files into your working directory from
   `http://getbootstrap.com/getting-started/#download`.

2. Open the `less/variables.less` file and look up the variables starting with
   `@navbar-inverse`.

3. Change the variables starting with `@navbar-inverse` according to the following:
   ```
   @navbar-inverse-color:         black;
   @navbar-inverse-bg:            yellow;
   @navbar-inverse-border:        darkgreen;
   ```

   Instead of editing `less/variables.less`, you can also write down the variables at the end of the `less/bootstrap.less` file.

4. Then, recompile Bootstrap's CSS by running the following command in your console:
   grunt dist

5. Now you can include the newly generated CSS code into a HTML file with the following lines of code:

```
<link rel="stylesheet" type="text/css" href="bootstrap-master/
dist/css/bootstrap.css">The HTML file should also contain the
following snippet of HTML code:
<nav class="navbar navbar-inverse" role="navigation">
  <div class="container-fluid">
    <!-- Brand and toggle get grouped for better mobile
    display -->
    <div class="navbar-header">
      <button type="button" class="navbar-toggle collapsed"
      data-toggle="collapse" data-target="#bs-example-
      navbar-collapse-1">
        <span class="sr-only">Toggle navigation</span>
        <span class="icon-bar"></span>
        <span class="icon-bar"></span>
        <span class="icon-bar"></span>
      </button>
      <a class="navbar-brand" href="#">Brand</a>
    </div>

    <!-- Collect the nav links, forms, and other content
    for toggling -->
    <div class="collapse navbar-collapse" id="bs-example-
    navbar-collapse-1">
      <ul class="nav navbar-nav">
        <li class="active"><a href="#">Link</a></li>
        <li><a href="#">Link</a></li>
        <li class="dropdown">
          <a href="#" class="dropdown-toggle" data-
          toggle="dropdown">Dropdown <span
          class="caret"></span></a>
          <ul class="dropdown-menu" role="menu">
            <li><a href="#">Action</a></li>
            <li><a href="#">Another action</a></li>
            <li><a href="#">Something else here</a></li>
            <li class="divider"></li>
            <li><a href="#">Separated link</a></li>
            <li class="divider"></li>
            <li><a href="#">One more separated
            link</a></li>
          </ul>
        </li>
      </ul>
```

```
<form class="navbar-form navbar-left" role="search">
  <div class="form-group">
    <input type="text" class="form-control"
    placeholder="Search">
  </div>
  <button type="submit" class="btn btn-
  default">Submit</button>
</form>
<ul class="nav navbar-nav navbar-right">
  <li><a href="#">Link</a></li>
  <li class="dropdown">
    <a href="#" class="dropdown-toggle" data-
    toggle="dropdown">Dropdown <span
    class="caret"></span></a>
    <ul class="dropdown-menu" role="menu">
      <li><a href="#">Action</a></li>
      <li><a href="#">Another action</a></li>
      <li><a href="#">Something else here</a></li>
      <li class="divider"></li>
      <li><a href="#">Separated link</a></li>
    </ul>
  </li>
</ul>
</div><!-- /.navbar-collapse -->
</div><!-- /.container-fluid -->
</nav>
```

6. Your newly styled navigation bar should look like what's shown in the following screenshot:

How it works...

The setup of the navbar is the same as the button and panel components, as described in the *Making custom buttons* and *Making custom panels* recipes of this chapter; also, the navbar component has a base class and another class that adds the style rules for colors. By default, Bootstrap provides two style classes: the `.default-navbar` and `.inverse-navbar` classes.

In contrast to the button and panel components, there are no mixins to build the style class for the navbar. In this recipe, you redeclared the navbar variables that changed the `.inverse-navbar` class in the compiled CSS code. Because the navbar component was intended to be used only once in a page, compiling an extra style class and keeping the `.default-navbar` and `.inverse-navbar` classes intact makes no sense because you can only use one.

Bootstrap's navbar is responsive by default on screens with a small width; the navbar will be displayed vertically, as seen in the following screenshot:

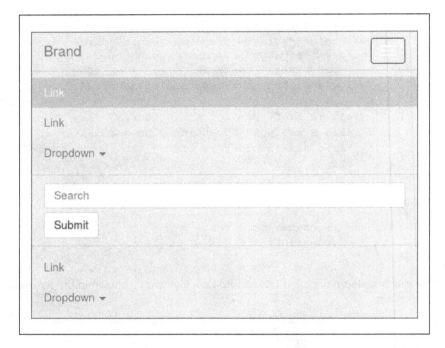

When the screen width is larger than the `@grid-float-breakpoint` variable, the navbar will collapse and become horizontal. You will find `@grid-float-breakpoint` in the `variables.less` file too; this variable can also be changed. The default value of the `@grid-float-breakpoint` variable has been set to `768px` (equal to the smallest width of the **small (sm)** grid intend for tablets).

Note that Bootstrap's JavaScript plugin is required for the navbar. Bootstrap JavaScript's plugin requires jQuery too. Discussing Bootstrap JavaScript plugins and jQuery is out of the scope of this book, but you can activate the plugin by adding the following files of code at the end of your HTML document:

```
<script src="//code.jquery.com/jquery-1.11.0.min.js"></script>
<script src="//code.jquery.com/jquery-migrate-
1.2.1.min.js"></script>
<!-- Latest compiled and minified JavaScript -->
<script src="https://maxcdn.bootstrapcdn.com/bootstrap/3.2.0/js/
bootstrap.min.js"></script>
```

There's more...

In this recipe, you only change the basic colors of the navbar. Other variables, such as the @navbar-inverse-link-color or @navbar-inverse-brand-color variables, are also available to change the look of the navbar.

You can also change the .inverse-navbar class by changing the CSS properties. You can, for instance, add a background gradient with the following Less code:

```
.navbar-inverse {
#gradient > .vertical(lighten(@navbar-default-
bg,10%),darken(@navbar-default-bg,10%));
}
```

The .vertical() mixin is part of Bootstrap's mixins and wrapped in the #gradient namespace.

The navbar with a background gradient will look like the following:

See also

▶ More information about Bootstrap jQuery plugins can be found at http://getbootstrap.com/javascript/

▶ Read more about jQuery at http://jquery.com/

▶ Test different navbar styles at http://twitterbootstrap3navbars. w3masters.nl/

Extending components using :extend

You can read more about the Less `:extend` pseudo class from the *Using extend to merge selectors* recipe of *Chapter 5, Extending and Referencing*. In this recipe, you will see how to use this pseudo class to make all the images in your Bootstrap project responsive by default.

Getting ready

Download the source version of Bootstrap from `http://getbootstrap.com/getting-started/#download`.

How to do it...

In Twitter's Bootstrap version 2, images (the `img` tag) were responsive by default. In Bootstrap version 3, an image can only be made responsive by adding the `.img-responsive` parameter to the `img` tag. You can use the following steps to make your images responsive by default again:

1. Install the source version of Bootstrap as described in *the Downloading and installing Bootstrap* recipe of this chapter.

2. Open the `less/bootstrap.less` file and add the following Less code at the end of this file:

```
img {
    &:extend(.img-responsive);
}
```

3. Recompile Bootstrap by running the following command in the console:

```
grunt dist
```

How it works...

Bootstrap has got a special class that makes images responsive. Responsive in this case means that you set the `width` property of the image to `100%`. All images will get the size of their parent. The `max-width` property is set to `100%` too; this prevents scaling a small image up to a larger size than the original size. The `.img-responsive` parameter can easily be applied on the `img` selector leveraging the `:exend` pseudo class. You can read more about extending the selector in the *Chapter 5, Extending and Referencing,* of this book.

There's more...

The compiled CSS code for the `img` selector will look like the following:

```
.img-responsive,
.thumbnail > img,
.thumbnail a > img,
.carousel-inner > .item > img,
.carousel-inner > .item > a > img,
img {
  display: block;
  width: 100% \9;
  max-width: 100%;
  height: auto;
}
```

When inspecting the preceding compiled CSS, you will find that the `display` property of the `img` selector has been set to block. Block-level elements occupy the entire space of its parent element, which seems to be the desired behavior of the responsive image. When you wrap you images inside p elements, where `display: inline-block` seems to fit better, you should consider making your image not responsive by default at all, or try the following Less code:

```
p img {
display: inline-block;
}
```

Maybe, you have also seen the `width: 100% \9;` declaration, the `\9;` code is part of a so called browser hack.

Finally, you will notice that you cannot easily extend all Bootstrap components. Bootstrap components are intended to be used with CSS classes in your HTML code.

Consider the following Less code:

```
.parent .btn { color: white}
.btn { color: blue; }
button:extend(.btn all){}
```

When compiling the preceding Less code into CSS code, you will find that it will contain the following selector:

```
.parent .btn,
.parent button {
  color: white;
}
```

In most cases, your custom HTML should not have defined the `.parent .btn` structure.

See also

▸ You can read more about inline versus block level in HTML at `https://developer.mozilla.org/en-US/docs/Web/HTML/Inline_elemente#Inline_vs._block-level`. W3C recommendations for the content of the `p` element can be found at `http://www.w3.org/TR/html-markup/p.html`

▸ An overview of CSS hacks can be found at `http://browserhacks.com/`

Reusing Bootstrap's grid

In the *Applying the flexbox grid on your design* recipe in *Chapter 8, Building a Layout with Less*, you can read how to use Bootstrap's grid as a fallback for the flexbox grid. In this recipe, you will see how to create a CSS file that contains the style rules for Bootstrap's grid.

Getting ready

The steps here are similar to the *Getting ready* section of the *Making custom buttons* recipe.

How to do it...

Perform the following steps:

1. Create a `bootstrapgrid.less` file that contains the following lines of Less code:

```less
@import (reference) "mixins.less";
@import (reference) "variables.less";
@import (reference) "mixins/vendor-prefixes.less";
* {
  .box-sizing(border-box);
}
*:before,
*:after {
  .box-sizing(border-box);
}
@import "grid.less";
```

2. Then, compile the `bootstrapgrid.less` file from the second step into CSS by running the following command in the console:

```
lessc  bootstrapgrid.less bootstrapgrid.css
```

3. Finally, you can test the grid with the HTML code from the *Applying the flexbox grid on your design* recipe of *Chapter 8, Building a Layout with Less*, and use it as a fallback for the flexbox layout.

How it works...

The code in the `bootstrapgrid.less` file defines Bootstrap's grid classes. These classes are intended to be used in your HTML code. You can, for instance, use the following HTML code to create a layout with two columns on small devices and four columns on larger devices:

```
<div class="container">
<div class="row">
<div class="col-xs-6 col-sm-3">Column 1</div>
<div class="col-xs-6 col-sm-3">Column 2</div>
<div class="col-xs-6 col-sm-3">Column 3</div>
<div class="col-xs-6 col-sm-3">Column 4</div>
</div>
</div>
```

Bootstrap uses a default grid of 12 columns and defines classes for different screen widths. The `.col-xs-6` class spans six columns on the extra small (xs) grid, while the `.col-sm-3` class spans three columns of the small (sm) grid. Because the grid uses a mobile-first approach, you don't have to explicitly set classes for larger grids, unless they span a different number of columns.

Notice that since Bootstrap 3.2, and also in version 4, vendor-prefix mixins are considered depreciated in favor of the autoprefixer postprocessor integrated in the build process. You can read more about using and integrating the autoprefixer postprocessor in your build process in the *Automatically prefix your code with Grunt* recipe.

There's more...

You may notice that the Bootstrap fallback for the flexbox grid does not give the exact same result, but on the other hand, your HTML code does not lose functionality in most cases. Both solutions are responsive, but for instance, Bootstrap's breakpoints are defined in pixels, while the flexbox grid defines its breakpoint in em units. Of course, you can try to fix all differences, but the graceful degradation strategy can help you here.

Criticism of Bootstrap will tell you that the Bootstrap grid will break the semantic features of HTML5. Bootstrap's grid mixins can be used to build a more semantic grid, however. You can read how to do this in the *There's more...* section of the *Building semantic grids with semantic.gs* recipe in *Chapter 7, Leveraging Libraries with Prebuilt Mixins*.

See also

► Read more about the graceful degradation strategy regarding support older browsers at `https://www.w3.org/community/webed/wiki/Optimizing_content_for_different_browsers:_the_RIGHT_way#Graceful_degradation`

Using Bootstrap classes and mixins

Although Bootstrap is a complete CSS framework, you can use some of its components for other non-Bootstrap projects. In this recipe, you will see how to reuse Bootstrap's pagination component. Also, refer to *Chapter 7, Leveraging Libraries with Prebuilt Mixins*, which describes how to use prebuilt mixin libraries.

Other examples of reusing Bootstrap's code can be found in other recipes of this book. In the *Declaring a class and mixin at once* recipe in *Chapter 3, Using Variables and Mixins*, you can read how to create a clearfix. The mixin for this clearfix can be found in the `less/mixins/ clearfix.less` file, which is included in Bootstrap's source files.

The *There's more...* section of the *Building semantic grids with semantic.gs* recipe in *Chapter 7, Using External Mixin Libraries*, describes how to use Bootstrap's grid mixins to build a semantic grid. Also, other recipes in this chapter describe how to use the grid, button, or panel components for your projects.

Getting ready

The steps here are similar to the *Getting ready* section of the *Making custom buttons* recipe.

How to do it...

You need to perform the following steps:

1. Create a `pagination.less` file and write the following Less code into it:

```
@import "variables.less";
@import  "mixins.less";
@import (reference) "pagination.less";

footer > ul {
.pagination;
.pagination-size(10px; 10px; 3em; 10px);
}
```

2. Compile the `pagination.less` file into CSS code with the following command:

   lessc pagination.less pagination.css

3. Finally, include the compiled `pagination.css` file into an HTML page that contains the following HTML code:

```
<footer>
  <ul class="pagination">
    <li><a href="#">&laquo;</a></li>
    <li><a href="#">1</a></li>
```

```
        <li><a href="#">2</a></li>
        <li><a href="#">3</a></li>
        <li><a href="#">4</a></li>
        <li><a href="#">5</a></li>
        <li><a href="#">&raquo;</a></li>
    </ul>
</footer>
```

4. Now, you will find that your pagination looks like the following:

How it works...

Bootstrap uses the files in the `less` directory to compile the CSS classes for the framework. The mixins to build these classes can be found in the `less/mixins` directory. The `mixins. less` file includes the mixins in the project. When building a custom version of Bootstrap, you can comment out the mixins you do not use in the `mixins.less` file.

Not all Bootstrap mixins are suitable for reuse without the corresponding CSS classes. In this recipe, you used the `pagination-size()` mixin, which can be found in the `less/mixins/ pagination.less` file. Without the `.pagination` class, the `pagination-size()` mixin makes no sense. On the other hand, you can use the .pagination class without the `pagination-size()` mixin. In this recipe, you combined both the `.pagination` class and the `pagination-size()` mixin into the `pagination-footer > ul` selector.

The `pagination-size()` mixin has to be called with four parameters: the first two parameters set the padding, the third parameter sets the font size, and the fourth parameter sets the border radius of the first and last element of the navigation.

The Less code used for this recipe imports the `mixins.less` file and also the files in the `less/mixins` directory, where you expected that only `less/mixins/pagination.less` would be sufficient. The `pagination-size()` mixin also makes use of the `.border- left-radius()` and `.border-right-radius()` mixins, which are defined in the `less/ mixins/border-radius.less` file. Importing all the files guarantees that the mixins from other files are also available. Notice that the `reference` keyword was used to ensure that no output of the imported files would be compiled in the CSS code, as also explained in the *Importing files with the @import directive* recipe of *Chapter 8, Building a Layout with Less*. This is mostly not needed for mixins. Mixins with parentheses after them do not generate output in the compiled CSS.

Also, the complete `variables.less` file was imported. The variables in this file gave default colors to Bootstrap's pagination. If you inspect the Less code in the `variables.less` file, you will find that all the colors for the pagination are prefixed with `@pagination`, as can also be seen in the following Less code:

```
//== Pagination
//
//##

@pagination-color:                  @link-color;
@pagination-bg:                     #fff;
@pagination-border:                 #ddd;

@pagination-hover-color:            @link-hover-color;
@pagination-hover-bg:               @gray-lighter;
@pagination-hover-border:           #ddd;

@pagination-active-color:           #fff;
@pagination-active-bg:              @brand-primary;
@pagination-active-border:          @brand-primary;

@pagination-disabled-color:         @gray-light;
@pagination-disabled-bg:            #fff;
@pagination-disabled-border:        #ddd;
```

You can change these variables or redeclare them in the `pagination.less` file before you compile them, so that they fit your needs.

There's more...

Bootstrap's gradient mixins are wrapped in a special namespace; see also the *Using namespaces to make your code reusable and portable* recipe in *Chapter 1, Getting to Grips with the Basic of Less*, for easy reuse. Note that you could also wrap the complete Bootstrap code in a namespace using the following code:

```
#bootstrap {
@import "bootstrap.less";
}
```

When reusing Bootstrap's code for your projects, you should keep in mind that you will have to prefix your properties, too. See the *Autoprefixing of Bootstrap's CSS* recipe in this chapter for more information about Bootstrap and the prefixing of CSS properties.

Extending Bootstrap with your own mixins

You can easily extend Bootstrap with your own mixins. In this recipe, you will see how to do this.

Getting ready

You will have to download the Bootstrap source code from `http://getbootstrap.com/getting-started/#download`. You can use a text editor to edit the Less code.

How to do it...

Perform the following steps:

1. Download and unzip the source files into your working directory from `http://getbootstrap.com/getting-started/#download`.

2. Create a Less file called `figures.less` and write the following Less code into this file:

```
.figures() {
article {

figure {
.center-block();
> img {
max-width:100%;
}
@media (min-width: @grid-float-breakpoint)
{
max-width:50%;
.pull-right();
}
}
.clearfix();
}
}

#maincontent {
.figures();
}
```

3. Then, open the `less/boostrap.less` file and add the following line of code at the end of this file:

```
@import "figures.less";
```

4. Now, recompile Bootstrap by running the following command in your console:

grunt dist

5. Create an `index.html` file that loads the compiled styles sheet from the `/dist/css/boostrap.css` file and contains the following snippet of HTML code:

```
<div id="maincontent">
<article>
<figure><img src="http://dummyimage.com/16:9x1080"></figure>
<p>Lorem ipsum dolor sit amet, consectetuer adipiscing elit.
Aenean commodo ligula eget dolor. Aenean massa. Cum sociis natoque
penatibus et magnis dis</p>
</article>
</div>
```

6. Finally, load the `index.html` file into your browser to inspect the results. Resize your browser window to see the effect of the media query.

How it works...

In this recipe, you wrote your own mixins, which leverage Bootstrap's variables and mixins. If you change `@grid-float-breakpoint` for the project, not only does the behavior of the Bootstrap code change, but the effect of the `.figures()` mixins is also adopted.

Also, the `.pull-right()` and `.clearfix()` mixins of Bootstrap are reused in the custom code.

There's more...

In *Chapter 7, Leveraging Libraries with Prebuilt Mixins*, of this book, you can read how to use mixin libraries for your project. You can also use these libraries together with Bootstrap. An interesting project, `AnimateLESSHat.less`, is found at `https://github.com/bluetidepro/AnimateLESSHat.less`; this project builds `animate.css`, as discussed in the *Creating animations with animations.css* recipe in *Chapter 7, Leveraging Libraries with Prebuilt Mixins*, with the mixins from the Less Hat library. You can read more about the Less Hat library in the *Building unlimited gradients with Less Hat* recipe of *Chapter 7, Leveraging Libraries with Prebuilt Mixins*. The `AnimateLESSHat.less` library can be easily integrated with Bootstrap, too.

To use `animate-lesshat.less` in your Bootstrap project, simply add this import into `bootstrap.less`, as follows:

```
@import "animate-lesshat.less";
```

Note that `AnimateLESSHat.less` also offers a version of prefixed mixins. The Less Hat mixins add vendor prefixes to the compiled CSS; this works well when compiling the Less code with the command-line `lessc` compiler. When bundled with Bootstrap, the code is not prefixed by the same or other mixins. Since version 3.2, Bootstrap has integrated the autoprefixer postprocessor in its build process; see also the *Autoprefixing Bootstrap's CSS* recipe in this chapter.

See also

▶ You can read more about autoprefixing your properties with Grunt in *Chapter 11, Compiling Less Real Time for Development Using Grunt.*

▶ The `AnimateLESSHat.less` mixin library can be found at `https://github.com/bluetidepro/AnimateLESSHat.less`

▶ Finally, the Less Hat library can be found at `http://lesshat.madebysource.com/`

Making custom color schemes with 1pxdeep

In the first recipe of this chapter, you read how to change the look and feel of your Bootstrap theme. Choosing the right color scheme for your project is not easy. The **1pxdeep** project will help you to choose the right color scheme for your project.

Getting ready

For this recipe, you will have to download the Bootstrap source files. You should also download the 1pxdeep files, which can be found at `https://github.com/rriepe/1pxdeep`. You can edit the source files with a text editor. The Less code in the recipe will be compiled with the Grunt build tool delivered with Bootstrap. Alternatively, you could also compile the Less code with the command-line `lessc` or client-side `less.js` compilers, as discussed in *Chapter 1, Getting to Grips with the Basic of Less.*

How to do it...

Perform the following steps:

1. Visit the 1pxdeep website at `https://github.com/rriepe/1pxdeep`.

2. Then, choose **Seed color**; in this recipe, the `#b97ec2` color will be used.

3. Download the 1pxdeep code after choosing your **Seed color** in the previous step.

4. The ZIP archive downloaded in the third step contains two files, `scheme.less` and `1pxdeep.less`. Copy these files to your Bootstrap directory.

5. Then, open `bootstrap.less` and write the following lines of Less code at the end of this file:

   ```
   @import "scheme.less"; // color scheme
   @import "1pxdeep.less"; // 1pxdeep theme
   ```

6. Next, recompile Bootstrap's CSS by running the following command in your console:

   ```
   grunt dist
   ```

7. Now, you can use the `dist/css/bootstrap.css` file in your HTML file, which will style your elements by confirming the chosen color scheme.

8. Download an example template at `http://getbootstrap.com/getting-started/#examples` to test your color scheme.

How it works...

The 1pxdeep project brings the concept of designing with colors schemes to Bootstrap. The color schemes contain colors that are related to each other based on their relative visual weight. This method makes your HTML independent of color choices. When you have to rebrand your project, you will only have to change your color scheme.

The 1pxdeep project not only changes the basic brand colors of Bootstrap; it also defines four basic colors with three variants. You can use the basic colors by adding an extra class to your HTML. The colors have the `.color1`, `.color2`, `.color3`, and `.color4` class names. Variant colors are named `.color1a`, `.color1b`, and `.color1c`.

The HTML code for a default button will look like the following code:

```
<button class="btn btn-default">
```

The preceding button can be compared with a default button, which will also color it according to your scheme:

```
<button class="btn btn-default color1">
```

The `scheme.less` file defines the color wheels used for your scheme. You can choose another wheel by uncommenting the corresponding variable. The variable for the color, as described in the preceding code, is also declared in the `scheme.less` file.

The `1pxdeep.less` file assigns the colors defined in the `scheme.less` file to color Bootstrap's classes and variables. Because of this file redeclare among other the basic brand color of Bootstrap, as discussed in the *Customizing Bootstrap with variables* recipe of this chapter, you should import this file after the `bootstrap.less` file. The last declaration wins rule will guarantee that all the Less code will use the newly defined colors.

There's more...

In *Chapter 10*, *Less and WordPress*, of this book, you will learn how to integrate Bootstrap and Less with WordPress. In the *Building a WordPress website with the JBST theme* recipe in *Chapter 10*, *Less and WordPress*, you will be introduced to the JBST WordPress theme. The JBST 1pxdeep theme is a child theme of JBST based on the 1pxdeep project. Edit your seed color in the setting found in your WordPress dashboard, recompile the required CSS (the compiler will start automatically after it saves the seedcolor), and you will have your WordPress website ready; its style will be based on the default color wheel settings of `@seedcolor` and 1px deep.

See also

▶   The JBST 1pxdeep theme can be found at `https://wordpress.org/themes/jbst-1pxdeep`

Autoprefixing Bootstrap's CSS

Since version 3.2, Bootstrap has integrated the autoprefixer postprocessor into its build process. This not only means that you have to compile Bootstrap with Grunt, but also that the prefix mixins become depreciated. The prefix mixins found in the `less/mixins/vedor-prefixes.less` file of the Bootstrap source file are not up to date since version 3.2, and only add for backward compatibility reasons.

You can read more about using the autoprefixer postprocess in the *Automatically prefix your code with Grunt* recipe in *Chapter 11*, *Compiling Less Real Time for Development Using Grunt*.

In some situations, you are not able to run Grunt and the autoprefixer. Some projects use alternative compilers such as `less.php` (`http://lessphp.gpeasy.com/`) to compile the Bootstrap Less files. This recipe will show you some alternatives; you can try these when you are not able the run the default prefixing process.

Getting ready

If you cannot run the autoprefixer postprocessor for your Bootstrap project, first try to change your workflow.

How to do it...

Here, you will find some alternatives to the autoprefixer. Each of them is a separate alternative.

The first alternative is if you are working on an existing project, you should consider why you should update to a newer Bootstrap version in the first place. Note that support for the autoprefixing mixins has been depreciated since version 3.2.

The second alternative or solution is you can maintain your own version of the autoprefixing mixins, which also means you will have to replace property declarations, which requires prefixing, by mixin calls in all Bootstrap Less code.

The third alternative deals with mixins and prefixes. Consider a declaration in the Bootstrap Less code, as follows:

```
box-shadow: 0 5px 15px rgba(0,0,0,.5);
```

When the Bootstrap Less code contains such a declaration, you should replace it with the mixin call, as shown here:

```
.box-shadow(0 5px 15px rgba(0,0,0,.5));
```

You will have to repeat this replacement for every property that requires prefixing. You should keep the mixins in `less/vendor-prefixes.less` up to date and repeat the entire process when updating to a newer version of Bootstrap. Of course, you can automate the process described in the preceding step.

An example result of such a process can be found at `https://github.com/bassjobsen/Bootstrap-prefixed-Less/`.

The next alternative is using the -prefix-free project found at `http://leaverou.github.io/prefixfree/`. The -prefix-free project is a JavaScript library, which enables you to write prefix-free Less/CSS code. Prefixes are added with JavaScript only when needed. To use `prefixfree.js`, you simply include the script anywhere in your HTML document, as follows:

```
<script src="prefixfree.js"></script>
```

How it works...

The second solution requires that you change the complete code of Bootstrap; you should also keep the mixins in the `less/vendor-prefixes.less` file up to date. You can easily write a test that compares your prefixed version with the version created with the autoprefixer.

The `prefixfree.js` solution runs client-side JavaScript, although the minified version is small and compact. You could argue that client-side JavaScript has a negative effect on the performance, and hence, user experience. Bootstrap 3 supports the Internet Explorer 8 browser, while `prefixfree.js` does not.

There's more...

Since version 2 of Less, you can use plugins with Less. The Less autoprefix plugin can be found at `https://github.com/less/less-plugin-autoprefix`. Autoprefix plugins are not available for every alternative Less compiler.

Autoprefixers such as **autoprefixer-php**, which can be found at `https://github.com/vladkens/autoprefixer-php`, still requires Node.js to be installed.

See also

▶ A complete list of alternative compilers can be found at `http://lesscss.org/usage/#third-party-compilers`

▶ Read how to compile Bootstrap with Less v2 and the autoprefix plugin at `http://bassjobsen.weblogs.fm/compile-bootstrap-less-v2-autoprefix-plugin/`

10
Less and WordPress

In this chapter, you will learn the following topics:

- ▶ Installing WordPress
- ▶ Developing your WordPress theme with Less
- ▶ Integrating Bootstrap into your WordPress theme
- ▶ Using Semantic UI to theme your WordPress website
- ▶ Customizing `Roots.io` with Less
- ▶ Building a WordPress website with the JBST theme

Introduction

WordPress is the most popular **content management system (CMS)** around the Web. Over 60 million people have already chosen to build their website or blog with WordPress. WordPress was written in PHP and is available for free. Although the WordPress core and many themes and plugins are published under the GPL V2 license, some components may be charged according to their policies. Components that are not free of charge are often called premium or business components.

The first version of WordPress in 2003 was designed so you could create your own web blog. Nowadays, WordPress is a complete CMS that enables you to build a website, or even a web shop, with ease. WordPress has been based on PHP and MySQL and runs on many different platforms. There are differences between `WordPress.com` and `WordPress.org`. The `WordPress.com` blogging software is a host for your blog, while `WordPress.org` refers to blogging software. In this book, we've been talking about the `WordPress.org` blogging software.

Setting up a website with the WordPress software is easy and well-documented. Your website will be up and running directly after the installation process. Once you install the website, you can install plugins and themes to customize your website via the built-in dashboard.

In this chapter, you will learn how to improve your WordPress workflow by leveraging Less. Note that this chapter will guide you through the process of integrating Less in to your WordPress workflow. You will find many useful tools and resources. Because this book is about Less, won't be able to discuss WordPress in detail. To learn more about WordPress, you can read one of the many books on the subject published by Packt Publishing. These books can be found at `https://www.packtpub.com/all/?search=wordpress`.

Installing WordPress

WordPress has a core that can be easily installed. Besides the core, WordPress has themes for visual representation and plugins for additional functionalities.

Getting Ready

You can install WordPress on any server that supports PHP and MySQL. At the time of writing this book, the minimal requirements for PHP and MySQL are as follows:

- ▶ PHP Version 5.2.4 or greater
- ▶ MySQL Version 5.0 or greater

You can download the latest version of WordPress from `https://wordpress.org/download/`.

The installation process of WordPress has been refined and improved over the last few years. Installing WordPress is really easy now. WordPress provides you with a 5-minute installation guide at `http://codex.wordpress.org/Installing_WordPress#Famous_5-Minute_Install`.

How to do it...

Globally, you will have to follow the ensuing steps:

1. Download and unzip the WordPress package.
2. Create a database for WordPress on your web server.
3. Upload the WordPress files to a public folder on your web server.
4. Run the WordPress installation script in your web browser.

You can also find these steps in the 5-minute installation guide mentioned in the preceding section.

How it works

After installing WordPress, your website will run one of the default themes. A theme defines the look and feel of your WordPress website. Each theme has at least one CSS file called `style.css`. This file will not only define the CSS rules for your website, but also set the theme name and version. The `style.css` file will look like the following code:

```
/*
Theme Name: Twenty Fourteen
Theme URI: http://wordpress.org/themes/twentyfourteen
Author: the WordPress team
Author URI: http://wordpress.org/
Description: In 2014, our default theme lets you create a
responsive magazine website with a sleek, modern design. Feature
your favorite homepage content in either a grid or a slider. Use
the three widget areas to customize your website, and change your
content's layout with a full-width page template and a contributor
page to show off your authors. Creating a magazine website with
WordPress has never been easier.
Version: 1.1
License: GNU General Public License v2 or later
License URI: http://www.gnu.org/licenses/gpl-2.0.html
Tags: black, green, white, light, dark, two-columns, three-
columns, left-sidebar, right-sidebar, fixed-layout, responsive-
layout, custom-background, custom-header, custom-menu, editor-
style, featured-images, flexible-header, full-width-template,
microformats, post-formats, rtl-language-support, sticky-post,
theme-options, translation-ready, accessibility-ready
Text Domain: twentyfourteen

This theme, like WordPress, is licensed under the GPL.
Use it to make something cool, have fun, and share what you've
learned with others.
*/
```

To customize your theme with Less, you should compile CSS that will replace the content of `style.css` or load after `style.css` and overwrite and extend it. The `functions.php` file in your theme folder also plays an important role. In this file, you can add or remove the loading of style sheet files, among others. In the See also section of this recipe, you will find a reference to the `wp_enqueue_style` function that can be used to add style sheets.

There's more...

The WordPress plugins add new functionalities to your WordPress installation. Both plugins and themes can add style sheets to your website and are therefore suitable to be integrated with Less.

See also

  ▶ The free WordPress themes can be found in the WordPress theme directory at `https://wordpress.org/themes/`.

  ▶ The WordPress plugin directory contains over 30,000 plugins to extend WordPress. You will find the plugin directory at `https://wordiness/plugins/`.

  ▶ You can use the `wp_enqueue_style` function in the `functions.php` file to safely add a CSS-style file to the generated WordPress page. You can read more about this function at `http://codex.wordpress.org/Function_Reference/wp_enqueue_style`.

Developing your WordPress theme with Less

In this recipe, you will learn how to extend and customize the **Twenty Fourteen** WordPress theme with Less.

Getting ready

The Twenty Fourteen theme is a free WordPress theme shipped with the default WordPress installation. For a fresh installation, this theme has been set as the default theme. However, if you have activated another theme already, you will have to reactivate the Twenty Fourteen theme in your dashboard. Navigate to **Appearance | Theme Options** in your dashboard and do this now.

This recipe also requires that the command-line `lessc` compiler, as described in *Chapter 1, Getting to Grips with the Basics of Less*, is installed. If the web server used for production does not have the command-line `lessc` compiler installed, you can compile the Less code on your local machine and upload only the results to your web server.

How to do it...

  1. In the `main` directory of your WordPress installation, navigate to `wp-content/themes/twentyfourteen/` and create a new subdirectory called `less/` inside it.

2. Open `wp-content/themes/twentyfourteen/functions.php` and find the line of code under the `// Load our main stylesheet` comment; replace this with the following code:

    ```
    wp_enqueue_style( 'twentyfourteen-style',
      get_template_directory_uri() . '/css/main.css', array(
        'genericons' ) );
    ```

3. Then, create a new `wp-content/themes/twentyfourteen/less/main.less` file and write the following Less code in it:

    ```
    @import (less) "../style.css";
    //your custom Less code here
    ```

4. Finally, compile the Less code by running the following command in your console:

    ```
    lessc less/main.less css/main.css
    ```

How it works...

Importing the original styles sheet with the `@import` directive and the `less` keyword imports the CSS code as the Less code and enables you to combine the original class and ID selectors. This way, extending the original selectors will also be possible. In your code, you can, for instance, use the following snippet:

```
.newselector {
  &:extend(.secondary-navigation ul ul);
  color: red;
}
```

Of course, you can also import any other library here, such as the mixin libraries, which is described in *Chapter 4, Leveraging the Less Built-in Functions*. Alternatively, import Bootstrap's Less code using the following `@import` directive:

```
@import "bootstrap.less";
```

You can read more about the `@import` directive in the *Importing files with the @import directive* recipe in *Chapter 8, Building a Layout with Less*.

There's more...

In this recipe, you used the command-line `lessc` compiler, as described in *Chapter 1, Getting to Grips with the Basics of Less*, to compile the Less code. The `WP Less to CSS` plugin enables you to compile the Less code in your dashboard. This plugin can be found at `https://wordpress.org/plugins/wp-less-to-css/`. When you have the plugin installed, you can find the Less compiler in your dashboard under the **Settings | WP CSS to Less** option. Instead of `less/main.less`, you should create a `wpless2css/wpless2css.less` file in your `themes` directory.

Note that this plugin compiles the Less code with the Less PHP compiler; this compiler may differ or not be up to date with the regular Less compiler.

The compiler will look like what is shown in the following screenshot:

Less.php enables you to compile your Less code with PHP using the following code:

```php
<?php
$parser = new Less_Parser();
$parser->parseFile( '/var/www/mysite/bootstrap.less', '/mysite/'
  );
$parser->parse( '@color: #4D926F; #header { color: @color; } h2 {
  color: @color; }' );
$css = $parser->getCss();
```

Note that you cannot use an autoprefix based on Node.js when compiling your code with a PHP Less processor. Alternatively, you could use the -prefix-free JavaScript library with your non-prefixed CSS code. The -prefix-free JavaScript library can be found at http://leaverou.github.io/prefixfree/.

Currently, there are two PHP Less compilers, as follows:

 ▶ Less.php is a Less compiler written in PHP, which can be found at http://leafo.net/lessphp/.
 ▶ Also, Less.php is a PHP port of the official Less processor. Less.php can be found at http://lessphp.gpeasy.com/.

See also

 ▶ The Twenty Fourteen theme can be found at https://wordpress.org/themes/twentyfourteen, and a demo can be found at https://twentyfourteendemo.wordpress.com/

Integrating Bootstrap into your WordPress theme

Plugins add additional functionalities to your WordPress website. The WordPress Twitter Bootstrap CSS plugin adds, as its name tells you already, the Bootstrap CSS to your website. This plugin ships with a built-in Less compiler that enables you to configure Bootstrap to fit your needs by setting up the Bootstrap variables.

Getting ready

You can read more about Bootstrap and how to extend and configure it with Less in *Chapter 9, Using Bootstrap with Less*. You need to download and install the WordPress Twitter Bootstrap CSS plugin, which can be found at `https://wordpress.org/plugins/wordpress-bootstrap-css/`. For this recipe, you need to activate a theme that does not use Bootstrap already. You can use the Twenty Fourteen theme shipped with WordPress by default.

How to do it...

1. After installing the plugin, you will find a Twitter Bootstrap option in the side menu of your dashboard. You should enable **shortcodes and Less** under the **Bootstrap CSS** option. Also, choose the latest version of Bootstrap for this recipe. Then, start a new blog post and write the following code inside the blog post text area:

   ```
   [TBS_BUTTON color="success" type="submit" value="y"]My
      Lovely Twitter Button[/TBS_BUTTON]
   ```

2. After this, inspect the blog post from step 1 in your browser and you will find a button appearing in the Bootstrap style in your post. Your button should look like what is shown in the following screenshot:

Optionally, you can carry out the next four steps, which will show you how to extend and configure Bootstrap by leveraging the WordPress Twitter Bootstrap CSS plugin:

1. Configure the upgrade constants for your system using the `ftpext` method, which will enable the plugin to use your filesystem. Instructions on how to do this can be found at `http://codex.wordpress.org/Editing_wp-config.php#WordPress_Upgrade_Constants`.

2. Then, edit the `/plugins/wordpress-bootstrap-css/resources/`
   `bootstrap-3.2.0/less/bootstrap.less` file and write the following code at
   the end of this file:

```
.btn-custom {
  .button-variant(white; darkblue; green);
}
```

   You can read more about this Less code snippet in the *Making custom buttons* recipe
   in *Chapter 9, Using Bootstrap with Less*.

3. Make sure you have the Less compiler section of the plugin enabled, and then click
   on the **Save all settings** button under the Bootstrap Less section. Clicking on this
   button will recompile the CSS code.

4. Now, you will be able to use the following shortcode in your post:

```
[TBS_BUTTON color="custom" type="submit" value="y"]My Lovely
Twitter Button[/TBS_BUTTON]
```

5. The preceding shortcode will now show a custom button in your post, like the one
   shown in the following screenshot:

How it works...

The WordPress Twitter Bootstrap CSS plugin loads Bootstrap's CSS (and JavaScript) into
the HTML of your theme. You can use this plugin for any theme, but you should not use it
for themes that already load Bootstrap.

The built-in Less compiler recompiled the CSS code using the settings in the editor. These
settings are equal to the Bootstrap variables. When you edit the Less code yourself, as was
done in step 5 of this recipe, your custom code will also be compiled in CSS. You can (re)use
the Bootstrap variables and mixins in your custom code.

The button was added to the blog post with `[TBS_BUTTON] [/TBS_BUTTON]`, which is
a WordPress shortcode. You can read more about these shortcodes at `http://codex.`
`wordpress.org/Shortcode`.

There's more...

You can also use this plugin together with the `WP Less to CSS` plugin, as described in the *There's more...* section in the *Developing your WordPress theme with Less* recipe.

This recipe shows you how to integrate a Bootstrap-styled button into your blog post. This button has only been used as an example. You can use the same process to use other components of Bootstrap in your WordPress website. You can even build themes with Bootstrap's grid layout.

To integrate Bootstrap and Less without the WordPress Twitter Bootstrap CSS plugin, read the *Developing your WordPress theme with Less* recipe.

After downloading and uploading Bootstrap's Less code from the source code, which can be downloaded from `http://getbootstrap.com/getting-started/#download` to your `themes` directory, you can add the `@import "bootstrap.less"` directive to your project file. You can do the same when using the `WP Less to CSS` plugin by adding the `@import "bootstrap.less"` directive to the `wpless2css/wpless2css.less` file in your `themes` directory.

Using Twitter's Bootstrap Shortcodes Ultimate Add-on plugin can provide you with a shortcode for Bootstrap 3. The Shortcodes Ultimate plugin can be found at `http://gndev.info/shortcodes-ultimate/`, and the Twitter's Bootstrap Shortcodes Ultimate Add-on plugin can be found at `https://wordpress.org/plugins/twitters-bootstrap-shortcodes-ultimate`.

 Note that Twitter's Bootstrap shortcodes have a parameter help option, where by if you set it equal to `y` (`help='y'`), it will print a list of all the parameters available in that shortcode.

See also

▸ A complete list of shortcodes for the WordPress Twitter Bootstrap CSS plugin can be found at `https:///www.icontrolwp.com/our-wordpress-plugins/wordpress-shortcodes-demo/`

Using Semantic UI to theme your WordPress website

Semantic UI helps you to build user interfaces for your web project. Semantic is tag-agnostic, meaning you can use any HTML tag with UI elements.

For instance, a grid with three columns will look like the following code:

```
<main class="ui three column grid">
  <aside class="column">1</aside>
  <section class="column">2</section>
  <section class="column">3</section>
</main>
```

Semantic UI consists of different components. These components are split up into elements, collections, views, and modules.

The Semantic UI theme is a developer theme for WordPress designed to be developed for your specific application. It sets the basics, but you should tweak it so it meets your requirements.

Getting Ready

In this recipe, you will install a WordPress theme based on Semantic UI. Download this theme from `https://github.com/ProjectCleverWeb/Semantic-UI-WordPress`, activate it in your WordPress dashboard, and perform the following steps:

1. Download `https://github.com/projectcleverweb/Semantic-UI-wordpress/archive/master.zip`.

2. Unzip the theme file from step 1 to your `wp-content/themes` directory.

3. Navigate to the `wp-content/themes/Semantic-UI-wordpress-master` directory and run the following command in your console:

   `npm install && npm install  gulp`

4. Then, run the following command in the console:

   `Gulp build`

5. Next, set the theme to `active` in your WordPress dashboard. When you have the theme already activated before running the build process, you should deactivate it (set another theme active) and then activate it again to make sure your theme files load from the `build` directory.

6. Turn the introduction page off. After activating the theme, you will find the theme options in your dashboard under **Appearance | Theme Options**. In the following screenshot, you will see the **Misc..** section of the theme's option:

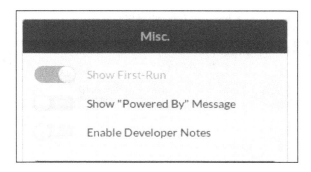

You should turn the **Show First-Run** option off.

This recipe requires that you have Node and npm installed, as described in *Chapter 11, Compiling Less Real Time for Development Using Grunt*. In case your web server for production runs in a different environment without Node installed, you can perform the steps in this recipe on your local machine and upload the compiled code to your web server.

Visit the Semantic UI website at http://semantic-ui.com/ to get an impression of the possibilities that Semantic UI has to offer. You can, for instance, inspect the comment view at http://semantic-ui.com/views/comment.html.

How to do it...

1. Navigate to the wp-content/themes/Semantic-UI-wordpress-master/src/assets/styles directory.
2. Remove the semantic.min.css file.
3. Rename the semantic.css file to semantic.tpl.
4. Create a new file called semantic.less.
5. Open the semantic.less file you created in step 2 with your text editor and write the following Less code into it:

```
@import (less) "semantic.tpl";
#main-header-grid {
h1.ui.inverted.header {color:red;}
}
```

6. Finally, run the following command in the console:

```
gulp build
```

7. You will find that the `header` text of your website will be colored red now. Your website should now look like the following screenshot:

How it works...

The Semantic UI theme uses Gulp instead of Grunt to run the tasks of the build process. Both Gulp and Grunt are JavaScript task managers. Gulp uses streams and code-over-configuration, which should make the tasks more intuitive. You can read more about automatic tasks and build systems in *Chapter 11, Compiling Less Real Time for Development Using Grunt*.

Gulp tasks compile any file with the `.less` extension found in the `src/assets/styles` directory by default. The theme comes with an already compiled version of `semantic.css`. In this recipe, you imported this code using the `less` keyword; see also the *Importing files with the @import directive* recipe in *Chapter 8, Building a Layout with Less*. Importing the CSS code as the Less code enables you to reuse the classes by extending a mixin in them. This method does not enable you to reuse the mixins and variables used in Semantic UI's Less code.

The Gulp task compiles the `semantic.less` file into `build/assets/styles/semantic.css` and also creates a minified version of this file called `semantic.min.css` at `build/assets/styles/`. This minified version of the CSS code will load into the HTML code of the theme.

There's more...

The complete Less code base of Semantic UI can be found and downloaded from `https://github.com/Semantic-Org/Semantic-UI`. Note that you can compile the Less code of each Semantic UI component independent of the other components.

After downloading Semantic UI's code base, you can copy the Less code into your `themes` directory. Then, in `semantic.less`, you can import the components you need and compile them into the `semantic.min.css` file.

▶ At `https://github.com/bassjobsen/Semantic-UI-WordPress`, you can find an example that shows you how to compile the `semantic.min.css` file with the latest version of the Semantic UI Less code.

Customizing Roots.io with Less

Roots is a WordPress starter theme that helps you to make better themes with HTML5 Boilerplate, Bootstrap, and Grunt. You can use a starter theme to build your own WordPress theme.

After installing the Roots theme and visiting your website, you will probably recognize the top navigation bar. Roots uses Bootstrap's default navigation bar. You can read more about Bootstrap in *Chapter 10, Less and WordPress* of this book. In this recipe, you will customize the navigation bar of the Roots theme.

Getting ready

You can download the Roots theme from `https://github.com/roots/roots`. Download and unzip this file into the `wordpress/wp-content/themes` directory of your WordPress installation, or alternatively, follow the ensuing steps.

To install the Roots theme, you should run the following commands in your console. Run these commands in the `wordpress/wp-content/themes` directory of your WordPress installation:

```
git clone git@github.com:roots/roots.git
npm install
grunt build
```

To run the first command, you need to create an account on Github first. You should also have an SSH key generated. More information on this can be found at `https://help.github.com/articles/https-cloning-errors/`.

 More information about npm and Grunt can be found in *Chapter 11, Compiling Less Real Time for Development Using Grunt*.

After the installation of the theme, as described in the preceding step, you should activate the theme in WordPress, too. Log in to your WordPress Dashboard (`http://localhost/wordpress/wp-admin/`). Then, choose **Appearance | Theme Options**, find the Roots theme, and activate it.

When you visit your website after the preceding steps, you will find that it will look like the following screenshot:

The `wp-config.php` file is located in the root of your WordPress file directory and contains your website's base configuration details. Before starting development with Roots, you should add the following line of code to your `wp-config.php` file; you will find this file in the main directory of your WordPress installation, that is, `define('WP_ENV', 'development');`. Add the code before the `/* That's all, stop editing! Happy blogging. */` comment. Setting this constant allows the theme to load the uncompressed CSS files, which are compiled with the `grunt dev` command.

How to do it...

1. Navigate to the Roots `themes` folder and open the `main.less` file under `/wordpress/wp-content/themes/roots/assets/less/` with your favorite text editor. Then, write the following line of Less code at the end of this file:

   ```
   @import "custom/_navbar.less";        // Navbar styling
   ```

2. Then, create a new `_navbar.less` file under the `wordpress/wp-content/themes/roots/assets/less/ custom/` file and write the following three lines of the Less code into it:

   ```
   @navbar-default-color:          black;
   @navbar-default-bg:             yellow;
   @navbar-default-border:         darkgreen;
   ```

3. Now, recompile your CSS code by running the following command in the command line:

   grunt dev

   Don't forget to set `define('WP_ENV', 'development');` in your `wp-config.php` file.

4. Finally, reload your WordPress site and find that the navigation bar has become yellow and will look like what is shown in the following screenshot:

How it works...

The Roots theme uses the Bootstrap frontend framework as the basis for their CSS. The `/wordpress/wp-content/themes/roots/assets/less/main.less` path, which also imports all Bootstrap Less code, will compile into the `assets/css/main.css` file and the final theme will load this file into the website, as follows:

```
<link rel='stylesheet' id='roots_css-css'
  href='http://localhost/wp-
    content/themes/roots/assets/css/main.css' type='text/css'
      media='all' />
```

Through the last declaration win strategy of Less, you can easily redeclare Bootstrap's variables to change the look and feel of your Roots theme.

You can read more about the customization of the Bootstrap navigation bar in the *Making custom navigation bars* recipe in *Chapter 9, Using Bootstrap with Less*.

There's more...

When you are happy with your result and want to take the website into production, you will have to make WP_ENV available for production in the wp-config.php file and run the following command:

```
grunt dist
```

In contrast to the grunt dev command, the grunt dist command also creates minified versions of your CSS code, runs the autoprefixer postprocessor, and prepares JavaScript.

See also

▸ More information about installing, configuring, and customizing the Roots theme can be found at http://roots.io/roots-101/.

▸ HTML5 Boilerplate can be found at http://html5boilerplate.com/. HTML5 Boilerplate is a professional frontend template that builds fast, robust, and adaptable web apps or sites.

▸ You can read more about Bootstrap in *Chapter 9, Using Bootstrap with Less*.

▸ In *Chapter 11, Compiling Less Real Time for Development Using Grunt*, you can read how to set up your build process with Grunt.

Building a WordPress website with the JBST theme

The JBST WordPress theme that can be found at https://wordpress.org/themes/jbst/. It can be used as a starter to build your own custom theme. JBST has been built with Bootstrap and has a built-in Less compiler.

Getting ready

Install and activate the JBST theme. Log in to the WordPress Dashboard of your demo website, choose **Appearance** | Theme **Options** and then **New**, and search for JBST. After installing the theme, your website will look like the following screenshot:

How to do it...

1. Download the `Bearpaw` `@font-face` kit from `http://www.fontsquirrel.com/fonts/Bearpaw`. Unzip this file and copy the `BEARPAW_-webfont.ttf`, `BEARPAW_-webfont.eot` `BEARPAW_-webfont.woff` and `BEARPAW_-webfont.svg` font files into the `wp-content/themes/jbst/assets/fonts` directory.

2. Go to your WordPress Dashboard, choose **Appearance | Less Compiler**, and enter the following Less code into the text area:

```
@custom-font-dir:"../themes/jbst/assets/fonts/";
.include-custom-font('Bearpaw','BEARPAW_-webfont');
@font-family-sans-serif: "Bearpaw", "Helvetica Neue",
    Helvetica, Arial, sans-serif;
```

3. Then, click on the **recompile Less code** button and reload your website. You will find that the font of the pages will have changed to Bearpaw, which will look like the following screenshot:

4. Optionally, you can also try to style the footer with the following variables:

```
@footer-bg-color
@footer-text-color
@footer-link-color
@footer-link-hover-color
```

How it works...

Just like the Roots starters theme, as discussed in the *Customizing Roots.io with Less* recipe, JBST has been built with Bootstrap. You can read more about Bootstrap in *Chapter 9, Using Bootstrap with Less*. The built-in Less compiler of JBST allows you to overwrite any of the Less variables of Bootstrap. You can find a complete list of these variables at http:// getbootstrap.com/customize/#less-variables. Besides the default Bootstrap variables, JBST also defines a set of themes for the Less variables and mixins. The @ footer-* variable and the .include-custom-font() mixin do not exist in Bootstrap, but enable you to style every piece of your theme with Less.

Note that you are not restricted to variables and mixins to style your site. You can, for instance, style the navigation bar using the following Less code in the Less editor:

```
.include-custom-font('Bearpaw','BEARPAW_-webfont');
#jbst-top-nav {
  #gradient > .vertical(lighten(@navbar-default-bg,10%),
    darken(@navbar-default-bg,10%));
  font-family: Bearpaw;
  font-size:2em;
  .nav > li {
    padding: 10px 0;
    &:hover,&.active,&:focus {
      #gradient > .vertical(lighten(@navbar-default-link-hover-
        bg,10%),darken(@navbar-default-link-hover-bg,10%));
      a {
        background: none;
      }
    }
    a {
      border-left: 1px solid lighten(@navbar-default-bg,10%);
      border-right: 1px solid darken(@navbar-default-bg,10%);
      padding: 10px 30px;
    }

    &:first-child a {  border-left: 0 solid;}
    &:last-child a {  border-right: 0 solid;}
  }
  .container-fluid {
    padding-left: 100px;
  }
}
```

After compiling the preceding Less code with the built-in Less editor, the navigation bar of your website should look similar to what is shown in the following screenshot:

The Less code used to style the navigation bar contains not only JBST selectors, such as the #jbst-top-nav selector, but also the Bootstrap mixins, such as the #gradient > .vertical() mixin, and much other advanced Less code.

There's more...

To prevent overwriting customizations when updating a WordPress theme, creating a child theme is a best practice. A Boilerplate for a JBST child theme can be found at `https://github.com/bassjobsen/Boilerplate-JBST-Child-Theme`. Other JBST child themes can be downloaded from the WordPress theme directory or from `http://themes.jbst.eu/`.

The Less code and settings of JBST are saved in the database and are not overwritten when updating.

See also

▶   In the *Making custom color schemes with 1pxdeep* recipe in *Chapter 9, Using Bootstrap with Less*, you can read about the **1pxdeep** project.

▶   The JBST 1pxdeep theme is a child theme of JBST based on the 1pxdeep project. You can download the JBST 1pxdeep theme from `https://wordpress.org/themes/jbst-1pxdeep`.

▶   In this recipe, the Bearpaw font has been used as an example; you can download the `@font-face` kit of this font from `http://www.fontsquirrel.com/fonts/Bearpaw`.

11
Compiling Less Real Time for Development Using Grunt

In this chapter, we will cover the following recipes:

- ► Installing Node and Grunt
- ► Installing Grunt plugins
- ► Utilizing the `Gruntfile.js` file
- ► Loading Grunt tasks
- ► Adding a configuration definition for a plugin
- ► Adding the Less compiler task
- ► Creating CSS source maps with the Less compiler task
- ► Cleaning and minimizing your code
- ► Adding the watch task
- ► Adding the connect and open task
- ► Adding the concurrent task
- ► Analyzing your code with CSS Lint
- ► Removing unused CSS code
- ► Compiling style guides with Grunt
- ► Automatically prefix your code with Grunt
- ► Installing the Grunt LiveReload plugin

Introduction

This chapter introduces you to the Grunt Task Runner and the features it offers to make your development workflow a delight. You will learn how to take advantage of its plugins to set up your own flexible and productive Less workflow. Although there are many applications available for compiling Less, Grunt is a more flexible, versatile, and cross-platform tool that allows you to automate many development tasks, including Less compilation. It can not only automate the Less compilation tasks, but it can also wrap any other mundane jobs, such as linting and minifying and cleaning your code, into tasks and run them automatically for you.

By the end of this chapter, you will become comfortable using Grunt and its plugins to establish a flexible workflow when working with Less. Using Grunt in your workflow is vital, as you are first shown the installation requirements of the three major operating systems. You will then be shown how to combine Grunt's plugins to establish a workflow for compiling Less in real time. Grunt becomes a tool to automate integration testing, deployments, builds, and development in which you can use. Finally, by understanding the automating process, you will also learn how to use alternative tools such as Gulp (which is another frontend build tool that runs on Node.js).

Installing Node and Grunt

Grunt is essentially a Node.js module and therefore requires Node.js to be installed. The goal of this recipe is to show you how to install Node.js and Grunt on the three major operating systems. This recipe will first show you how to gather the information needed before you install Node.js. Then, it will explain how to install it along with Grunt on your chosen operating system.

Getting ready

Before you download Node.js, you need to gather some information about your operating system (OS) kernel. This information will help you to install the correct version of Node.js for your OS architecture. The decision boils down to deciding whether to download and install the 32-bit version or the 64-bit version of Node.js. Follow these steps to find out how.

If you are using Mac OS X, follow these steps:

1. First access the Terminal at `Applications/Utilities/Terminal.app` or directly through the spotlight using the *command* + Space bar keyboard shortcut and typing in `terminal`.

2. Once the Terminal is open, type the `uname -a` command in order to print out the OS information. Look at the end of the output to see whether it reads `RELEASE_I386 i386` or `RELEASE_X86_64 x86_64`. If it is the latter, then it means that you are running a 64-bit OS. Otherwise, it is a 32-bit kernel.

If you are using Windows 7 or Windows 8, follow these steps:

1. Use the Windows logo + *Pause/Break* keyboard shortcut to open the **System Properties** dialog box.

2. Under **System**, look for **System type**. It will tell you whether you are running a 32-bit or 64-bit Windows operating system. Use this information to decide whether to download and install the 32-bit or the 64-bit version of Node.js.

If you are running a Linux distribution, such as Debian, Fedora, Ubuntu, Mageia, Mint Linux, SUSE, or Red Hat, first open the Terminal using the *Ctrl +Alt + T* keyboard shortcut. Once the Terminal is open, type the `uname -a` command to print your OS architecture. If the end of the output reads `x86_64 GNU/Linux`, it indicates that you are running a 64-bit OS. If it reads `i386`, `i486`, `i586`, or `i686`, it means that you are running a 32-bit version of the kernel and you would need to download the 32-bit version of Node.js.

Now that you have gathered the necessary information about your OS, continue to the next section that explains how to install Node.js and Grunt on your operating system in detail.

How to do it...

If you are using a Mac or Windows system, you can use the Node.js installer. Simply go to `http://nodejs.org/download` and download the installer for your system. For example, if you use the 64-bit version of Mac OS X, download the 64-bit Mac OS X Installer (`.pkg`). If you are using the 64-bit version of Windows, then download and install the 64-bit Windows Installer (`.msi`). Once you have downloaded the installer, open it and go through the installation process. The installation process is almost the same as that of installing any other application and will not take more than a couple of minutes. Once the installation is complete, open the command line or Terminal and run the `node -v` and `npm -v` commands to make sure that Node.js and its package manager have been successfully installed. If you see the output for both commands, it means that you have successfully installed Node.js and its package manager on your system.

If you are using a Linux distribution, however, the easiest way to install Node.js is to use the Linux Binaries (`.tar.gz`) for your OS kernel's architecture. In order to install the binaries, first go to `http://nodejs.org/download` and copy the Linux Binaries (`.tar.gz`) download link for your OS kernel architecture by right-clicking on the link and choosing **Copy link address**. At the time of writing this book, the URL for the 64-bit version reads `http://nodejs.org/dist/v0.10.24/node-v0.10.24-linux-x64.tar.gz` and `http://nodejs.org/dist/v0.10.24/node-v0.10.24-linux-x86.tar.gz` for the 32-bit version of Node.js.

1. Open the Terminal and first add yourself to the `/usr/local` folder, which will require the administrator password:

    ```
    $ ME=$(whoami) ; sudo chown -R $ME /usr/local
    ```

2. Then go to the `/usr/local/bin` folder, make a folder called _node and navigate to it:

```
$ cd /usr/local/bin && mkdir _node && cd $_
```

3. The next step is to download and unarchive Node.js. Make sure to use the URL that you copied from the download page in the `wget` command as shown here:

```
$ wget http://copied/url/from/nodejs.tar.gz -O - | \ tar zxf -
--strip-components=1
```

4. The final step is to create the symbolic links for Node.js and npm:

```
$ ln -s "/usr/local/bin/_node/bin/node" ..
$ ln -s "/usr/local/bin/_node/lib/\ node_modules/npm/bin/npm-
cli.js" ../npm
```

5. Check and see whether Node.js and npm are installed and run `node -v && npm -v` in the Terminal. If the installation is successful, the output should print the versions of Node.js and npm:

```
v0.10.24
1.3.21
```

Now that you have installed Node.js and npm, you are finally ready to install Grunt. Installing Grunt is as simple as running a single command, regardless of the operating system that you are using. Just open the command line or the Terminal and execute the following command:

```
$ npm install -g grunt-cli
```

That's it! This command will install Grunt globally and make it accessible anywhere on your system. Run the `grunt --version` command in the Terminal or the command line in order to confirm that Grunt has been successfully installed. If the installation is successful, you should see the version of Grunt in the Terminal's output:

```
$ grunt --version
grunt-cli v0.1.11
```

After installing Grunt, the next step is to set it up for your project:

1. Make a folder on your desktop and call it `chapter1`, then navigate to it and run `npm init` to initialize the setup process:

```
$ mkdir ~/Desktop/chapter1 && cd $_ && npm init
```

2. Press *Enter* for all the questions and accept the defaults. You can change the settings later. This should create a file called `package.json` that contains some information about the project and the project dependencies. In order to add Grunt as a dependency, install the Grunt package as follows:

```
$ npm install grunt --save-dev
```

3. Now, if you look at the `package.json` file, you should see that Grunt is added to the list of dependencies:

```
..."devDependencies": {"grunt": "~0.4.2"
}
```

 In addition, you should see an extra folder created called `node_modules` that contains Grunt and other modules that you will install later in this chapter.

How it works...

In the preceding section, you installed Grunt (`grunt-cli`) with the `-g` option. The `-g` option installs Grunt globally on your system. Global installation requires superuser or administrator rights on most systems. Only the globally installed packages that you have need to be run from the command line. Everything that you will use with the `require()` function in your programs should be installed locally in the root of your project. Local installation makes it possible to solve your project's specific dependencies. More information about global versus local installation of npm modules can be found at `https://www.npmjs.org/doc/faq.html`.

There's more...

Node package managers are available for a wide range of operation systems, including Windows, OSX, Linux, SunOS, and FreeBSD. A complete list of package managers can be found at `https://github.com/joyent/node/wiki/Installing-Node.js-via-package-manager`. Notice these package managers are not maintained by the Node.js core team. Instead, each package manager has its own maintainer.

Installing Grunt plugins

Grunt plugins are the heart of Grunt. Every plugin serves a specific purpose and can also work together with other plugins. In order to use Grunt to set up your Less workflow, you need to install several plugins. You can find more information about these plugins in the following *How it works...* section.

Getting ready

Before you install the plugins, you should first create some basic files and folders for the project. Navigate to the root of the project using `cd ~/Desktop/chapter1` and run the following to create the files and folders:

```
$ a="app/dev" ; mkdir -p $a/css ; mkdir $a/less
$ touch $a/less/app.less && touch $a/index.html
```

This simply creates some files that you are going to work with throughout the chapter. You do not need to use the command line to create them, but in the end, you should end up with the following folder and file structure:

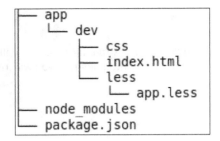

```
├── app
│   └── dev
│       ├── css
│       ├── index.html
│       └── less
│           └── app.less
├── node_modules
└── package.json
```

How to do it...

Grunt plugins are essentially Node.js modules that can be installed and added to the `package.json` file in the list of dependencies using npm. To do this, follow the ensuing steps:

1. Navigate to the root of the project.

2. Install the modules using npm, as follows:

```
$ cd ~/Desktop/chapter1 && npm install \
  grunt-contrib-less \
  grunt-contrib-watch \
  grunt-contrib-connect \
  grunt-contrib-less \
  grunt-open grunt-concurrent \
  load-grunt-tasks \
  grunt-contrib-csslint \
  grunt-uncss \
  grunt-styleguide \
  grunt-autoprefixer \
--save-dev
```

> Notice the single space before the backslash in each line. For example, on the second line, `grunt-contrib-less \`, there is a space before the backslash at the end of the line. The space characters are necessary because they act as separators. The backslash at the end is used to continue the commands on the next line. Also, notice the logical and (`&&`). Using the logical `&&`, you can run two commands in one line. This guarantees that the second command will run only if the first one succeeds.

The `npm install` command will download all the plugins and place them in the `node_modules` folder, in addition to including them in the `package.json` file. The next step is to include these plugins in the `Gruntfile.js` file.

How it works...

Grunt plugins can be installed and added to the `package.json` file using the `npm install` command followed by the name of plugins separated by a space, followed by the `--save-dev` flag:

```
$ npm install nameOfPlugin1 nameOfPlugin2 --save-dev
```

The `--save-dev` flag adds the plugin names and a tilde version range (see `https://www.npmjs.org/doc/misc/semver.html` for more information on the version's syntax) to the list of dependencies in the `package.json` file so that the next time you need to install the plugins, all you need to do is run `npm install`. This command will look at the directory from which it was called, look for the `package.json` file, and will automatically download all the specified plugins. This makes porting workflows very easy; all it takes is copying the `package.json` file and running npm install. Finally, the `package.json` file contains a JSON object with metadata.

It is also worth explaining the long command that you have used to install the plugins in this recipe. This command has two parts: the first part changes the directory to the `chapter1` folder on your desktop and the second part installs the plugins that are continued on to the next line by the backslash. The second part of the command is essentially equivalent to the following:

```
npm install grunt-contrib-less --save-dev
npm install grunt-contrib-watch --save-dev
npm install grunt-contrib-connect --save-dev
...
npm install load-grunt-tasks --save-dev
```

As you can see, it is very repetitive. However, both yield the same results; it is up to you to choose the one that you feel more comfortable with.

The `node_modules` folder contains all the plugins that you install with npm. Every time you run `npm install name-of-plugin`, the plugin is downloaded and placed in the folder. If you need to port your workflow, you do not need to copy all the contents of the folder. In addition, if you are using a version control system such as `git`, you should add the `node_modules` folder to the `.gitignore` file so that the folder and its subdirectories are ignored.

There's more...

Each Grunt plugin also has its own metadata set in a `package.json` file, and so plugins can have different dependencies. For instance, the `grunt-contrib-less` plugin, as described in the *Adding the Less compiler task* recipe, has set its dependency of the Less compiler, which can be seen as follows:

```
"dependencies": {
    "less": "^1.7.0"
    }
```

In the following list, you will find the plugins used in this chapter followed by a brief description:

- `load-grunt-tasks`: This loads all the plugins listed in the `package.json` file
- `grunt-contrib-watch`: This watches your files for changes
- `grunt-contrib-connect`: This runs a simple, static local server
- `grunt-contrib-less`: This compiles Less files
- `grunt-open`: This opens URLs and files from a Grunt's task
- `grunt-concurrent`: This allows the execution of multiple tasks concurrently
- `grunt-contrib-csslint`: This analyzes your CSS code
- `grunt-uncss`: This removes unused CSS
- `grunt-styleguide`: This compiles style guides with Grunt
- `grunt-autoprefixer`: This parses CSS and adds vendor-prefixed CSS properties using the *Can I use* database (see `http://caniuse.com/` for more information)

In addition to installing plugins, you can remove them as well. You can remove a plugin using the `npm uninstall name-of-plugin` command where `name-of-plugin` is the name of the plugin that you wish to remove. For example, if a line in the list of dependencies of your `package.json` file contains `grunt-concurrent": "~0.4.2`, then you can remove it using the following command:

`npm uninstall grunt-concurrent`

Then you just need to make sure to remove the name of the plugin from your `package.json` file so that it is not loaded by the `load-grunt-tasks` plugin the next time you run a Grunt task. Running `npm prune` after removing the items from the `package.json` file will also remove the plugins. The `prune` command removes "extraneous" packages that are not listed in the parent package's dependencies list.

Utilizing the Gruntfile.js file

The Gruntfile.js file is the main configuration file for Grunt that handles all the tasks and task configurations. All the tasks and plugins are loaded using this file. In this recipe, you will create this file and will learn how to load Grunt plugins using it.

Getting ready

First, you need to install Node and Grunt as described in the *Installing Node and Grunt* recipe of this chapter. You will also have to install some Grunt plugins as described in the *Installing Grunt plugins* recipe of this chapter.

How to do it...

Once you have installed Node and Grunt, follow these steps:

1. In your Grunt project directory (the folder that contains the package.json file), make a file, save it as Gruntfile.js, and add the following lines to it:

```
module.exports = function(grunt) {
        grunt.initConfig({
                pkg: grunt.file.readJSON('package.json'),
                app: {
                        dev: 'app/dev'
                },
    //Add the Tasks configurations here.
  });
    // Define Tasks here
};
```

   This is the simplest form of the Gruntfile.js file that only contains two information variables.

2. The next step is to load the plugins that you installed in the *Installing Grunt plugins* recipe. Add the following line at the end of your Gruntfile.js file:

```
grunt.loadNpmTasks('grunt-contrib-less');
```

   In the preceding line of code, grunt-contrib-less is the name of the plugin you want to load.

3. Finally, your `Gruntfile.js` file will look like this:

```javascript
module.exports = function(grunt) {
    grunt.initConfig({
        pkg: grunt.file.readJSON('package.json'),
        app: {
            dev: 'app/dev'
        },
    //Add the Tasks configurations here.
    });
        // Define Tasks here
    grunt.loadNpmTasks('grunt-contrib-less');
    grunt.loadNpmTasks('grunt-contrib-watch');
    grunt.loadNpmTasks('grunt-contrib-csslint');
    grunt.loadNpmTasks('grunt-autoprefixer');
    grunt.loadNpmTasks('grunt-styleguide');
    grunt.loadNpmTasks('grunt-uncss');
};
```

That is all it takes to load all the necessary plugins. The next step is to add the configurations for each task to the `Gruntfile.js` file.

How it works...

Any Grunt plugin can be loaded by adding a line of JavaScript to the `Gruntfile.js` file, as follows:

```javascript
grunt.loadNpmTasks('name-of-module');
```

This line should be added every time a new plugin is installed so that Grunt can access the plugin's functions. However, it is tedious to load every single plugin that you install. In addition, you will soon notice that as your project grows, the number of configuration lines will increase as well. As described in the *Loading Grunt tasks* recipe of this chapter, you can also use the `load-grunt-tasks` plugin to load your plugins automatically, based on the information in your `package.json` file.

The `Gruntfile.js` file should be written in JavaScript or CoffeeScript. Grunt tasks rely on configuration data defined in a JSON object passed to the `grunt.initConfig` method. **JavaScript Object Notation** (**JSON**) is an alternative for XML and used for data exchange. JSON describes name-value pairs written as `"name" : "value";`. All the JSON data is separated by commas, with JSON objects written inside curly brackets and JSON arrays inside square brackets. Each object can hold more than one name/value pair with each array holding one or more objects.

You can also group tasks into one task. You alias groups of tasks using the following line of code:

```
grunt.registerTask('alias',['task1', 'task2']);
```

Loading Grunt tasks

Instead of loading all the required Grunt plugins one by one, you can load them automatically with the `load-grunt-tasks` plugin.

Getting ready

For this recipe, you need to install the `load-grunt-tasks` plugin. You can install this by using the following command in the root of your project:

```
$ npm install load-grunt-tasks --save-dev
```

How to do it...

Add the following line at the very beginning of your `Gruntfile.js` file after `module.exports`:

```
require('load-grunt-tasks')(grunt);
```

Now your `Gruntfile.js` file should look like this:

```
module.exports = function(grunt) {
    require('load-grunt-tasks')(grunt);
    grunt.initConfig({
        pkg: grunt.file.readJSON('package.json'),
        app: {
            dev: 'app/dev'
        },
    //Add the Tasks configurations here.
  });
    // Define Tasks here
};
```

How it works...

The `load-grunt-tasks` plugin loads all the plugins specified in the `package.json` file. It simply loads the plugins that begin with the `grunt-` prefix or any pattern that you specify. This plugin will also read the `dependencies/devDependencies/peerDependencies` in your `package.json` and load the Grunt tasks that match the provided patterns.

A pattern to load specifically can be added as a second parameter. The can load, for instance, all the `grunt-contrib` tasks with the following code in your `Gruntfile.js` file:

```
require('load-grunt-tasks')(grunt, {pattern: 'grunt-contrib-*'});
```

Adding a configuration definition for a plugin

Any Grunt task needs a configuration definition. The configuration definitions are usually added to the `Gruntfile.js` file itself and are very easy to set up. In addition, it is very convenient to define and work with them because they are all written in JSON format. This makes it very easy to spot the configurations in the plugin's documentation examples and add them to your `Gruntfile.js` file.

In this recipe, you will learn how to add the configuration for a Grunt task.

Getting ready

For this recipe, you will first need to create a basic `Gruntfile.js` file and install the plugin you want to configure. If you want to install the `grunt-example` plugin, you can install it using the following command in the root of your project:

```
$ npm install grunt-example --save-dev
```

How to do it...

Once you have created the basic Grunt file, follow these steps:

1. A simple form of the task configuration is shown in the following code. Start by adding it to your `Gruntfile.js` file wrapped inside `grunt.initConfig{}`:

```
example: {
subtask: {
  files: {
      "app/dev/css/app.css":
"app/dev/less/app.less"
        }
     }
  }
```

2. Also, add a name and path for your project by adding to following code, also wrapped inside `grunt.initConfig{}`, to the `Gruntfile.js` file:

```
app: {
        dev: 'app/dev'
}
```

After following these steps, your `Gruntfile.js` file should look like this:

```
module.exports = function(grunt) {
    require('load-grunt-tasks')(grunt);
    grunt.initConfig({
            pkg: grunt.file.readJSON('package.json'),
            app: {
                    dev: 'app/dev'
            }
            example: {
                subtask: {
                files: {
                    "app/dev/css/app.css": "app/dev/less/app.less"
                }
              }
            }
    //Add the Tasks configurations here.
    });
    // Define Tasks here
};
```

The **Don't Repeat Yourself** (**DRY**) principle can be applied to your Grunt configuration too. If you look closely at the configuration definition, you will see the paths for the Less source and compiled CSS are hardcoded. A better approach would be to use templates to specify the paths. After you replace the values with template variables, your Less configuration will look like this:

```
less: {
  dev: {
    files: {
      "<%= app.dev %>/css/app.css": "<%= app.dev %>/less/app.less"
    }
  }
}
```

If you decide to change the name of your development directory, for example, all you need to do is change the `app` variable that is defined at the top of your `Gruntfile.js` file.

How it works...

If you look closely at the task configuration, you will notice the `files` field that specifies what files are going to be operated on. The `files` field is a very standard field that appears in almost all Grunt plugins simply due to the fact that many tasks require some or many file manipulations.

In addition, you should have noticed the template has been used using the `<%= %>` delimiter to expand the value of the development directory:

```
"<%= app.dev %>/css/app.css": "<%= app.dev %>/less/app.less"
```

The `<%= %>` delimiter essentially executes inline JavaScript and replaces values, as you can see in the following code:

```
"app/dev/css/app.css": "app/dev/less/app.less"
```

So, put simply, the value defined in the `app` object at the top of the `Gruntfile.js` file is evaluated and replaced. It is also worth mentioning that the value for the template does not necessarily have to be a string and can be a JavaScript literal.

See also

> ▶ Using the templates is key in order to avoid hardcoded values and inflexible configurations; you can read more about templates in the *Templates* section of Grunt's documentation at `http://gruntjs.com/configuring-tasks#templates`

Adding the Less compiler task

The Less task is the core task that you will need for your Less development. It has several features and options but at the heart of it is the Less compiler that can compile your Less files to CSS. By the end of this recipe, you will have a good understanding of this plugin, how to add it to your `Gruntfile.js` file, and how to take advantage of it.

Getting ready

The only requirement for this recipe is to have the Less plugin installed and loaded in your `Gruntfile.js` file. If you have not installed this plugin in the *Installing Grunt plugins* recipe of this chapter, you can do this using the following command in the root of your project:

```
$ npm install grunt-contrib-less --save-dev
```

How to do it...

The simplest form of the Less task configuration is shown in the following code. Start by adding it to your Gruntfile.js file after app: {dev: 'app/dev'},:

```
less: {
  dev: {
    files: {
      "app/dev/css/app.css": "app/dev/less/app.less"
    }
  }
}
```

Now, your Gruntfile.js file should look like this:

```
module.exports = function(grunt) {
    require('load-grunt-tasks')(grunt);
    grunt.initConfig({
        pkg: grunt.file.readJSON('package.json'),
        app: {
            dev: 'app/dev'
        },
        less: {
        dev: {
            files: {
            "app/dev/css/app.css": "app/dev/less/app.less"
            }
          }
        }
    //Add the Tasks configurations here.
  });
    // Define Tasks here
};
```

In the preceding code, the first file path (field's key) is the destination of the compiled CSS and the second is the Less source files.

How it works...

In addition to setting up the task configuration, you should run the `grunt` command to test the Less task. When you run the `grunt less` command, Grunt will look for a configuration called `less` in the `Gruntfile.js` file. Once it finds it, it will run the task with some default options if they are not explicitly defined. Successful tasks will end with the following message:

```
Done, without errors.
```

There's more...

In order to quickly test the current configuration, open the `app.less` file at `app/dev/less/app.less` and add the following Less lines to it:

```
@bg-color : #000;
@text-color : #bada55;

body {
    background-color:@bg-color;
    font-size: 1em;
    color: @text-color;
}
```

Then, open the Terminal in the directory that contains your `Gruntfile.js` file and run the following `grunt less` command:

```
$ cd ~/Desktop/chapter1/ && grunt less
```

If the execution is successful, you should get the following message:

```
Running "less:dev" (less) task
File app/dev/css/app.css created.
Done, without errors.
```

In addition, you should be able to see the compiled CSS at `app/dev/css/app.css`:

```
body {
  background-color: #000000;
  font-size: 1em;
  color: #bada55;
}
```

The Less task, similar to any other Grunt task, allows you to define options for your task. For example, if you need to include another folder that contains your Less source files, you can use the `paths` option that specifies directories to look for `@import` directives:

```
less: {
  dev: {
    options: {
      paths: ["<%= app.dev %>/less/src"]
    },
    files: {
      "<%= app.dev %>/css/app.css": "<%= app.dev %>/less/app.less"
    }
  }
}
```

By default, the Less task sets the paths to the directory of the source but you can change it if you choose to.

There are several other options that you can include in the Less task. Please refer to Grunt's documentation for a full list of options, which is available at `https://github.com/gruntjs/grunt-contrib-less#options`. An option can also be set at the global Less task level so the option will be applied in all subtasks of Less.

In addition to options, Grunt also provides targets for every task to allow you to set different configurations for the same task. In other words, if, for example, you needed to have two different versions of the Less task with different source and destination folders, you could easily use two different targets. Adding and executing targets are very easy. Adding more builds just follows the JSON notation, as shown here:

```
less: {
  dev: {
    options: {
      paths: ["dev-assets/css"]
    },
    files: {
      "path/to/dev-result.css": "path/to/dev-source.less"
    }
  },
  dist: {
    options: {
      paths: ["dist-assets/css"],
      cleancss: true
    },
    files: {
      "path/to/result.min.css": "path/to/dist-source.less"
    }
  }
}
```

In the preceding example, two builds are defined. The first one is named `dev` and the second is called `dist`. Each of these targets belongs to the Less task but they use different options and use different folders for the source and the compiled Less.

Moreover, you can run a particular target using `grunt less:nameOfTarget`, where `nameOfTarget` is the name of the target that you are trying to use. So, for example, if you needed to run the `dist` target, you will have to run `grunt less:dist`. However, if you needed to run both targets, you could simply run `grunt less` and it would run both the targets sequentially. Refer to Grunt's documentation at `http://gruntjs.com/configuring-tasks#task-configuration-and-targets` for more details.

Creating CSS source maps with the Less compiler task

In the *Adding the Less compiler task* recipe, you installed the Less task and read how to configure this task. In the *Using CSS source maps to debug your code* recipe from *Chapter 2, Debugging and Documenting Your Less Code*, you can read how to create a v3 CSS source map and use this source map to debug your code. This recipe describes how to create these source maps automatically with the Less compiler task.

Getting ready

The only requirement for this recipe is to have the Less plugin installed and loaded in your `Gruntfile.js` file. You can check the *Adding the Less compiler task* recipe of this chapter to find out how to install this plugin.

How to do it...

Open the `Gruntfile.js` file that contains your Less task configuration. The `grunt-contrib-less` task has options to turn the source maps on and set the output path. The `sourceMap` option is Boolean, which can be set to `true` to enable source maps. With only the `sourceMap` option set to `true`, the source map will be included inside the CSS file. With the `sourceMapFilename` option, you can write the source map to a separate file with the given filename. When setting both the options, the Less task configuration in your `Gruntfile.js` file will look as follows:

```
less: {
  dev: {
    files: {
      "<%= app.dev %>/css/app.css": "<%= app.dev %>/less/app.less"
    }
    options: {
```

```
                    sourceMap: true,
                    sourceMapFilename: "<%= app.dev
%>/css/style.css.map"
        }
}
```

For production, your final CSS code should be as short as possible in order to help your website load faster. For this reason, you should not inline Less code in your CSS files for production.

 In the *Adding the Less compiler task* recipe of this chapter, you can read how to define Grunt targets; you can define different targets that add CSS source maps or not, depending of the type of the target.

How it works...

Since Less v1.5, creating CSS v3 source maps are an option of the Less compiler. CSS helps you to debug your Less code by creating a mapping between the output of your CSS code and the original Less code. When inspecting your source with, for instance, Google Chrome, you will see your CSS selectors refer to the Less file of the origin, including line numbers. The following screenshot shows you an example of the additional information from the source map. Here, you can see that the **Styles** tab shows the CSS selectors with references to the Less files, including the line numbers.

```
Styles   Computed   Event Listeners   DOM Breakpoints   Properties

element.style {                                          +  ▦  ▲
}

div.other p {                                       style.less:14
   -webkit-transform: rotate(180deg);
   -ms-transform: rotate(180deg);
⚠  transform: rotate(180deg);
}

body p {                                             style.less:1
   font-size: 32px;
   border-radius:▶10px;
}

p {                                          user agent stylesheet
   display: block;
   -webkit-margin-before: 1em;
   -webkit-margin-after: 1em;
   -webkit-margin-start: 0px;
   -webkit-margin-end: 0px;
}
```

Other options to set the output of your CSS source map include `sourceMapURL` and `sourceMapBasepath` among others, which are described in more detail at `https://github.com/gruntjs/grunt-contrib-less#sourceMap`. Also note that these options of the `grunt-contrib-less` task do not exactly match the options of the Less compiler.

There's more...

The cleaning and minimizing your code recipe of this chapter shows you how to clean and minify your code. Unfortunately, the default code compressor of Less, `clean-css`, also removes the reference to the source map in your CSS. Future versions of Less will solve this problem, however. For now, you can use the alternative compressor by setting compress instead of `clean-css` in your task options.

The `grunt-recess` Grunt task is an alternative for compiling, linting, and minifying your Less and CSS code. More information about this plugin, which you can download, can be found at `https://www.npmjs.org/package/grunt-recess`. At the time of writing this book, neither `grunt-recess` nor the newer `gulp-less` have support for CSS source maps. The `grunt-recess` Grunt task does not support source maps at all, and `gulp-less` offers inline source maps only. Also, note that `gulp-less` won't work with Grunt but uses the alternative frontend builder Gulp.

Cleaning and minimizing your code

The Less compiler has two options for compressing and minimizing. The first option (`-x` or `--compress`) removes some whitespaces, and the second option (`--clean-css`) uses `clean-css`, which you can access at `https://github.com/GoalSmashers/clean-css`. Note that you cannot use both the options together.

Getting ready

The only requirement for this recipe is to have the Less plugin installed and loaded in your `Gruntfile.js` file. You can check the *Installing Grunt plugins* and *Adding the Less compiler task* recipes of this chapter to find out how to install this plugin.

How to do it...

Open the `Gruntfile.js` file that contains your Less task configuration. Edit the `grunt-contrib-less` options to set the `compress` or `clean-css` to `true`, as follows:

```
less: {
  dev: {
    files: {
      "<%= app.dev %>/css/app.css": "<%= app.dev %>/less/app.less"
    }
    options: {
            cleancss: true
    }
  }
}
```

Cleaning and compressing your final CSS is important to load the website faster. Also, you can remove unused code, as discussed in the *Removing unused CSS using Grunt* recipe of this chapter, to make the CSS code smaller and load your website faster.

There's more...

The Less compiler also has the possibility to pass an option to `clean-css` with `clean-option`. On the other hand, you will find that `grunt-contrib-less` does not support this option.

Adding the watch task

In this recipe, you will add the `watch` plugin. This plugin enables you to watch files and folders for any changes and execute certain tasks upon any change. In this recipe, you will add the watch task to watch for changes in the development folder and trigger the Less task every time any of the Less files is changed.

Getting ready

The only requirement for this recipe is to have the `watch` plugin installed and loaded in your `Gruntfile.js` file. If you have not installed this plugin in the *Installing Grunt plugins* recipe of this chapter, you can do this using the following command in the root of your project:

```
$ npm install grunt-contrib-watch --save-dev
```

How to do it...

In order to add the watch configuration, add the following lines to your `Gruntfile.js` file after the Less task configuration:

```
watch: {
    dev: {
            options: {
                    livereload: true
            },
            files: ['<%=app.dev%>/**', '!<%= app.dev %>/css/**'],
            tasks: ['less']
    },
},
```

Now your `Gruntfile.js` file will look like the following code:

```
module.exports = function(grunt) {
    require('load-grunt-tasks')(grunt);
    grunt.initConfig({
            pkg: grunt.file.readJSON('package.json'),
            app: {
                    dev: 'app/dev'
            },
            less: {
              dev: {
                  files: {
                  "<%= app.dev %>/css/app.css": "<%= app.dev
%>/less/app.less"
                  }
              }
            },
            watch: {
                    dev: {
                            options: {
                                    livereload: true
                            },
                            files: ['<%=app.dev%>/**', '!<%=
app.dev %>/css/**'],
                            tasks: ['less']
                    },
            }
    //Add the Tasks configurations here.
  });
    // Define Tasks here
};
```

Notice that the Less and the watch tasks are separated by commas. As a matter of fact, you can add as many tasks as you like as long as they are separated by commas. Also, if you read the *Utilizing the Gruntfile.js file* recipe of the chapter, you will get a brief description of the JSON format.

Now you can ask Grunt to watch your development folder and compile it every time you make a change. Navigate to the root of the project directory and run the watch task, as follows:

```
$ grunt watch
```

If everything is successful, you should see the following message in the terminal or the command line:

```
Running "watch" task

Waiting...
```

Now every time you make a change to any of the files in the `app/dev/` folder (except the `css` folder), the watch task will trigger the Less task to compile your Less file. You can try it by opening the `app/dev/less/app.less` file and adding a simple line and saving it. You will see a message as soon as you save the file:

```
>> File "app/dev/less/app.less" changed.

Running "less:dev" (less) task
File app/dev/css/app.css created.


Done, without errors.
Completed in 0.587s at Sun Jan 12 2014 22:03:16 GMT-0500 (EST) -
Waiting...
```

It is as simple as that! Now, if you want to stop the watch task, just use the *Ctrl + C* keyboard shortcut to terminate the process.

How it works...

The watch task can continuously monitor files and folders specified in the task configuration for changes and run other defined Grunt tasks upon any change. Grunt tasks can be easily passed in to the watch task as an array, which is one of the reasons why working with the watch task is such a breeze.

Similarly, the watched files and folders can also be listed in an array and included in the task configuration.

Use globing patterns to effectively specify the files and folders that you want Grunt to watch. For example, if you need to watch all the `.less` files in the Less directory, use the `less/*.less` pattern. However, if you need to watch all the Less files in the `less` folder and all the `less` subdirectories, use the `less/**/*.less` pattern. Refer to Grunt's documentation at `http://gruntjs.com/configuring-tasks#globbing-patterns` for more details.

The `livereload` option enables you to dynamically refresh all the files that have changed. This is very useful when combined with the connect task since the connect task also has a `livereload` option that enables Grunt to refresh the browser upon any file change.

There's more...

The watch plugin is versatile and has many options and features that will take couple of pages to fully explore. Make sure to visit its documentations at `https://github.com/gruntjs/grunt-contrib-watch` for more details on the options and frequently asked questions.

Adding the connect and open task

The next tasks that you are going to add are the connect and open tasks. The `connect` plugin provides a simple static development server that you can use to serve your static files. You can use the `livereload` option provided by the `connect` plugin along with the watch task (see the *Adding the watch task* recipe) to automatically reload your browser as you work on your project. In addition to the connect task, you will also add a small task using the open plugin to open a URL that is unsurprisingly called the open task.

This recipe will show you how to set the connect task along with the open task to automatically open served folders as you work on your project.

Getting ready

The only requirement for this recipe is to have the open and the connect plugins installed and loaded in your `Gruntfile.js` file. If you haven't installed these plugins in the *Installing Grunt plugins* recipe of this chapter, you can do this now using the following command in the root of your project:

```
$ npm install grunt-contrib-connect grunt-open --save-dev
```

How to do it...

Add the following configuration to your `Gruntfile.js` file after the watch task (make sure to add the comma after the end of the watch task configuration):

```
connect: {
    server: {
        options: {
            port: 9001,
            base: ['<%= app.dev %>'],
            keepalive: true,
            livereload: true
        }
    }
}
```

Now, in your `Gruntfile.js` file, the watch and the connect configurations should look like this:

```
...
watch: {
    dev: {
        options: {
            livereload: true
        },
        files: ['<%=app.dev%>/**', '!<%= app.dev %>/css/**'],
        tasks: ['less']
    }
},
connect: {
    server: {
        options: {
            port: 9001,
            base: ['<%= app.dev %>'],
            keepalive: true,
            livereload: true
        }
    }
}
```

Next, add the configuration for the open task to your `Gruntfile.js` file after the connect task configuration:

```
...
connect: {
    server: {
        options: {
            port: 9001,
            base: ['<%= app.dev %>'],
            keepalive: true,
            livereload: true
        }
    }
},
open: {
    all: {
        path: 'http://localhost:<%= connect.server.options.port%>'
    }
}
...
```

The last step is to group the connect and open tasks into one task. You alias groups of tasks use the following line of code:

```
grunt.registerTask('serve',['connect', 'open']);
```

Although the preceding code is correct, it is not going to run both tasks. This is because of the fact that the connect task keeps running (because of the `keepalive: true` option) and will block the open task to open the URL. The *Adding the concurrent task* recipe will show you how to solve this issue using the concurrent plugin.

How it works...

The connect plugin, similar to any other Grunt plugin, has several options. The options used in this recipe are given in the following list along with a short description:

- ▶ `port: 9001`: This specifies the port on which the server will be listening on.
- ▶ `base: ['<%= app.dev %>']`: This defines the directory from which files will be served. Different base directories can be passed into the array but only the last one will be able to be browsed.
- ▶ `keepalive: true`: This keeps the server running after Grunt's tasks have been completed and it will not allow any other tasks to run after it.

▶ `livereload: true`: This injects a live reload script into the page. Also, it enables live page reloading when used with the `livereload` option from the watch task.

There are several other options available that you can explore by visiting the project's repository at `https://github.com/gruntjs/grunt-contrib-connect`.

Adding the concurrent task

The concurrent task enables you to run several tasks concurrently. This is particularly useful when working with tasks such as the connect or watch task that stay active and block the tasks after them.

In this recipe, you will learn how to use the concurrent plugin to run the connect, open, and watch tasks at the same time. This will allow you to run one command to start the server and automatically open the browser window and watch the files for changes to reload the browser as you save any of the files.

Getting ready

The only requirement for this recipe is to have the concurrent plugin installed and loaded in your `Gruntfile.js` file. If you have not installed this plugin in the *Installing Grunt plugins* recipe of this chapter, you can do this using the following command in the root of your project:

```
$ npm install grunt-concurrent --save-dev
```

How to do it...

Add the following configuration for the concurrent task to the `Gruntfile.js` file after the open task:

```
open: {
    all: {
        path: 'http://localhost:<%= connect.server.options.port%>'
    }
},
concurrent: {
    dev: ['connect', 'open', 'watch'],
    options: {
        logConcurrentOutput: true,
        limit: 3
    }
}
```

Next, group the connect, open, and watch tasks using the `registerTask` function and call it `dev`:

grunt.registerTask('dev', ['concurrent']);

Then, add it to the end of the `Gruntfile.js` file before the last closing curly brace (`}`). So, the collapsed version of your `Gruntfile.js` file will look this:

```
module.exports = function(grunt) {
    require('load-grunt-tasks')(grunt);
    grunt.initConfig({
        pkg: grunt.file.readJSON('package.json'),
        app: {
            dev: 'app/dev'
        },
        less: { ... },
        watch: { ... },
        connect: { ... } ,
        open: { ... },
        concurrent { ... }
    });
    grunt.registerTask('dev', ['concurrent']);
};
```

In order to test the server and the concurrent plugin, let's add some content to the `app/dev/index.html` file:

```
<!DOCTYPE html>
<html>
    <head>
        <meta charset="utf-8">
        <meta http-equiv="X-UA-Compatible" content="IE=edge,chrome=1">
        <title>WebProject</title>
        <meta name="viewport" content="width=device-width, maximum-scale=1.0" />
        <link rel="stylesheet" type="text/css" href="css/app.css">
    </head>
    <body>
        <h1>The server is running successfully !</h1>
    </body>
</html>
```

Now change the directory to the root of your project and run the `dev` task:

$ cd ~/Desktop/chapter1 && grunt dev

Once you do this, after a couple of seconds a new browser window will open at `http://localhost:9001` serving the `index.html` file. Now, if you change and save any file in the `app/dev` folder, the page will automatically be refreshed. Try it by changing the `app.less` file at `app/dev/less/app.less`. You should see that the file gets automatically reloaded and refreshed in the browser, as shown in the following screenshot:

Finally, as always, you can stop the task using the *Ctrl + C* keyboard shortcut to stop the running process.

How it works...

The concurrent plugin is very similar to another plugin called the parallel plugin that enables you to run blocking tasks. In addition, these plugins are also useful to speed up the building processes that require several tasks to be executed at the same time. Please make sure to visit the project's repository at `https://github.com/sindresorhus/grunt-concurrent` to learn more about the plugin and the features that it has to offer.

Analyzing your code with CSS Lint

Less compiles into valid CSS, but note that "valid" does not always mean you will have compiled code of the highest quality. Lint your final CSS code with CSS Lint; this will help you to find possible issues and prevent you from making common mistakes. It not only checks your code for possible errors, such as double or empty properties, but also checks for compatibility and looks for problematic patterns or signs of inefficiency.

CSS Lint applies a set of rules to your code; all rules are optional and you can even write your own rules. It also has rules to check the maintainability and accessibility of your code. Finally, CSS Lint applies some rules that are based on the principles of **Object Oriented CSS** (**OOCSS**). More information about OOCSS can be found at http://www.smashingmagazine.com/2011/12/12/an-introduction-to-object-oriented-css-oocss/.

Getting ready

The only requirement for this recipe is to have the CSS Lint plugin installed and loaded in the Gruntfile.js file. If you have not installed this plugin in the *Installing Grunt plugins* recipe of this chapter, you can do so using the following command in the root of your project:

```
$ npm install grunt-contrib-csslint --save-dev
```

How to do it...

All you need to do is add the following configuration for the CSS Lint task to your Gruntfile.js file:

```
csslint: {
            src: ['css/style.css']
    }
```

How it works...

The CSS Lint task lints your CSS code and checks a wide range of rules to validate it. You can ignore some rules by setting it to false or even defining your own rules. A complete list of rules can be found at https://github.com/CSSLint/csslint/wiki/Rules.

To start with, your Less code may look as follows:

```
header {
        h1 {
                color: darkgreen;
        }
    }
```

Running the grunt csslint command will give you the result illustrated here:

Running "csslint:src" (csslint) task

```
Linting css/style.css ...ERROR
```

```
[L1:C8]
```

```
Heading (h1) should not be qualified. Headings should not be qualified
(namespaced). (qualified-headings)
```

```
Warning: Task "csslint:src" failed. Use --force to continue.
```

```
Aborted due to warnings.
```

The `qualified-headings` rule checks whether your code defines all the heading elements (`h1-h6`) as top-level styles, which is a requirement of OOCSS. Some Less features can break OOCSS rules. Note that you can visit `http://blog.mediumequalsmessage.com/guidelines-using-oocss-and-css-preprocessors` to find out more about this issue.

Set `qualified-headings` to `false` as follows:

```
        csslint: {
                        options: {
                                "qualified-headings": false
                        },
                        src: ['css/style.css']
        }
```

By running the grunt `csslint` command, you will get the following result:

```
Running "csslint:src" (csslint) task
```

```
>> 1 file lint free.
```

```
Done, without errors.
```

The preceding message shows you that CSS Lint did not find any more errors. The `Done, without errors` message is Grunt's default message when all tasks have run successfully.

There's more...

Alternatively, you can use the Less Lint plugin called `Grunt-lesslint`, which is a Grunt task to validate the Less files with CSS Lint. More information about this plugin can be found at `https://www.npmjs.org/package/grunt-lesslint/`.

Removing unused CSS using Grunt

When your project grows or when you are using CSS frameworks, such as Bootstrap, your compiled CSS code can contain many selectors that are never used. This unused CSS code will have a negative effect on the performance of your website. The unused CSS plugin can remove this unused selector from your CSS code.

Getting ready

The only requirement for this recipe is to have the unused CSS plugin installed and loaded in your `Gruntfile.js` file. If you have not installed this plugin in the *Installing Grunt plugins* recipe of this chapter, you can do so using the following command in the root of your project:

```
$ npm install grunt-uncss -save-dev
```

How to do it...

You can add the following configuration for the watch task to your `Gruntfile.js` file:

```
uncss: {
  dist: {
  files: {
    'css/style.css' : ['index.html']
   }
  }
 }
```

The preceding code only checks the `index.html` file for unused selectors. You can add a list of HTML to check using and array as follows:

```
    'css/style.css' :
['index.html','aboutus.html','blog.html']
```

How it works...

The unused CSS plugin loads HTML by PhantomJS, and JavaScript is also executed. However, you need to realize that the plugin cannot detect code that has been injected by JavaScript, triggered by user interactions. Style sheet for this dynamically injected HTML code should be added to the ignore option of this task. The unused CSS plugin also handles media queries, but by default, UnCSS processes only style sheets with media queries such as all, screen, and those without a media query. Other media queries can be set using the media option.

See also

▸ You can find a complete list of options at `https://github.com/addyosmani/grunt-uncss#options`

Compiling style guides with Grunt

In the *Building style guides with StyleDocco* recipe in *Chapter 2, Debugging and Documenting Your Less Code*, you can see how style guides can help you, and content developers can directly see the effect of your work. With the Grunt style guide plugin, you can automate the process of creating style guides.

Getting ready

For this recipe, you need to have the style guide plugin installed and loaded in the `Gruntfile.js` file. If you have not installed this plugin, which requires you to read the *Installing Grunt plugins* recipe of this chapter, you can do so using the following command in the root of your project:

```
$ npm install grunt-styleguide --save-dev
```

In this recipe, the style guide will be built with StyleDocco, which requires your Less code to be commented with comments written in the Markdown syntax. Markdown is a plain text formatting syntax, designed such that it can be easily converted in to HTML.

 At `http://stackoverflow.com/`, the popular question and answer website, users are required to use Markdown to edit their questions, answers, and comments. Visit `http://stackoverflow.com/editing-help` or read *Instant Markdown, Arturo Herrero, Packt Publishing*, to learn more about writing in Markdown.

How to do it...

Firstly, add the following configuration for the concurrent task to your `Gruntfile.js` file:

```
styleguide: {
    styledocco: {
        options: {
            framework: {
                name: 'styledocco'
            },
            name: 'Style Guide',
            template: {
                include: ['plugin.css', 'app.js']
            }
        },
        files: {
            'docs': 'less/*.less'
        },
    }
}
```

By including Markdown-styled comments, your Less code will look this:

```
/*  Base
===============

    This is a simple Base CSS

    <div class="h1">H1 type headers</div>

*/

.h1 {
    font-size:30px;
    font-weight:normal;
}
```

Running the `grunt styleguide` task will write your style guide files to `docs/index.html`. The following screenshot shows you how the style guide will look after running the preceding tasks:

Automatically prefix your code with Grunt

Browser-specific prefixes can make CSS3, and therefore Less code, complex and more difficult to maintain. Mixins (prebuilt) offer you the opportunity to write single-line declarations for properties such as gradients and shadows. The autoprefixer plugin can prefix your code automatically, which uses the *Can I use* database (available at `http://caniuse.com/`) in order to find the prefixes that meet your requirements.

Getting ready

The only requirement for this recipe is to have the autoprefixer plugin installed and loaded in your `Gruntfile.js` file. If you have not installed this plugin in the *Installing Grunt plugins* recipe of this chapter, you can do so using the following command in the root of your project:

```
$ npm install grunt-autoprefixer  --save-dev
```

How to do it...

Add the following configuration for the concurrent task to the `Gruntfile.js` file:

```
autoprefixer: {
single_file: {
  src: '<%=app.dev%>css/style.css',
  dest: '<%=app.dev%>css/style.css'
  }
}
```

Notice that the preceding code will overwrite the original file. Multiple files can be prefixed with the `multiple_files` option.

How it works...

The autoprefixer plugin parses CSS and adds vendor-prefixed CSS properties using the *Can I use* database. This database contains information for each browser version and also includes statics about the current usage of the different browser versions.

With the browser option, you can set the browser you will have to support. By default, the browser option is set to an array, as follows:

['> 1%', 'last 2 versions', 'Firefox ESR', 'Opera 12.1']

The autoprefix task can also be updated to your CSS source map files. Creating a CSS source map with Grunt is described in the *Creating CSS source maps with the Less compiler task* recipe. You can set the path to your source map using the map option. If you do not set the map option, then autoprefixer will look for the source map files automatically.

As an example, consider the following Less file:

```
p {
   transform: rotate(180deg);
}
```

After compiling and running the autoprefixer task, your CSS code will look this:

```
p {
   -webkit-transform: rotate(180deg);
   -ms-transform: rotate(180deg);
   transform: rotate(180deg);
}
```

There's more...

When using the autoprefixer task, you can define all your properties with a single declaration using the official W3C rules, described at http://www.w3.org/Style/CSS/specs.en.html.

Installing the Grunt LiveReload plugin

In the *Adding the connect and open task* and *Adding the concurrent task* recipes of this chapter, you can find how to get a live preview of your changes to your code. Instead of using grunt-concurrent, you can also achieve the same with the browser extensions from LiveReload. Currently, extensions are available for Safari, Google Chrome, and Firefox. Notice that the extension for Safari does not work with file URLs.

Getting ready

This recipe requires you to have the watch plugin, as described in the *Adding the watch task* recipe, and the Less plugin, as described in the *Adding the Less compiler task* recipe, installed. You will also need Safari, Google Chrome, or Firefox browser, and the free LiveReload extension installed. More information about installing the browser extension can be found at http://feedback.livereload.com/knowledgebase/articles/86242-how-do-i-install-and-use-the-browser-extensions.

How to do it...

Add the following configuration for the watch task to your Gruntfile.js file:

```
watch: {
  css: {
    files: ['less/*.less'],
    tasks: ['less:dev'],
    options: {
      livereload: true,
    }
  }
}
```

For the Less task, you will have to add the following configuration code:

```
less: {
        dev: {
        files: {
        "<%= app.dev %>/css/app.css": "<%= app.dev
%>/less/app.less"
            }
        }
    }
```

Now you can create the following folder and file structure:

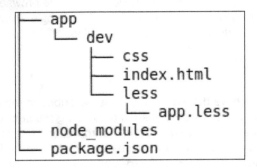

Finally, load the index.html file in your browser with LiveReload enabled. The index.html file should include your style sheet as follows:

```
<link rel="stylesheet" type="text/css" href="css/app.css">
```

Try the index file of the *Adding the concurrent task* recipe or add some content to it by yourself. Add, for instance, an h1 tag and style this in the app.less file with the following code:

```
h1 {
color:red;
}
```

Now after changing and saving your app.less file, your browser will reload automatically and show the results of your changes.

How it works...

The `livereload` option of the watch task fires a signal to port `35729` after running the `less:dev dev` task, evoked by a file change of a `.less` file in the `less` folder. The LiveReload browser extension injects some JavaScript code into the HTML source as follows:

```
<script
src="http://127.0.0.1:35729/livereload.js?ext=Firefox&extver=2.0.8
">
```

The JavaScript code in the `livereload.js` file reloads the browser triggered by signals on port `35729`. This process of reloading is very similar to the `livereload` option of the connect plugin, as described in the *Adding the connect and open task* recipe of this chapter.

Index

F

files
  importing, @import directive used 253-255
flexbox
  about 202, 204
  URL 208
flexbox grid
  applying, on design 266-270
  in CSS specification, URL 273
  URL 256, 257
  using, for page layout 246
flexbox grid library
  unofficial Less version, URL 276
  URL 266, 274, 276
flexbox library
  URL 256
fluid grids
  alternative building, Frameless used 236-239
fluid responsive grid system
  building 240-243
Font Awesome 213
font-face declarations
  generating, Clearless used 211-214
Frameless
  used, for building alternative for
      fluid grids 236-239
  URL 240
functions
  mixins used as 156-161

G

GIMP
  URL 112
GitHub
  Cardinal, URL 250
  Twitter' Bootstrap, URL 250
GNU Image Manipulation Program (GNU) 112
graceful degradation
  versus progressive enhancement, URL 79
graceful degradation strategy
  URL 295

gradient functions
  URL 198
gradients
  unlimited gradients, building with
      Less Hat 199-201
grid
  building, grid classes used 256-260
Grunt
  code, prefixing 361-363
  documentation, URL 340, 343
  installing 328-331
  plugins, installing 331-334
  tasks, loading 337, 338
  unused CSS, removing 358
grunt-autoprefixer plugin 334
grunt-concurrent plugin 334
grunt-contrib-connect plugin 334
grunt-contrib-csslint plugin 334
grunt-contrib-less plugin 334
grunt-contrib-watch plugin 334
Gruntfile.js file
  utilizing 335, 336
grunt-open plugin 334
grunt-recess Grunt task 346
grunt-styleguide plugin 334
grunt-uncss plugin 334
guards
  applying, to CSS selectors 173-175
GulP
  URL 16
Gulp Less plugin
  URL 16

H

hsla() function 104
HTML5 Boilerplate
  URL 322
HTML5 doctor
  URL 266
HTTP
  compression, URL 88
hue, saturation, lightness (HSL) 103

Thank you for buying
Less Web Development Cookbook

About Packt Publishing

Packt, pronounced 'packed', published its first book, *Mastering phpMyAdmin for Effective MySQL Management*, in April 2004, and subsequently continued to specialize in publishing highly focused books on specific technologies and solutions.

Our books and publications share the experiences of your fellow IT professionals in adapting and customizing today's systems, applications, and frameworks. Our solution-based books give you the knowledge and power to customize the software and technologies you're using to get the job done. Packt books are more specific and less general than the IT books you have seen in the past. Our unique business model allows us to bring you more focused information, giving you more of what you need to know, and less of what you don't.

Packt is a modern yet unique publishing company that focuses on producing quality, cutting-edge books for communities of developers, administrators, and newbies alike. For more information, please visit our website at www.packtpub.com.

About Packt Open Source

In 2010, Packt launched two new brands, Packt Open Source and Packt Enterprise, in order to continue its focus on specialization. This book is part of the Packt open source brand, home to books published on software built around open source licenses, and offering information to anybody from advanced developers to budding web designers. The Open Source brand also runs Packt's open source Royalty Scheme, by which Packt gives a royalty to each open source project about whose software a book is sold.

Writing for Packt

We welcome all inquiries from people who are interested in authoring. Book proposals should be sent to author@packtpub.com. If your book idea is still at an early stage and you would like to discuss it first before writing a formal book proposal, then please contact us; one of our commissioning editors will get in touch with you.

We're not just looking for published authors; if you have strong technical skills but no writing experience, our experienced editors can help you develop a writing career, or simply get some additional reward for your expertise.

**Less Web Development
Essentials**

ISBN: 978-1-78398-146-5 Paperback: 202 pages

Use CSS preprocessing to streamline the development
and maintenance of your web applications

1. Produce clear, concise, and well-constructed code
   that compiles into standard compliant CSS.

2. Explore the core attributes of Less and learn how
   to integrate them into your site.

3. Optimize Twitter's Bootstrap to efficiently develop
   web apps and sites.

**Instant LESS CSS
Preprocessor How-to**

ISBN: 978-1-78216-376-3 Paperback: 80 pages

Practical, hands-on recipes to write more efficient CSS,
with the help of the LESS CSS Preprocessor library

1. Learn something new in an Instant! A short, fast,
   focused guide delivering immediate results.

2. Use mixins, functions, and variables to
   dynamically autogenerate styles, based
   on minimal existing values.

3. Use the power of LESS to produce style sheets
   dynamically, or incorporate precompiled versions
   into your code.

4. Learn how to use existing mixin libraries, or to
   create your own that you can reuse in future
   projects.

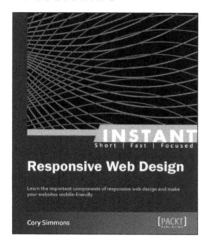

Instant Responsive Web Design

ISBN: 978-1-84969-925-9   Paperback: 70 pages

Learn the important components of responsive web design and make your websites mobile-friendly

1. Learn something new in an Instant! A short, fast, focused guide delivering immediate results.

2. Learn how to make your websites beautiful on any device.

3. Understand the differences between various responsive philosophies.

4. Expand your skill set with the quickly growing mobile-first approach.

Responsive Web Design with HTML5 and CSS3

ISBN: 978-1-84969-318-9   Paperback: 324 pages

Learn responsive design using HTML5 and CSS3 to adapt websites to any browser or screen size

1. Everything needed to code websites in HTML5 and CSS3 that are responsive to every device or screen size.

2. Learn the main new features of HTML5 and use CSS3s stunning new capabilities including animations, transitions, and transformations.

3. Real world examples show how to progressively enhance a responsive design while providing fall backs for older browsers.

Please check **www.PacktPub.com** for information on our titles